Youth and Substance Use

Advisory Editor
Thomas M. Meenaghan, *New York University*

Related books of interest

Youth and Substance Use
Prevention, Intervention, and Recovery

LORI HOLLERAN STEIKER
University of Texas at Austin

LYCEUM
BOOKS, INC.

5758 South Blackstone Avenue
Chicago, Illinois 60637

Published by
LYCEUM BOOKS, INC.
5758 S. Blackstone Avenue
Chicago, Illinois 60637
773-643-1903 fax
773-643-1902 phone
lyceum@lyceumbooks.com
www.lyceumbooks.com

6   5   4   3   2   1   15   16   17   18   19

ISBN 978-1-935871-63-7

Printed in the United States of America.

The art on the cover, #4, 2014, was created by noted Chicago artist Richard Hull, using crayon on paper.

Library of Congress Cataloging-in-Publication Data

Steiker, Lori Holleran.
   Youth and substance use : prevention, intervention, and recovery / Lori Holleran Steiker.
      pages cm
    ISBN 978-1-935871-63-7 (pbk. : alk. paper)
    1. Youth—Substance use—United States.   2. Substance abuse—United States—Prevention.   3. Substance abuse—Treatment—United States.   4. Drug abusers—Rehabilitation—United States.   5. Social work with drug addicts—United States.   I. Title.
HV4999.Y68S74   2016
362.290835'0973—dc23
                                                            2015007833

This book is dedicated to my parents,
Beverly & Alan Koenigsberg,
who brought love, recovery, and hope into my life.

CONTENTS

Contents

Part IV: Evidence-Based Treatment Interventions

Chapter 7: Different Approaches to Evidence-Based Treatment

Chapter 8: Support Groups, Twelve-Step, and Other Paths to Recovery

Contents

PREFACE

This book translates the best of what we know from research and practice into a "how to" book—how to understand, how to interact and intervene, how to maximize your impact, and how to transform societal perceptions beyond your practice. Although numerous texts address substance misuse in general, this book allows specializing undergraduates, graduate students, and practitioners to acquire knowledge and skills related to substance misuse specifically among youth populations. This text will meet the needs of practitioners in social work and other mental health fields who desire a living, *practical guide* to the latest information on working with this population in their clinical practice. It provides a comprehensive overview of the critical issues related to child and adolescent substance misuse and covers a spectrum of topics from assessment to prevention and intervention. Grounded in the evidence, the book aims to illustrate adolescent substance misuse, intervention, and recovery "where the rubber hits the road." Although theoretical frames are offered as a foundation, there will always be practical implications and concepts directly relevant to working with youth around drug and alcohol issues. Corresponding with trends showing youth risk behaviors, experimentation, and substance misuse occurring at younger ages, the text has a developmental approach, considering factors related to the initiation of this behavior among children and adolescents.

The author braids personal, professional, and research perspectives on the topic to produce a heartfelt, honest, narrative-grounded, and empirically sound compendium. The book includes easy-reference boxes, checklists, bulleted points, case scenarios, and other visual aids. Each chapter incorporates key terms and queries to prompt critical thought and discussion, case scenarios to illustrate main points, and/or exercises to practice relevant skills. In addition, it is the hope of the author that students will find and read the research referenced in the text— information literacy is key to being a responsible and effective practitioner.

In line with cutting-edge research, this book employs a Transtheoretical Model, based specifically on motivational enhancement and interviewing, Stage of Change–based interventions, and harm reduction and dissonance-based models of prevention and intervention. But rather than focusing *solely* on the research, the book is framed as a practical guide to working with adolescents with substance misuse issues. It acts as a bridge between the research and practice—a form of "technology transfer." It provides step-by-step directions on the use of evidence-based interventions in various settings, with a discussion of cultural adaptation based on the agency, cultural group including the influence of peers, and the experiences of the unique population under consideration (e.g., incarcerated youth, homeless youth, LGBTQ youth, youth on the Mexican border, collegiate youth, and emerging adults in a variety of life situations).

Another thing that makes this text unique in the cadre of publications about adolescent substance misuse is that it is strengths based. The focus of this text shifts from the nightmare of substance misuse to the hope for recovery, being witnessed in larger and larger numbers of youth nationally and internationally. Young Peoples' recovery program meetings are filling up, sometimes standing room only. Youth with genetic predispositions by virtue of their parents' addictions are "seeing the writing on the wall" early enough to "raise the bottom," averting some of the worst consequences of substance misuse and introducing them into a new life. Youth recovery organizations such as Young People in Recovery (youngpeopleinrecovery.org) are spreading like fire, advocating, and reframing the disease in light of what has been recognized as a true Recovery Movement (Best & Lubman, 2012).

Recently, the ONDCP (Office of National Drug Control Policy) launched a vitalized National Youth Anti-Drug effort to alert parents to the rising trend of teen prescription drug misuse in America (ONDCP, 2008). These efforts resulted in a 19-percent increase in youth awareness and a 28-percent increase in anti-drug beliefs, which correlates with behavior change. As youths' awareness of such media campaigns as "Above the Influence" has increased, their beliefs about the risks of drug use and the importance of staying drug free have strengthened as well. Parent awareness of teen prescription-drug misuse more than doubled, and more than 75 percent of parents reported that they intended to take actions indicated in campaign messages, such as securing medications. Another initiative, the Anti-Meth Campaign, highlights the dangers associated with methamphetamine use—for individuals, families, and communities—and provides a message of hope that people can and do recover from methamphetamine addiction.

But perhaps the biggest challenge is combating the stigma attributed to drug and alcohol addictions, as well as to those in recovery. Stigma-based biases and stereotypes are the most insidious and deadly aspects of the disease. Denials, embraced by youth who believe that the face of addiction couldn't possibly be their own, and reinforcement from parents who often would rather have their child diagnosed with any health problem other than substance dependence are the hallmarks of alcoholism and drug addiction. Stigma breeds a million versions of fear and shame, blocking the doors of treatment and greasing the rails to jails, homelessness, and death. Once a young person finds peers in recovery and a new sense of self and purpose for living, the shame melts away and doors open. Recovery is out of hiding and "in" popular culture. As noted in the independent feature documentary "The Anonymous People," there are over 23 million Americans living in long-term recovery from alcohol and other drug addictions. Addiction has been likened to a national epidemic; in the film, Patrick Kennedy states boldly, "If we could ever tap those 20+ million people in long-term recovery, we'd change this overnight." (*The Anonymous People*, 2013). The addiction conversation is shifting from problems to solutions. Young people in recovery are, as the movie notes, "stepping from the shadows and into the light." This book is written to illuminate adolescent substance use—prevention, intervention, and recovery. It moves from well-established foundations and protocols to the present innovations in the creation and augmentation of peer recovery networks (CSAT, 2009). It aims to cause dissonance with what readers think and to push against the stereotypes.

The landscape changes every day. Use this book as a jumping off place a springboard for your curiosity, conviction, and inquiry. Fill in the blanks. Ask the hard questions. Think critically. And find a way to help and contribute to the unfolding picture. Every detail helps helpers to save and transform the young clients and families with whom they work.

REFERENCES

Best, D., & Lubman, D. I. (2012). The emergence of a recovery movement for alcohol and drug dependence. *Australian & New Zealand Journal of Psychiatry*, *46*(6), 586.

CSAT—Center for Substance Abuse Treatment (2009). What Are Peer Recovery Support Services? HHS Publication No. (SMA) 09–4454. Rockville, MD:

Substance Abuse and Mental Health Services Administration, U.S. Department of Health and Human Services.

ONDCP—The Office of the National Drug Control Policy (2008). National Youth Anti-Drug Media Campaign. Accessed April 15, 2015: https://www.white house.gov/ondcp/anti-drug-media-campaign

Williams, G., Director (2013). *The anonymous people*. Documentary film, accessed April, 2015 on the Faces and Voices website: 2manyfaces1voice .org, http://manyfaces1voice.org

PART I

Conceptualization of Adolescence, Substance Use, Addiction, and Theory

The problem of substance misuse among young people has been deemed an epidemic (SAMHSA, 2014). But what does that mean in terms of operationalizing interventions? That question is a prime focus of this book.

When studying the problem of youth and substance misuse, the first question students, practitioners, clients, and families tend to ask is this: How do you discern substance use from misuse and from addiction? To get at the best answer to this question, Part I explores the physiological aspects of drug use and misuse, laying the groundwork for more in-depth discussion of the holistic aspects that must be considered when working with young people who are involved with substance use. The biological, psychological, social, and spiritual aspects start with the developing brain.

Part I investigates the big pictures related to adolescents. Although adolescence used to be thought to blend into adulthood at about eighteen years old, research is showing definitive plasticity of young people's brains well until the age of twenty-five or beyond (Arain et al., 2013). Part I explores the changes in a young person's body, mind, and cultural and social existence, and how young people make meaning in the world. All of these factors must be understood before turning to the methods and mechanisms for intervening.

REFERENCES

Arain, M., Haque, M., Johal, L., Mathur, P., Nel, W., Rais, A., Sandhu, R., & Sharma, S. (2013). Maturation of the adolescent brain. *Neuropsychiatric Disease and Treatment, 9,* 449–461.

SAMHSA (Substance Abuse and Mental Health Services Administration), Center for Behavioral Health Statistics and Quality. (September 4, 2014). *The NSDUH Report: Substance Use and Mental Health Estimates from the 2013 National Survey on Drug Use and Health: Overview of Findings*. Rockville, MD: SAMHSA.

Chapter 1

Overview of Substance Misuse

EPIDEMIOLOGY AND ETIOLOGY

Use of tobacco, alcohol, and illicit substances costs society dearly, in economic, health, and social realms. Tobacco, alcohol, and illicit drug use are among the most important global public health problems, with their genesis in adolescence. Their long-term adverse health consequences are well documented, but short-term outcomes among adolescents are important and include associations with injury, violence and suicide, teenage pregnancy, sexually transmitted diseases, and adverse mental health (diClemente, Hansen, & Ponton, 1996).

Despite considerable efforts to minimize use of legal substances and prevent use of illicit substances, more than 400,000 Americans die yearly from cigarette smoking, and one in every five deaths in the United States are smoking related (National Center for Disease Prevention and Health Promotion, 2001). Alcohol and illicit substance misuse have dire consequences including cirrhosis, suicide, employment disruptions, and criminal behaviors (Voss et al., 2013.) The economic costs of substance misuse were estimated as $400 billion yearly in the United States in 1999 (McGinnis & Foege, 1999).

Substance use is associated with a wide range of risk behaviors. Substance use has some risks for those that use recreationally as well as those experiencing problematic substance misuse and those with dependence. For example, in 2002, 4.7 percent of the population reported driving under the influence of an illicit drug and 14.2 percent reported driving under the influence of alcohol at least once during the past year (SAMHSA, 2002). Due to the loosening of inhibitions experienced under the influence, inebriated or high individuals make riskier choices with regard to relationships, sex, money, crime, health, driving, and the like.

A hallmark of the transition from childhood to adolescence is the increase in risk-taking behaviors (Nargiso, Friend, & Florin, 2013; Schulenberg, Bryant, & O'Malley, 2004; Windle, 2000; Windle et al., 2008). Alcohol continues to be the most commonly used drug among youth. For example, 2012 data from the Monitoring the Future Survey indicates that 72 percent of twelfth graders (nearly three out of four) have tried alcohol, and 39 percent of eighth graders have reported some alcohol use in their lifetime (Johnston, O'Malley, Bachman, & Schulenberg, 2014).

• •

The Problem

- 75 percent (10 million) of all high school students have used addictive substances including tobacco, alcohol, marijuana, or cocaine; one in five of them meets the medical criteria for addiction (CASA, 2011).

- 46 percent (6.1 million) of all high school students currently use addictive substances; one in three of them meets the medical criteria for addiction (CASA, 2011). Alcohol remains the substance most widely used by today's teenagers: seven out of every ten students (68 percent) have consumed alcohol (more than just a few sips) by the end of high school, and three out of ten (2 percent) have done so by eighth grade (Johnston et al., 2014). Over half (52 percent) of twelfth graders and one eighth (12 percent) of eighth graders in 2013 reported having been drunk at least once in their life (Johnston et al., 2014).

- Substance use increases with age, and the highest rate of current illicit drug use was among eighteen- to twenty-year-olds (23.8 percent) (SAMHSA, 2011).
- Nine out of ten Americans who meet the medical criteria for addiction started smoking, drinking, or using other substances before age eighteen (CASA, 2011).
- One in four Americans who began using any addictive substance before age eighteen are addicted, compared to one in twenty-five who started using at age twenty-one or older. The risk of being addicted is much higher among Americans who begin to use addictive substances at a younger age (CASA, 2011). In high school, those students who are not college-bound (a decreasing proportion of the total youth population) are considerably more likely to be at risk for using illicit drugs, drinking heavily, and particularly smoking cigarettes (Johnston et al., 2014).
- Death rates from prescription drug overdose in Americans aged fifteen to twenty-four more than doubled from 2000 to 2010 (CDC, 2010).
- Substances are the most prevalent cause of teen morbidity and mortality in the U.S. (SAMHSA, 2013).

• •

Of greater concern is the widespread occurrence of episodes of drunkenness and binge drinking. The rates of self-reported drunkenness in the past thirty days were 5 percent, 14 percent, and 25 percent, respectively, for grades 8, 10, and 12, and the prevalence rates of binge drinking (occasions of consuming five or more drinks in a row in the previous two weeks) were 8 percent, 16 percent, and 25 percent for the three grades, respectively. The most recent MTF (Monitoring the Future) study (2014) notes that in 1981, 41 percent of twelfth graders reported having five or more drinks in a row on at least one occasion in the two weeks prior to the survey; thus the recent two percentage-point increase to 24 percent in 2012 still leaves it well below peak levels of the 1980s.

Despite these alarming statistics, which have been consistently reported over the last two decades, there was little, if any, research prior to 1990 on the potential adverse consequences of underage drinking on social, emotional, behavioral, and neurobiological development or on future drinking patterns (Witt, 2010). The lack of research in this area was partly because adolescent drinking was viewed as a transient phenomenon, with the majority of high school and college students aging out (i.e., moving beyond the developmental stage in which this is common) of heavy drinking as they transitioned to new roles in adulthood (e.g., Bachman et al., 2002; Chen & Kandel, 1995; Donovan, Jessor, & Jessor, 1983; Grant, Harford, & Grigson, 1988; and Temple & Fillmore, 1985–6). However, more recent epidemiological data accent the high rates of risky drinking patterns, such as binge drinking, in youth and young adults as well as a surge in the prevalence of alcohol dependence between adolescence and adulthood that is unequaled at later ages (Li, Hewitt, & Grant, 2007). Therefore, looking at the harmful consequences of high-risk drinking during adolescence and early adulthood became a priority.

Historically, drug use, misuse, and dependence were issues for emerging adults and adults. However, trends have shown that drug use has become more and more common among adolescents and even children. Of particular importance are findings relating to relatively new synthetic drugs and some relating to the use of more traditional drugs of misuse, like marijuana and Ecstasy. According to the Monitoring the Future study (Johnston et al., 2014), perceived risk for marijuana has been falling for the past six years, and disapproval declined for the past three to four years. These changes foreshadow a further increase in teenage marijuana use. The trend towards legalization (especially if solid prevention interventions are not in place) may augment this trend (see the final chapter of this book for an in-depth discussion of this issue). It is therefore not surprising to those in the field that roughly one in fifteen high school seniors today is a current daily, or near-daily, marijuana user.

Synthetic marijuana (aka Spice and K-2) is a herbal drug mixture that usually contains "designer" chemicals that fall into the cannabinoid family. According to Johnston et al. (2014), until March of 2011 these drugs were not scheduled by the Drug Enforcement Administration (DEA), so they were readily and legally available on the Internet and in head shops, gas stations, and the like. The DEA did recognize them beginning March 1, 2011, making the possession and sale of their most commonly used ingredients no longer legal. However, despite this tactic by the DEA, common manufacturers of the synthetic drug consistently switch out the active ingredients with new unbanned materials, as quickly as the old ones are made illegal. This leads to increasingly dangerous and harmful synthetic substances on the open market. MTF added this to its 2011 survey, asking twelfth graders about use in the prior twelve months, and 11.4 percent indicated use in the prior twelve months. Despite the policy intervention of the DEA making it illegal, use among twelfth graders remained unchanged in 2012 at 11.3 percent, which suggests either that compliance with the new scheduling has been limited or that those who produce these products have succeeded in continuing to change their chemical formulas to avoid using the DEA recognized and scheduled chemicals. Perhaps the scariest statistic is this: in 2012, MTF researchers asked eighth and tenth graders about their use of synthetic marijuana, and their annual prevalence rates were 4.4 percent and 8.8 percent, respectively.

Recently, "synthetics," as the youth call them, have become more available in communities and online. "Bath salts" (named this because they were sold over the counter as safe products like bath salts despite the fact that they contain strong and dangerous stimulants) have received media attention in the past few years; however, there has been very little scientific information about the prevalence of their use. MTF has found relatively low prevalence rates, but clinicians should be aware of the presence of these drugs because of their availability, popularity, and potential to prompt psychoses. The most common name is "Spice," referring to a wide variety of herbal mixtures that produce experiences similar to marijuana (cannabis) and that are marketed as "safe," legal alternatives to that drug. Sold under many names, including K2, Fake Bake, Mojo, Scooby Snax, Yucatan Fire, Skunk, Moon Rocks, and others—and labeled "not for human consumption"—these products contain dried, shredded plant material and chemical additives that are responsible for their psychoactive (mind-altering) effects. The combination of dangerous chemicals is poured on leaves or even on tea bags and smoked to get a high. According to the National Institute of Health, this is a serious and emerging trend (http://www.drug abuse.gov/drugs-abuse/emerging-trends); in one recent month in the media, the crises of synthetic marijuana were ubiquitous: more than 120 emergency-room visits in New York City in one week; nearly 100 people sent to the hospital in Alabama; more than 30 hospitalizations in New Jersey; and over 100 overdose cases in Lincoln, Nebraska (Collins, 2015). Although marijuana is detected in a urine test, Spice is not, which is why some kids choose it—and it has resulted in numerous deaths due to cardiac arrest. Police, policy makers, and parents cannot keep up with its availability: When one chemical composition is outlawed, those who manufacture it just change the ingredients so it is no longer illegal.

MTF (2014) found that youth continue to misuse the following drugs at consistent levels: cocaine powder, crack, methamphetamine, crystal methamphetamine, Rohypnol, GHB, Ketamine, steroids, over-the-counter cough and cold medicines taken to get high, sedatives, and any prescription drug taken without medical supervision. MTF (2014) highlights the fact that prescription drugs, especially amphetamines (e.g., Adderall), anxiolytics (e.g., Xanax), and narcotic pain medications (e.g., Oxycontin, Vicodin, and Codeine), some of which are legitimately prescribed, some non-prescribed, and some overprescribed, now make up a larger part of the overall U.S. drug problem than was true ten to fifteen years ago, in part because use increased for many prescription drugs over that period, and in part because use of a number of street drugs has declined substantially since the mid-1990s. Perhaps the greatest cause of the high levels of misuse of prescriptions in this population is that youth perceive prescription drugs as low-risk. Doctors prescribe such drugs for legitimate reasons and, therefore, youth tend to underestimate the drugs' dangers and overestimate the safety of using them.

Also, the fact that drug companies now advertise increases kids' exposure to prescription drugs and decreases stigma about their use. Americans tend to be drug seeking in general. The now well established "direct to consumer" (DTC) advertising of medications advocates clear messages: "fix your problem quick," "get out of pain immediately," "demand a pill," and "be your own doctor." There is a literature on the impact of subliminal messages in cigarette and alcohol advertising, especially for teenagers. These messages—"use this pill to be sexy," "use this pill to be happy," and most recently, "use this pill to be smart and competitive" may perpetuate the societal drug epidemic. What do you think?

Take the instance of "study drugs." One drug class that showed sign of increasing use (by twelfth graders) in MTF (2014) was Adderall. The misuse (use outside of medical supervision) of Adderall may still be rising at grade 12—possibly because it is being used to enhance academic performance. These pills are becoming increasingly problematic on college campuses, and many students do not realize the risks (e.g., overdose, heart attacks, legal interventions, etc.). In addition, the research shows that, although study drugs may increase one's focus the first time someone uses them, or even several times depending upon body chemistry, there is a definite and measurable pattern of diminishing returns (i.e., the longer one uses the drug, the less effective it is in helping the person focus and retain information) and ultimately, those who utilize study drugs have lower GPAs than those who never use them (Arria et al., 2013).

An encouraging bit of news from the recent Monitoring the Future Study (2012) is that the percentage using any illicit drug other than marijuana has been declining gradually since about 2001. Ecstasy, Salvia, heroin used without a needle, inhalants, tranquilizers, Vicodin, and Oxycontin showed statistically significant declines in 2012. Therefore, those who work as adolescent substance misuse preventionists and interventionists have reason to celebrate.

Until recently, research on adolescent development focused primarily on physiological and behavioral transitions, such as the onset of puberty and associated behavioral increases in sensation seeking and risk taking, peer relationships, and a need to achieve parental independence (Spear, 2000). It wasn't until the mid-1990s that researchers began to recognize that adolescence is a period of rapid brain growth and neural remodeling, particularly in the prefrontal cortex (PFC), an area responsible for executive functions such as cognitive flexibility, self-regulation, and the evaluation of risk and reward. Because of the dramatic changes in brain, behavioral, and pubertal maturation, adolescence becomes a vulnerable time with regard to psychiatric disorders that begin to emerge, including depression, schizophrenia, violence, delinquency, and alcohol and substance misuse (Steinberg, 2005).

PHYSIOLOGY AND MECHANISMS OF SUBSTANCE MISUSE

It was once believed that a black and white dichotomy existed: Either you were an addict or you were not. However, research has made clear that there are many varied types and scenarios with regard to substance use, misuse, and dependence. In the upcoming re-release of the *Diagnostic and Statistical Manual of Mental Disorders* (DSM 5), this is depicted as a substance use disorder continuum. With assessment, various identifying predictors and manifestation of symptoms place an individual somewhere along the continuum, from misuse to dependency to the most elevated chronic level of the disease, addiction.

Addictions counselors used to joke, "Like being pregnant, either you are or you ain't." It is true that some people are "chemically predisposed" for alcoholism and/or addiction, and others are not. However, it is also clear that one can use enough substance or alcohol to shift brain chemistry and disrupt pleasure pathways permanently, leading to addictive use of substances. Although the term is widely used, "addiction" is an imprecise term; scientists in the field of substance misuse use "dependence" to indicate the disease. The switch from addiction as a

11

substance "abuse" model of diagnosis to a chronic continuum shows people's more enlightened understanding. Researchers are now gaining insight into the very nature and multi-level dynamics of substance use disorders and other compulsive disorders.

Also, it is important to remember that most people misunderstand "alcoholism," thinking of it as weakness of will or a moral failing when it is, in fact, dependence on alcohol. The most salient characteristic of dependence is simply the inability to stop once started. This is confusing, because people assume that with powerful and sufficient consequences, anyone can choose to stop, but this is where the "ism" comes in. Those who have the disease of alcoholism (sometimes cleverly referred to as dis-ease), instead of being able to take it or leave it, in actuality can't take it and can't leave it. They are compelled to drink by a neurologically centered compulsion. It is recommended that clinicians and professionals use proper terminology in all technical and clinical situations so as not to perpetuate the misconceptions and myths associated with the field (Erickson, 2007).

• •

- Misuse is intentional, voluntary.
- Dependence is pathological, an "impaired control over drug use."
- Dependence is an "I can't stop without help" disease.

• •

As highlighted by pharmacist, researcher, and addictionologist Carlton Erickson, withdrawal, blackouts, dose, and amount are not, in and of themselves, diagnostic of dependence (Erickson, 2007). In fact, mental health diagnosis is still considered as much an art as it is a science. That is to say it is based on subjective "criteria" (i.e., verbal and written assessment of data). Scientists are researching the possibilities of biomarkers for dependence, but at present, drug screens, urine tests, and blood markers give clues in the big picture but are not diagnostic. However, it is clear that neuroscience is likely going to make powerful contributions to the future of diagnosing use, misuse, and dependence via brain scans and genetic testing.

Although it may appear that dependence is a linear process in which people evolve from misuse to dependence, it is clear, anecdotally, that some people experience becoming "instantly dependent." One cannot attend a number of twelve-step meetings without hearing stories of "magical" first experiences with alcohol or other substances in which individuals experienced a sensation of a "fix"—a literal feeling of an internal adjustment from being broken to being aligned. This is ironic in the sense that the "fix" is fleeting and the person then "chases that high," in the words of Alcoholics Anonymous, "into the gates of insanity or death" (*Big Book* of Alcoholics Anonymous, p. 30). Such individuals may consider themselves predisposed to alcoholism or dependence due to genetics, a factor which accounts for approximately 60 percent of the variance (Schuckit, 1999) with regard to who can stop using and who cannot stop without help. Also the National Institute of Alcohol Abuse and Alcoholism (NIAAA) epidemiology studies show that although some people become dependent during the first year of use, other misusers never become dependent. Carlton Erickson is fond of joking, "They just don't have what it takes."

It is erroneous to assume all drugs have the same level of addictiveness, or ability to elicit addiction. The lifetime "estimated prevalence of dependence" of nicotine is 32 percent, heroin is 23 percent, "sedatives" 9 percent, cocaine 17 percent, psychedelics 5 percent, alcohol 15 percent, inhalants 4 percent, and stimulants 11 percent (Anthony, Warner, & Kessler, 1994). On the other hand, it is also a mistake to assume that non-synthetic drugs like marijuana are not addictive; cannabis has an estimated prevalence of dependence of 9 percent (Erickson, 2007)

• •

- Dependence occurs because of neurochemical disregulations of the mesolimbic dopamine system (MDS) (also known as the Medial Forebrain Bundle (MFB), reward pathway, or pleasure pathway).
- Drugs are associated with specific neurotransmitters. Genetics affect how the brain regulates (or disregulates) the problematic pathways.
- The drugs essentially connect to the problematic neurotransmitter system, which is why many people have a sensation of feeling better (self-medicating) when they use, particularly their "drugs of choice."
- The key fact is that some people's craving is genuinely physical, not psychological.

• •

In defining addiction, behavioral or process disorders, such as gambling, "sex addiction," compulsive spending, gaming, and eating disorders, are actually impulse control disorders. They most resemble obsessive-compulsive disorders, and it is important to separate them from chemical dependence (Erickson, 2007). When people, especially professionals, lump all compulsive behaviors into the category of addiction, they lose sight of the way the brain disease is related to chemical pathway deregulation. This is not only a disservice to the field, but a dangerous and erroneous message to send to helping professionals.

Contrary to the aforementioned mistaken public belief, the problem is not one of will power. This is true for two reasons: (1) The main problem with dependence lies in the subconscious brain processes. (2) Problems with the frontal cortex produce a pathological impairment of decision-making (Erickson, 2007). It is critical that clinicians recognize that dependence is not primarily under conscious control. This can help reduce stigma and judgment of the person misusing or dependent on substances.

BIO-PSYCHO-SOCIAL-SPIRITUAL MODEL

The bio-psycho-social-spiritual model is a holistic conceptualization of the important aspects of addiction assessment and intervention (Flanzer, Gorman, & Spence, 2001). It serves as a valuable frame for this discussion of adolescent addictions. After providing a little more detail regarding the biological aspects (i.e., addiction as a brain disease), this chapter examines the psychological, social, and spiritual aspects of substance misuse and dependence. Figure 1.1 highlights the issues that one must understand and explore in order to have an accurate picture of an adolescent's relationship with substances.

This bio-psycho-social-spiritual paradigm will be used throughout this book to help maintain a holistic perspective, always remembering that people are complex due to their biochemistry, their intrapersonal feelings/thoughts (which of course influence behaviors), their interpersonal relationships, and their spiritual existence in the world (i.e., how they make meaning out of their existence). Although the new diagnostic criteria for substance use disorders contain a continuum with varying levels of severity of misuse, this book focuses on the far end of the spectrum concerned with clinical addiction. Note, however, that the framework of intervention, prevention, and treatment detailed in

Figure 1.1: Bio-Psycho-Social-Spiritual Model

BIO	PSYCHO	SOCIAL	SPIRTUAL
• Genetics	• Low self	• "Love you, go	• Loss in belief
• Cravings	esteem	away"	in good things
• Blackouts	• Grandiosity	• Isolation	• Lack of sense
• Tolerance	• Warped sense	(even in gp.)	of meaning
• Body harm	of self/others	• Fear of being	• Fear and lack
• Accidents	• Faulty social	found out	of trust,
• Dual Dx	interpretation	• Lack of trust	existentially
• Process Dis.	• Sub. Priority	• Seeking like	• Demoraliza-
• Anticipatory	• Justifying &	peers	tion
highs	Rationalizing	• Social	• "Spiritual
• Retention of	• Manipulate/lie	consequence	Malady"
memory of the	• Loneliness	(work, family,	• Question or
high	• Self-loathing	legal, school)	reject religion

this book can and should be used to assist in the betterment of all instances of substance use disorder. Preventing escalation of a substance use disorder is paramount to long-lasting wellness of all individuals, if it is possible to do so. It should also be noted that this book is written from a social worker's perspective—that is, there are three underlying tenets that undergird the entire work:

1. All individuals have strengths, value, and the capacity for growth and change; it naturally follows that they should be engaged with dignity, curiosity, and hope.
2. Human beings are unique and complex parts of systems and do not act the way they do in vacuums. This implies both that therapeutic alliances should be judgment-free and that consideration of the client's system is critical.

3. It is the responsibility of helping professionals to support, advocate, and facilitate the emergence of an individual's authentic self, acknowledging and whenever possible celebrating their unique character, culture, talents, abilities, and vulnerabilities.

This book begins with explanations of the relationship between adolescent substance use and the brain. Once one understands the power of the brain chemistry piece, it is easier to grasp the social and psychological aspects of choices that young people make regarding drugs and alcohol. Although some may bristle at the addition of the spiritual piece in the model, rest assured that it is included due to the scientific evidence that this area of research is instrumental in explanations of adolescent drug- and alcohol-related behaviors as well as risks, resilience, and recovery mechanisms. This research began over a decade ago and has now been fully incorporated into the profession. It should be noted that, in the context of this work, spirituality and religion are not synonymous and should not be used interchangeably. It is entirely possible for spirituality to exist for religious believers, agnostics, and atheists concurrently.

The book will refer back to this framework as it traverses prevention, screening, intervention, and policy issues, keeping the holistic picture of the adolescent and his/her system in mind throughout. This will be one of your challenges, just as it is the challenge of all of those who work in the field of substances. It will serve you well to concern yourself with the individual, his/her family, neighborhood, state, region, country and world (e.g., micro, meso, and macro realms of existence.) Think of the interplay of person and community as well as community and agency. And never underestimate the complexity and beauty of individuals—their minds, bodies, and spirits all capable of growth and healing.

KEY TERMS

MTF (Monitoring the Future Study)

Binge drinking

Synthetics

Study drugs

Diminishing returns

Addiction

Dependence

Alcoholism

Compulsion

Withdrawal

Blackouts

Fix

Craving

Self-medicating

Mesolimbic dopamine system (MDS)

Reward pathway/pleasure pathway

Neurotransmitters

Behavioral or process disorders

Impulse control disorders

Stigma

DISCUSSION QUESTIONS

1. List as many consequences of the following substances as you can:

   a. Tobacco use

   b. Underage alcohol consumption

   c. Prescription drug misuse

   d. Illicit drug use and misuse

2. List some of the primary findings of the Monitoring the Future Study (MTF). In addition to the notes in this chapter, go to http://www.drug abuse.gov/related-topics/trends-statistics/monitoring-future/ monitoring-future-survey-overview-findings-2014 and gather additional information to flesh out this chapter's overview. Pay particular attention to the charts and graphs. Then think critically and, in discussion, make sense of the findings from biological, psycho-social, political, and spiritual perspectives.

3. An entire text could be written about epidemiology (i.e., patterns, causes, and effects of health and disease conditions in defined populations) and youth substance use/misuse. What have you learned in

this chapter about the epidemiology of adolescent drug and alcohol misuse?

4. What societal messages contribute to youth substance use and misuse, and how do these influences impact young people?

5. Are all substances equally addiction-prompting? Is marijuana potentially dependence-forming? How it that different from heroin's addictiveness?

6. Is gambling, overeating, or sex an addiction like substance dependence? Why or why not?

REFERENCES

Anthony, J. C., Warner, L. A., & Kessler, R. C. (1994). Comparative epidemiology of dependence on tobacco, alcohol, controlled substances, and inhalants: Basic findings from the National Comorbidity Survey. *Experimental and Clinical Psychopharmacology, 2*(3), 244–268.

Arain, M., Haque, M., Johal, L., Mathur, P., Nel, W., Rais, A., Sandhu, R., & Sharma, S. (2013). Maturation of the adolescent brain. *Neuropsychiatric Disease and Treatment. 9*, 449–461.

Arria, A. M., Wilcox, H. C., Caldeira, K. M., Vincent, K. B., Garnier-Dykstra, L. M., & O'Grady, K. E. (2013). Dispelling the myth of "smart drugs": Cannabis and alcohol use problems predict nonmedical use of prescription stimulants for studying. *Addictive Behaviors, 38* (3), 1643–1650.

Bachman, J. G., O'Malley, P. M., Schulenberg, J. E., Johnston, L. D., Bryant, A. L., & Merline, A. G. (2002). *The decline of substance use in young adulthood: Changes in social activities, roles, and beliefs.* Mawah, NJ: Lawrence Erlbaum Associates, Inc.

CASA (2011). *National survey of American attitudes on substance abuse XVI: Teens and parents.* New York, NY: National Center of Addiction and Substance Abuse at Columbia University.

Chen, K., & Kandel, D. B. (1995). The natural history of drug use from adolescence to mid-thirties in a general population sample. *Am. J. Public Health, 85*, 41–47.

Collins, D. (May 8, 2015). There's been a sudden, alarming spike in hospitalizations caused by synthetic marijuana. *Huffington Post Healthy Living,*

retrieved from http://www.huffingtonpost.com/2015/05/08/synthetic
-marijuana-hospitalizations_n_7241772.html

DiClemente, R. J., Hansen, B., & Ponton, L. E. (1996). *Handbook of adolescent health risk behavior*. New York, NY: Springer.

Donovan, J. E., Jessor, R., & Jessor, L. (1983). Problem drinking in adolescence and young adulthood: A follow-up study. *J. Stud. Alcohol, 44,* 109–137.

Erickson, C. K. (2007). *The science of addiction: From neurobiology to treatment.* New York, NY and London: W. W. Norton & Company.

Flanzer, J. E., Gorman, M., & Spence, R. T. (2001). Fear of Neuroscience. *Journal of Social Work Practice in the Addictions, 1*.3: 103–12.

Grant, B. F., Harford, T. C., & Grigson, M. B. (1988). Stability of alcohol consumption among youth: A national longitudinal study. *J. Stud. Alcohol, 49,* 253–260.

Johnston, L. D., O'Malley, P. M., Bachman, J. G., & Schulenberg, J. E. (2014). *Monitoring the Future national results on drug use: 2012 Overview, Key Findings on Adolescent Drug Use.* Ann Arbor: Institute for Social Research, The University of Michigan.

Li, T. K., Hewitt, B. G., & Grant, G. F. (2007). Is there a future for quantifying drinking in the diagnosis, treatment, and prevention of alcohol use disorders? *Alcohol. Clin. Exp. Res., 41,* 57–63.

McGinnis, J. M., & Foege, W. H. (1999). Mortality and morbidity attributable to use of addictive substances in the United States. *Proceedings of the Association of American Physicians, 111*(2), 109–18.

Nargiso, J. E., Friend, K., & Florin, P. (2013). Family and community context risk factors for alcohol use and alcohol use intentions in early adolescents. *Journal of Early Adolescence, 33,* 973–993.

National Center for Disease Prevention and Health Promotion. (2001). Tobacco information and prevention source (TIPS). (http://www.cdc.gov/tobacco/ research_data/health_consequences/mortali.htm)

Schuckit, M. A. (1999). New findings in the genetics of alcoholism. *JAMA, 281*(20), 1875–1876.

Schulenberg, J. E., Bryant, A. L., & O'Malley, P. M. (2004). Taking hold of some kind of life: How developmental tasks relate to trajectories of well-being during the transition to adulthood. *Development and Psychopathology, 16,* 1119–1140.

Spear, L. P. (2000). The adolescent brain and age-related behavioral manifestations. *Neuroscience Biobehavioral Review, 24(4),* 417–463.

Steinberg, L. (2005). Cognitive and affective development in adolescence. *Trends in Cognitive Science, 9,* 69–74.

Substance Abuse and Mental Health Services Administration (SAMHSA), Center for Behavioral Health Statistics and Quality. (2014). The NSDUH Report: Substance Use and Mental Health Estimates from the 2013 National Survey on Drug Use and Health: Overview of Findings. Rockville, MD.

Substance Abuse and Mental Health Services Administration (SAMHSA) (2002). Results from the 2002 National Survey on Drug Use and Health: national findings. Rockville, MD: Office of Applied Studies, NHSDA series H-22, DHHS publication no. SMA 03–3836.

Temple, M. T., & Fillmore, K. M. (1985–1986). The variability of drinking patterns and problems among young men age 16–31: A longitudinal study. *Int. J. Addict, 20,* 1595–1620.

Voss, W. D., Kaufman, E., O'Connor, S. S., Comtois, K. A., Conner, K. R., Ries, R. K. (2013). Preventing addiction related suicide: A pilot study. *Journal of Substance Abuse Treatment, 44*(5), 565–569.

Windle, M. (2000). Parental, sibling, and peer influences on adolescent substance use and alcohol problems. *Applied Developmental Science, 4*(2), 98–110.

Windle, M., Spear, L. P., Fuligni, A. J., Angold, A., Brown, J. D., Pine, D., & Dahl, R. E. (2008). Transitions into underage and problem drinking: Developmental processes and mechanisms between 10 and 15 years of age. *Pediatrics, 121,* S273-S289.

Witt, E. D. (2010). Research on alcohol and adolescent brain development: opportunities and future directions. *Alcohol, 44*(1), 119–124.

Chapter 2

Substance Misuse Implications for Children and Adolescents

DEVELOPMENTAL ISSUES

Adolescence is a tough time, no matter how you define it. Although some adolescents have a tougher time than others, there is no getting away from the fact that the main tasks of this developmental period are ones of self-discovery, differentiation from parents, and attempts to feel a part of something while trying desperately to feel unique and special. This is all done in the midst of developing brain chemistry, a growing body, new awareness of pheromones, puberty, and hormones. Some might call it "the perfect storm."

Research from the National Institute of Health's (NIH) National Institute on Drug Abuse (NIDA, 2003) has shown that key risk periods for substance misuse occur during such transitions as adolescence. A subset of youth demonstrates problem behaviors in early adolescence and these youth are at an especially high and generalized risk for developing adult psychopathology. Therefore, substance use assessment, prevention, and intervention are particularly critical for adolescents. In order to be comprehensive, the counseling approach should encompass the physical, mental, emotional, social, cultural, and cognitive-behavioral aspects of the adolescent.

Culture is complex and potentially curative (Santiago-Irizarry, 1996). To understand this definition of culture, one must imagine layers and layers of details creating the holographic human. You might describe culture by using the image of an overhead projector, on which you layer transparency after transparency until the full image is portrayed—family, region, religion, gender, sexual identity, personality, talents, appearance, life experiences, socio-economic status (SES); every aspect of human beings affects their culture. Consequently, it is important to gather as much information as possible before determining a plan for any individual. If the clinician is doing the screening and intake as well as the counseling, it is recommended that the adolescent be interviewed first. Then the parents should be interviewed with the client present. This helps to build trust that is critical in establishing rapport, otherwise known as the therapeutic alliance.

At the beginning of the screening process, it is important to spell out the policy of confidentiality and the limits or exceptions to it. Many late adolescent clients (and some of the younger ones) may arrive at the screening interview without their parents. Still, collateral data should be obtained if possible. Screening the whole family together provides important information, protects the counselor legally, and can be therapeutic if done with compassion, care, and consistency. It is important to assess techniques and directions on a case-by-case basis. For example, if the youth has been physically or sexually abused, and the clinician is aware of it, the parents (if they are the perpetrators) should not be interviewed in the standard fashion. Having the parents present may even put the child at risk. In other cases, as with runaway or homeless youth, identified parents are not always available. When counseling with an adolescent in the presence of his or her parents, clinicians should make it clear that whatever the client says in individual counseling will be held strictly confidential unless his or her security is at risk. During this same meeting, counselors should advise the parents, in front of the client, that the parents' verbalizations will be held confidential as well.

According to the National Institute of Health (2011), the development of children through adolescence (i.e., ages twelve through eighteen years old) is expected to include the following anticipated physical and mental milestones:

- Understand abstract ideas and develop their values and moral philosophies.
- Establish and maintain satisfying relationships by learning to share intimacy without feeling worried or inhibited.
- Move toward a more mature sense of themselves and their purpose.
- Question old values without losing their identity (this is often part of the process of individuating from their parents).

Physical development consists of the development of the body structure, including muscles, bones, and organ systems. Physical development is generally composed of sensory development, dealing with the organ systems underlying the senses and perception; motor development, dealing with the actions of the muscles; and the nervous system's coordination of both perception and movement. In adolescence, puberty marks drastic changes in the physical self and sexual awareness and related social imperatives.

Cognitive development is sometimes referred to as "intellectual" or "mental" development. Cognitive activities include thinking, perception, memory, reasoning, concept development, problem-solving ability, and abstract thinking. According to Blakemore and Choudhury (2006), most early adolescents still think predominantly in concrete terms as opposed to abstract thoughts. They relate information and experiences to what they currently know and have a hard time thinking about the future or about things they have never been exposed to. Their ability to think abstractly—to project into the future and to understand intangible concepts—develops as adolescence progresses. The fact that most early adolescents cannot think abstractly has important implications for program planning and necessitates different program approaches than would be created for older adolescents. For example, drug prevention programs that ask early adolescents to picture what future opportunities would be lost by using substances will not be very effective with young people (Blakemore & Choudhury, 2006). For many high school aged youth, for example, when asked about the future, their first thought might be after school or the weekend, rather than a five- or ten-year plan.

Social development includes the child's interactions with other people and the child's involvement in social groups (peer groups). The earliest social task is attachment and the presence or absence of effective parental attachment is a strong predictor of the health and resilience of the adolescent (Taylor-Seehafer, Jacobvitz, & Holleran Steiker, 2008). The development of relationships with adults and peers, the assumption of a moral system, and eventually assuming a productive role in society are all social tasks.

Emotional development includes the development of personal traits and characteristics, including a personal identity, self-esteem, the ability to enter into reciprocal emotional relationships, and mood and affect (feelings and emotions) that are appropriate for one's age and for the situation. Although each of these four developmental domains can be examined individually, it is misleading to suggest that development occurs separately in each of the four domains. Development in any domain affects, and is affected by, development in all of the other domains; that is to say they occur concurrently. The primary developmental milestones of adolescence include: puberty (drastic maturing in physical and sexual self), a shift from parents to peer groups as the primary influence, and growing independence in thoughts and actions.

Even though middle stage adolescents typically have developed intellectually to a degree comparable to an adult, their erroneous beliefs and perceptions such as thinking that they are immortal (or "bulletproof" as some have called it) often contributes to high-risk behaviors including the following: experimenting with drugs, breaking laws, and engaging in frivolous or even dangerous sexual encounters (e.g., without protection from STDs or pregnancy) (Blakemore & Choudhury, 2006). These high-risk behaviors are often synonymous with sensation seeking that is seen in later adolescence and into emerging adulthood. During these times, life events such as family problems of divorce, separation, and drug use can further affect the experiences of the adolescent.

The sudden and rapid physical, mental, cognitive, and emotional changes that adolescents go through make them very self-conscious, sensitive, and worried about their changes. They may make painful comparisons about themselves with their peers. Individuation (or identity separation, making themselves distinct from parents), in some families, may manifest in adolescent rebellion, which may lead to conflict as the parents try to keep control. As adolescents pull away from their parents in a search for their own identity, they shift to their peer group as their locus of control. Their peer group may become a safe haven, in which the adolescent can test new ideas. Or their peer group (depending upon the level of risk-based activities of the group) can be a

Figure 2.1: Peers

dangerous place disguised as a sanctuary. As the youth moves into mid-adolescence, the peer group expands to include romantic friendships. In mid- to late adolescence, young people often feel the need to establish their sexual identity by dating and experimenting sexually. Young people who do not have the opportunity to break away from their parents or experience intimacy with their peers may have more difficulty with relationships when they are adults. On the other hand, youth who experiment sexually in the midst of drug and alcohol use may find themselves with consequences that they did not intend or anticipate. Pregnancy, STDs, sexual abuse—all of these risks are more prevalent when alcohol and drugs are in the picture (Eaton et al., 2011).

Adolescents who are moving into higher levels of abstract thinking also may experience some altered and inaccurate senses of self. If clinicians know of these cognitive misperceptions, they can more effectively and sensitively help adolescents navigate and alter what have been referred to as myths of adolescence (NIH, 2011):

27

- The spotlight. This erroneous perception is that they are "on stage" and other people's attention is constantly centered on their appearance or actions. This normal self-centeredness may appear (especially to adults) to border on paranoia, self-love (narcissism), or even hysteria.

- Not me! This erroneous perception is the idea that "it will never happen to me, only the other person." "It" may represent becoming pregnant or catching a sexually-transmitted disease after having unprotected sex, causing a car crash while driving under the influence of alcohol or drugs, or any of the many other negative effects of risk-taking behaviors.

Ideally, adolescents should become more and more independent, developing good decision-making skills, and learning from scrapes along the way. Their inherent strong need for peer approval may entice them to try dangerous feats or take part in risk-taking behaviors. In addition, adolescents who tend more towards sensation seeking, insecurity, depression, or biochemical predisposition to addiction may have much more pressure towards risk behaviors than seeking approval of their peers.

In order to recognize warning signs early, there is a recent trend toward integrating alcohol and drug screening and education in primary care settings. A federally funded screening program, including brief interventions and referral to treatment (SBIRT), was initiated by the Substance Abuse and Mental Health Services Administration (SAMHSA) in a wide variety of medical settings. SBIRT (which stands for Screening, Brief Intervention, and Referral to Treatment) is defined as "a comprehensive and integrated approach to the delivery of early intervention and treatment services through universal screening for persons with substance use disorders and those at risk" (Babor et al., 2007: p. 7). The limited evidence from SBIRT outcome research with adolescents suggests that brief interventions may be effective with youth, but a number of gaps in the literature were identified (Mitchell, Gryczynski, O'Grady, & Schwartz, 2013). This evidence-based method has been used in emergency rooms, but findings are still not definitive as to whether the brief intervention techniques using motivational interviewing were effective with young adults. In fact, according to Mitchell and others (2013), there have been six large random-assignment studies of adolescent patients (age range twelve to twenty-one) in urban U.S. emergency departments (EDs). None of these found significant group differences in reducing drinking or binge drinking at any of their follow-up interviews at three, six, or twelve months for groups assigned to MI-based brief interventions compared to assessment only (Bernstein et al., 2010; Maio et al., 2005; Spirito et al., 2011; & Walton et al., 2010).

• •

Adolescent SBIRT

Screening, Brief Intervention, & Referral to Treatment

The Council on Social Work Education (CSWE) is presently partnering with the Hilton Adolescent SBIRT Project and Learning Collaborative, creating resources and modules to educate practitioners in the most effective ways to utilize SBIRT techniques with adolescents. To learn more and see some of the role plays, case studies, tools, simulations, and other resources, see http://www.sbirteducation.com/

• •

There were fewer studies conducted in primary care clinics, schools, and other community settings, and none addressed referral to treatment. Thus, there is a need for additional research to fill these gaps in the evidence base. It is theoretically sound that pediatricians provide early, relationship-based assessment for substances along with other health-oriented areas including healthy sexual behavior choices (e.g., teen pregnancy prevention, HPV vaccines, etc.). However, in the *Annals of Internal Medicine*, Patnode and others (2014) reviewed all recent research and found that the body of evidence was small and included mostly adolescents without substance use problems. They conclude that "evidence is inadequate on the benefits of primary care–relevant behavioral interventions in reducing self-reported illicit and pharmaceutical drug use among adolescents" (p. 612). However, it is clear that more research is needed in this area.

As will be fleshed out later in this text, when evidence-based prevention techniques are discussed, some adolescents are naturally more resilient than others and there are things that can be done to bolster the protective factors and reduce risk among adolescents who do not naturally embody such instincts. However, all young people have powerful vulnerabilities whether they are explicit and evident or disguised. It is important that clinicians not think of the young person's responses as "resistance" but instead as protective mechanisms that can be identified, embraced, and shifted in the midst of trusting therapeutic connections.

CULTURAL ISSUES

Maladaptive relationships with substances start well before substance experimentation. Young children witness parents' use or nonuse of substances, attitudes towards substances, reasons and justifications, consistency or inconsistencies. Cultural and social influences can be viewed through two distinct lenses:

1. the culture of the individual
2. the culture of substance(s)

• •

The Language of Drugs

Try these phrases and see if you can translate:

1. I am so into Batman right now.
2. Who wants to go on a Robotrip?
3. Seriously cafeteria-style!
4. I never realized skiing could be so much fun!
5. She so tripped with a bad rib.

For those less familiar with the language of drugs on campus, here are your simplified translations:

1. Some Ecstasy comes in tablets with the bat symbol on the tablet, and this phrase refers to being interested in this version of the drug.
2. Robotripping is a slang term for using cough medicine containing dextromethorphan to get "high" or experience the hallucinogenic effects that are associated with higher dose dmx use.
3. Cafeteria-style refers to having a wide variety of drugs (usually in pill form) to choose from. Just pick what you want and use it. Often associated with "pharming" or improper use/ abuse of prescriptive drugs.
4. Skiing is a slang term for using cocaine. This term is widely used in online communities to refer to cocaine use so as not to openly admit to using an illegal drug.
5. Rib is a slang term for Rohypnol, a hypnotic sedative that is related to Valium and not legal in the United States.

I Said No to Drugs . . . But the Drugs Wouldn't Listen!, Michael P. McNeil, Columbia University (2008: 93)

• •

Youth grow up with many complex messages. In a micro realm, they are impressed by parents, family, siblings, peers, friends' parents, friends' siblings, other relatives, neighbors, and other local entities. On a meso level, they are impacted by teachers, school administrators, clergy, law enforcers, health professionals, local businesses, local policies, mores, and politics. On a macro level, they are influenced by societal norms and media, as well as U.S. and global political, legal, and policy issues.

But it is also critical to recognize that there is a culture to the world of substance use and misuse as well. It has its own mores, traditions, even language. It often has a powerful allure for youth who are hungry for a sense of individuation from parents, a sense of rebellion, a sense of creative self.

● ●

Celebrity Deaths Due to Drugs/Alcohol

- Whitney Houston
- Amy Winehouse
- Michael Jackson
- Heath Ledger
- Mitch Hedberg

● ●

Youth are deeply susceptible to cues and influences in "pop culture" that they deem as "cool" (note: this is still a term that is considered timely; however, the more recent terms, which adolescents use more readily are "sweet," "rad," and "dope"). Many "styles" have grown from related drug culture practices. For example, baggy pants originated from a need for camouflage for drugs and bottles in big pockets. Another example is a style known as "heroin chic," which emerged in the 1990s in the American high fashion scene. Heroin chic was characterized by dark heavy circles underneath the eyes, pale skin, and a fragile figure. This "look" was coupled with high priced clothing lines, and the fashion industry glamorized the drug related aesthetics. This text will uncover many layers of culture as it illuminates the complexities of adolescent addiction.

RESEARCH-SUPPORTED RISK FACTORS

Age of Onset

"Childhood drug use"—this term shocks many who hear it. Trends have shown earlier and earlier experimentation and use of substances as norms in our society (Swendsen et al., 2012). According to Parents' Resource Institute for Drug Education (PRIDE, 2003), it is not uncommon for elementary school children to experiment with various substances. The PRIDE survey analyzing data collected from 72,025 fourth through sixth grade students reported that 2.7 percent of fourth graders, 4.4 percent of fifth graders, and 5.6 percent of sixth graders smoked cigarettes during the past year. The proportion of the elementary school students who drank beer or wine coolers in the previous year ranges from 6.3 (beer consumption among fourth graders) to 11.2 percent (wine cooler consumption among sixth graders). Substance use by elementary school children is not limited to tobacco or alcohol beverages. Three percent of fourth graders, 3.3 percent of fifth graders, and 3.9 percent of sixth graders reported inhalant use in the prior year. The percentages of the students using marijuana in the past year ranges from 0.7 percent for fourth graders to 1.8 percent for sixth graders.

Early age of onset is associated with higher dependence liability. Most studies suggest the greatest risk lies with youth who start before age fourteen. Also, the age of alcohol and cannabis use onset mediates the association of risk in childhood and development of alcohol and cannabis disorders (Kirisci et al., 2013). In addition, early alcohol use or other substance use may have grave and potentially long-lasting consequences during this developmental period. Drinking alcohol in adolescence often has profound effects on brain structure, function, and neurocognition (Bava & Tapert, 2010). Heavy drinking has been shown to affect the neuropsychological performance (e.g., memory functions) of young people and may impair the growth and integrity of certain brain structures. Furthermore, alcohol consumption during adolescence may alter measures of brain functioning, such as blood flow in certain brain regions and electrical brain activities. Not all adolescents and young adults are equally sensitive to the effects of alcohol consumption, however. Moderating factors—such as family history of alcohol and other drug use disorders, gender, age at onset of first use, drinking patterns, use of other drugs, and co-occurring psychiatric disorders—may influence the extent to which alcohol consumption interferes with an adolescent's normal brain development and functioning.

Early onset of alcohol or other drug use is one of the strongest predictors of later alcohol dependence (Grant, 1998). There is substantial evidence that drug problems surface more quickly when use starts before adulthood, even when length or duration biases are taken into account (Chen, O'Brien, & Anthony, 2005). Some observers even express a view that preventing or delaying onset of drug use (until adulthood) might be sufficient to prevent occurrence of drug dependence syndromes. King & Chassin (2007) take a more sobering perspective; their evidence supports the idea that early-onset alcohol use is simply a marker and not a cause of later alcohol problems. Animal research provides the strongest evidence for causation because the age of exposure can be randomly assigned; in these studies, of course, the external validity is harder to establish (Spear, 2000).

In terms of human data, some people have tried to use covariates to test whether the effect is causal or just a marker (King &

Chassin, 2007). Some have used genetically informed designs (Kendler & Prescott, 2006; McGue & Irons, 2013). Matt McGue started his groundbreaking longitudinal Twin Studies in the 1990s. His research indicated that genetic factors wielded a substantial influence on alcoholism risk, more in males than females. His work has also demonstrated that the age at which an individual first experiments with alcohol is predictive of a wide range of adult behavioral problems, including alcoholism, drug misuse, academic underachievement, and antisocial personality disorder. His work showed that the age of one's first drink is familial and, at least in males, heritable. The implication is that an early age of first drink is an indicator of vulnerability to disinhibitory behavior and psychopathology (McGue & Irons, 2013).

After propensity-score matching, early-exposed adolescents remained at an increased risk for a number of poor outcomes; approximately 50 percent of adolescents exposed to substances prior to age fifteen had no conduct-problem history, but were at heightened risk for adult substance dependence, herpes infection, early pregnancy, and crime (Odgers et al., 2008). Ultimately, the research points towards the need for efforts to reduce or delay early substance exposure in order to prevent a wide range of adult health problems. The experts note that this should not be restricted to adolescents who are already at risk (Odgers et al., 2008).

Alcohol and drug use tends to begin in mid-to-late adolescence, though it is greater among individuals who experience early puberty (O'Connell, Boat, & Warner, 2009). The earlier the age at which people start drinking, the greater the risk that they will develop alcohol-related problems later in life. A delay in drinking until twenty to twenty-one years old reduces the risk of developing alcohol-related problems (Chou & Pickering, 1992).

The Four "A's": Attitudes, Approval from Parents, Associations with Peers, and Access

The majority of alcohol consumed by youth is obtained through social sources, such as parents and friends, at underage parties and at home (Birckmayer, Holder, Yacoubian, & Friend, 2004). Availability of alcohol or illicit drugs leads to increased use (Treno, Grube, and Martin, 2003). In addition, low perception of harm towards alcohol and drug use is a risk factor for use (Henry & Slater, 2005). Individuals with attitudes or values favorable to alcohol or drugs are more likely to initiate substance use (Hawkins, Catalano, & Miller, 1992).

It is clear that a family history of alcoholism/addiction is a significant risk factor for the development of adolescent alcohol use disorders (Warner & White, 2003). Although the issue of genetics has already been discussed, it is important to also note the "nurture" piece of the nature-nurture argument. Parent or older sibling drug use (or perception of use) has a powerful impact on adolescents as well as biological factors. Familial alcohol-using behaviors are strong predictors of adolescent alcohol use (Birckmayer et al., 2004). Strong parent and adolescent relationships and family cohesion are undoubtedly protective; adolescents who have a close relationship with their parents are less likely to become alcohol involved (Birckmayer et al., 2004).

Approval from parents is one of the most salient factors in whether a child experiences a substance use disorder. Parental involvement and connections with youth are some of the most tangible and strongly documented risk or protective factors, depending upon the presence or absence of a caring adult relationship in the adolescent's life. Unconditional love and acceptance is a powerful factor; reported maternal care perception has been shown to be significantly lower among alcohol users and those who use multiple drugs (Gerra et al., 2004). Parental approval of substances, on the other hand, is a different story. Youth perception that parents approve of their alcohol or drug use can make or break their decisions about drugs and alcohol use. One of the most consistent risk factors for adolescent drinking is perceived parental approval (Donovan, 2004). Parents often err in this area when raising adolescents. Under the premise that they will model temperance, they unintentionally model approval of drinking or drugging by virtue of their own choices. Whereas negative messages and strict rule-based messaging tend to be associated with lower levels of alcohol use among adolescents, permissive parental messages (and even some harm reduction rule-based messages such as, "If you get drunk, get a ride home or sleep over your friend's house; you can drink, but you must do so at our home while I am here") have been shown to be associated with more frequent alcohol consumption (Reimuller, Hussong, & Emmit, 2011). Adolescents who report low parental monitoring are significantly more likely to use a variety of substances (Shillington et al., 2005). Positive parental style and close monitoring by parents are proven protective factors for adolescents' use of alcohol and other drugs (Ennett, Tobler, Ringwalt, & Flewelling, 1994; Reimuller et al., 2011).

Children and adolescents watch their parents carefully. They notice if their parents drink to unwind after a work day, take pills to get started in the morning, believe in avoiding pain at all costs, or drink to celebrate happy events. These associations cannot be minimized. It is easy to blame peers for youth initiation to drug and alcohol use, but interestingly, a 2003 study found that alcohol initiation most often occurred during family gatherings (Warner & White, 2003).

According to the Institute of Medicine's Committee on the Prevention of Mental Disorders and Substance Abuse among

Children, Youth and Young Adults, associating with drug- or alcohol-using peers, or being rejected by peers, can create problem behaviors and influence attitudes and norms related to substance use (O'Connell, Boat, & Warner, 2009). Exposure to peer problem behavior is correlated with increased alcohol and other substance use in the same month (Dishion & Skaggs, 2000). Those who drink in a social setting, or who have peers who do so, are more likely to misuse alcohol later in life (Beck & Treiman, 1996). Also, youth may choose peers, consciously or unconsciously, on the basis of who can give them easy access to the substances they want (or crave).

Whether young people date—and who they date—also can play a role in their choices and behaviors about drugs and alcohol. Although healthy social skills and interpersonal relationships have been shown to be protective in many ways (Hawkins, Catalano, & Miller, 1992), dating or having romantic relationships can be red flags for future problems in some cases as well. Pam Orpinas (2013) and her research group at the University of Georgia did a study to identify courses of dating from sixth to twelfth grade, and they identified four dating trajectories: low (16 percent), increasing (24 percent), high middle school (22 percent), and frequent (38 percent). The researchers found that students in the high and frequent dating groups had significantly worse study skills, were four times more likely to drop out of school, and reported twice as much alcohol, tobacco, and marijuana use than students in the low and increasing dating groups (Orpinas, Horne, Song, Reeves, & Hsieh, 2013). This study highlights the diversity of dating trajectories and some of the risks associated with early dating (Orpinas et al., 2013). Also, an association has been found between older boyfriends and depression and drug problems in adolescent girls (Haydon & Halpern, 2010).

Substance Misuse and School Drop-Out Prevention

Conversely, losing positive associations can also be problematic. School drop-out is also a strongly correlated risk of drug and alcohol use in adolescents. It should be noted that these issues are complex and it is difficult to discern what is causal in these scenarios. Dropping out tends to coincide with increased delinquency, teen pregnancy among females, and incidents of alcohol drug use and misuse. Marijuana initiation is positively related to dropping out of high school: The effect of marijuana initiation on the probability of high school dropout is stable, with marijuana users dropping out 2.3 times as often as non-users, regardless of frequency (Bray et al., 2000). Drug use, alcohol use, cigarette use, church going, and dropping out of high school all yielded strong evidence of peer-group effects at the school level for all activities (Gaviria & Raphael, 2001). The relationship between drug use and drop-out is reciprocal because, although the drug use is often concurrent or causal, it also is often perpetuated or worsened by the drop-out itself.

Engagement is key to both drop-out and drug prevention. A lack of engagement is a powerful risk factor: programs must resonate with youth and keep them interested and involved to mediate the risks of adolescence (Weissberg, Kumpfer, & Seligman, 2003; Holleran Steiker, 2008). Poor school achievement and low school bonding are salient pieces in the puzzle. Adolescents who have a low commitment to school or do poorly are more likely to become alcohol involved (Birckmayer et al., 2004). There are also many hidden relationships and complex connections between marijuana smoking and drop-out that are not immediately evident in research studies, such as subtle brain effects, attitude, behavior, activity interest, human connection, and relationship changes (McCaffrey, Pacula, Han, & Ellickson, 2010.)

It is important to consider "school climate" with regard to drug and alcohol cultures. This is a new and cutting edge area of study, and research supports the idea that the responsiveness of staff/faculty, policies, schools, and communities affects the substance culture (Clauss-Ehlers, Serpell, & Weist, 2013).

Other Risk and Protective Factors

Adolescents with early and persistent problem behaviors, risk-taking, and high sensation-seeking often demonstrate other risk factors in conjunction with the ones that have already been discussed. Other issues affecting risk include the following: temperament (e.g., novelty seeking, low harm avoidance); cognitive functioning (self-regulation, attention, reasoning, risk seeking); genetics; peer influence; the tendency to seek one's own kind; parental use; divorce/discord; parental nondirectiveness or inconsistency; lack of closeness or bonding with parents or mentors; and life events and/or trauma; (e.g., abuse or bereavement). In addition, early aggressiveness or antisocial behavior persisting into early adolescence predicts later adolescent aggressiveness and substance use disorders (Hawkins, Catalano, and Miller, 1992).

Research findings consistently support the fact that trauma affects substance choices. Childhood sexual abuse, suicidal behavior, post-traumatic stress disorder (PTSD), and substance use disorders are intimately linked with drug and alcohol decision making (Spooner, 1999). Adolescent substance use is concurrent with negative affect, behavioral lack of control, childhood victimization, sexual victimization, and, for females, adult boyfriends.

Resiliency and protective factors, also called mediators of risk (Glantz & Sloboda, 1999), include the following: intelligence, problem solving abilities, social skills, self-efficacy, supportive family/community, affect regulation, commitment/bonds at school, and religious affiliation/activity. It should be noted that self-efficacy (defined as "knowing one can do what one sets out to do") is more useful than self-esteem, which is defined as "how one feels about oneself."

• •

Warning Signs

- family substance misuse
- truancy or sudden grade drop
- change in peer group
- quitting important activities
- legal difficulties
- drug-related paraphernalia
- unknown source of income
- physical changes
- "hanging out" in strange places
- depression/suicidality (persons addicted to alcohol and drugs are at five to ten times higher risk for suicide than the general population
- no longer believing in good things like friendship, love, peace, and altruism

• •

Self- esteem is a particularly hard construct to define, measure, and alter, especially in adolescents with addictions, who have an unusual combination of grandiosity and low self worth. The kitschy metaphors used for this unusual style (which to some seems an oxymoron), are "king baby" and "egomaniacs with inferiority complexes." This is related to how teenagers tend to esteem themselves on the basis of whether they are "better or worse" than another in some way. This concrete assessment—

"smarter or dumber," "prettier or uglier," "more or less popular"—is clearly a black and white oversimplification, leaving teens feeling isolated, separate, and "terminally unique."

In addition, a number of powerful mediators have been determined to influence risk, including the contextual factors which follow: socio-economic status, settings (e.g., military, boarding school, fraternities/sororities, urban vs. rural, incarcerated youth, etc.), associations (e.g., religious activities, incarceration with delinquent youth), education, structural barriers, and poverty.

KEY TERMS

Adolescence	Sensation seeking
Physical and mental milestones	Moderating factors
Cognitive development	Risk and protective
Concrete vs. abstract thinking	factors
Attachment	Early onset
High-risk behaviors	The four "A's"
Individuation	Engagement
Locus of control	School climate

DISCUSSION QUESTIONS AND APPLICATION EXERCISE

1. What are the developmental tasks of the stage called adolescence?

2. Psychologist Erik Erikson (not to be confused with Pharmacist/Researcher/Scholar Carlton Erickson) believed that the psychosocial stage of adolescence occurs between twelve to eighteen years old, and that the primary task is moving from identity confusion to a solid sense of self. Some have argued that adolescence does not end where psychologist Erickson supposed it did. What is the evidence, in your experience as well as in the literature, for and against this definition?

3. What is the intersection of culture and adolescent development?

4. How does the particular stage of brain development affect adolescents and how does this overlap with substance use/misuse or other risky decisions?

5. List as many ways as you can think of that culture affects adolescent substance use decisions.

Application Exercise

Take the blank bio-psycho-social-spiritual table, below, and fill in where the risk factors and warning signs from this chapter belong. Do the same thing for protective factors (the opposite of the risk factors).

BIO	PSYCHO	SOCIAL	SPIRITUAL

REFERENCES

Babor, T. F., McRee, B. G., Kassebaum, P. A., Grimaldi, P. L., Ahmed, K., & Bray, J. (2007). Screening, brief intervention, and referral to treatment (SBIRT): Toward a public health approach to the management of substance abuse. *Substance Abuse, 28*(3), 7–30.

Bava, S., & Tapert, S. F. (2010). Adolescent brain development and the risk for alcohol and other drug problems. *Neuropsychol Rev., 4,* 398–413.

Beck, K., & Treiman, K. A. (1996). The relationship of social context of drinking, perceived social norms, and parental influence to various drinking patterns of adolescents. *Addictive Behaviors, 21*(5), 633–44.

Bernstein, J., Heeren, T., Edward, E., Dorfman, D., Bliss, C., Winter, M., & Bernstein, E. (2010) A brief motivational interview in a pediatric emergency department, plus 10-day telephone follow-up, increases attempts to quit drinking among youth and young adults who screen positive for prob-lematic drinking. *Academic Emergency Medicine, 17,* 890–902.

Birckmayer, J. D., Holder, H. D., Yacoubian, G. S., & Friend, K. B. (2004). A general causal model to guide alcohol, tobacco, and illicit drug prevention: Assessing the research evidence. *Journal of Drug Education, 34*(2), 121–153.

Blakemore, S. J., & Choudhury, S. (2006). Development of the adolescent brain: implications for executive function and social cognition. *Journal of Child Psychology and Psychiatry, 47*(3–4), 296–312.

Bray, J. W., Zarkin, G.A., Ringwalt, C., & Qi, J. (2000). The relationship between marijuana initiation and dropping out of high school. *Health Economics, 9,* 9–18.

Chen, C. Y. I., O'Brien, M. S., & Anthony, J. C. (2005). Who becomes cannabis dependent soon after onset of use? Epidemiological evidence from the United States: 2000–2001. *Drug and Alcohol Dependence, 79*(1), 11–22.

Chou, S. P., & Pickering, R. R. (1992). Early onset of drinking as a risk factor for lifetime alcohol-related problems. *British Journal of Addiction, 87*(8), 1199–1204.

Clauss-Ehlers, C. S., Serpell, Z. N., & Weist, M. D. (2013). Introduction: Making the case for culturally responsive school mental health. In *Handbook of Culturally Responsive School Mental Health,* pp. 3–15. New York, NY: Springer.

Dishion, T. J., & Skaggs, N. M. (2000). An ecological analysis of monthly 'bursts' in early adolescent substance use. *Applied Developmental Science, 4,* 89–97.

Donovan, J. E. (2004). Adolescent alcohol initiation: A review of psychosocial risk factors. *Journal of Adolescent Health, 35*(6), 529.

Eaton, D. K., Kann, L., Kinchen, S., Shanklin, S., Flint, K. H., Hawkins, J., Harris, W. A., Lowry, R., McManus, T., Chyen, D., Whittle, L., Lim, C., & Wechsler, H. (2011). Youth risk behavior surveillance—United States, 2011. *Morbidity and Mortality Weekly Report, Surveillance Summaries, 61*(4), 1–168.

Gaviria, A., & Raphael, S. (2001). School-based peer effects and juvenile behavior. *Review of Economics and Statistics, 83* (2), 257–268.

Gerra, G., Angioni, L., Zaimovic, A., Moi, G., Bussandri, M., Bertacca, S., Santoro, G., Gardini, S., Caccavari, R., & Nicoli, M. A. (2004). Substance use among high-school students: Relationships with temperament, personality traits, and parental care perception. *Substance Use & Misuse, 39*(2), 345–367.

Glantz, M., & Sloboda, Z. (1999). Analysis and reconceptualization of resilience. In M. Glantz & J. Johnson (Eds.) *Resilience and development: Positive life adaptations.* New York, NY: Kluwer Academic/Plenum, pp. 109–125.

Grant, G. F. (1998). The impact of a family history of alcoholism on the relationship between age at onset of alcohol use and DSM-IV alcohol dependence: Results of the National Longitudinal Alcohol Epidemiologic Survey. *Alcohol Health & Research World, 22*, 144–147.

Hawkins, J. D., Catalano, R. E., & Miller, J. Y. (1992). Risk and protective factors for alcohol and other drug problems in adolescence and early adulthood: Implications for substance use prevention. *Psychological Bulletin, 112,* 64–105.

Haydon, A. A., & Halpern, C. T. (2010). Older romantic partners and depressive symptoms during adolescence. *Journal of Youth and Adolescence, 39,* 1240–51.

Henry, K. L., & Slater, M. D. (2005). Alcohol use in early adolescence: The effect of changes in risk taking, perceived harm and friends' alcohol use. *Journal of Studies on Alcohol, 66*(2), 275–283.

Holleran Steiker, L.K. (2008). Making drug and alcohol prevention relevant: Adapting evidence-based curricula to unique adolescent cultures. *Family & Community Health, 31*(1S), S52–60.

Kendler, K. S., & Prescott, C. A. (2006). *Genes, environment and psychopathology: Understanding the causes of psychiatric and substance use disorders.* New York, NY: Guilford Press.

King, K. M., & Chassin, L. (2007). A prospective study of the effects of age of initiation of alcohol and drug use on young adult substance dependence. *Journal of Studies on Alcohol and Drugs, 68,* 256–265.

Kirisci, L., Tarter, R., Ridenour, T., Reynolds, M., Horner, M., & Vanyukov, M. (2015). Externalizing behavior and emotion dysregulation are indicators of transmissible risk for substance use disorder. *Addictive Behaviors, 42,* 57–62.

Maio, R. F., Shope, J. T., Blow, F. C., Gregor, M. A. Zakrajsek, J. S. Weber, J. E., & Nypaver, M. M. (2005). A randomized controlled trial of an emergency department-based interactive computer program to prevent alcohol misuse among injured adolescents. *Annals of Emergency Medicine, 45,* 420–429.

McCaffrey. D., Pacula. R. L., Han, B., & Ellickson, P. (2010). Marijuana use and high school drop out: The influence of unobservables. *Health Economics, 19*(11), 1281–1299.

McGue, M., & Irons, D. E. (2013). Etiology. In B. S. McCrady & E. S. Epstein (Eds.) *Addictions: A comprehensive guidebook* (pp. 36–72). New York: Oxford.

McNeil, M. P. (2008). I said no to drugs . . . but the drugs wouldn't listen! *Collegiate Drug Use,* 93.

Mitchell, S. G., Gryczynski, J., O'Grady, K. E., & Schwartz, R. P. (2013). SBIRT for adolescent drug and alcohol use: current status and future directions. *Journal of Substance Abuse Treatment, 44*(5), 463–72.

NIH (2011). Adolescent Development. Medline Plus. Accessed September 2, 2013. http://www.nlm.gov/medlineplus/ency/article/002003.htm

O'Connell, M. E., Boat, T., & Warner, K. E. (Eds.) (2009). *Preventing mental, emotional, and behavioral disorders among young people: Progress and possibilities.* Committee on the Prevention of Mental Disorders and Substance Use among Children, Youth and Young Adults, Institute of Medicine. Washington, DC: National Academies Press.

Odgers, C. L., Caspi, A., Nagin, D. S., Piquero, A. R., Slutske, W. S., Milne, B. J., Dickson, N., Poulton, R., & Moffitt, T. E. (2008). Is it important to prevent early exposure to drugs and alcohol among adolescents? *Psychological Science, 19*(10), 1037–44.

Orpinas, P., Horne, A. M., Song, X., Reeves, P. M., & Hsieh, H. (2013). Dating trajectories from middle to high school: Association with academic performance and drug use. *Journal of Research on Adolescence, 23*(4), 772–784.

Parents' Resource Institute for Drug Education. (2003). 2002–03 PRIDE Surveys national summary for grades 4 thru 6. Bowling Green, KY: the author.

Patnode, C. D., O'Connor, E., Rowland, M., Burda, B. U., Perdue, L. A., & Whitlock, E. P. (2014). Primary care behavioral interventions to prevent or reduce illicit drug use and nonmedical pharmaceutical use in children and adolescents: A systematic evidence review for the U.S. Preventive Services Task Force. *Annals of Intern Medicine,* 160(9), 612–20.

Reimuller, A., Hussong, A., & Ennett, S. T. (2011). The influence of alcohol-specific communication on adolescent alcohol use and alcohol-related consequences. *Prevention Science, 12*(4), 389–400.

Santiago-Irizarry, V. (1996). Culture as cure. *Cultural Anthropology, 11*(1), 3–24.

Shillington, A. M, Lehman, S., Clapp, J., Hovell , M. F., Sipan, C., & Blumberg, E. J. (2005). Parental monitoring: Can it continue to be protective among high-risk adolescents? *Journal of Child & Adolescent Substance Use, 15*(1), 1–15.

Spear, L. P. (2000). The adolescent brain and age-related behavioral manifestations. *Neuroscience Biobehavioral Review, 24*(4), 417–463.

Spirito, A., Sindelar-Manning, H., Colby, S. M., Barnett, N. P., Lewander, W., Rohsenow, D. J., & Monti, P. M. (2011). Individual and family motivational interventions for alcohol-positive adolescents treated in an emergency department: Results of a randomized clinical trial. *Journal of American Medical Association, Pediatrics, 165*(3), 269–274.

Spooner, C. (1999). Causes and correlates of adolescent drug abuse and implications for treatment. *Drug and Alcohol Review, 18*(4), 453–475.

Stewart, C. (2002). Family factors of low-income African-American youth associated with substance use: An exploratory analysis. *Journal of Ethnicity in Substance Use, 1*(1), 97–111.

Swendsen, J., Burstein, M., Case, B., Conway, K. P., Dierker, L., He, J., & Merikangas, K. R. (2012). Use and abuse of alcohol and illicit drugs in US adolescents: Results of the National Comorbidity Survey–Adolescent Supplement. *Archives of General Psychiatry, 69*(4), 390–398.

Taylor-Seehafer, M., Jacobvitz, D., & Holleran Steiker, L. K. (2008). Patterns of attachment organization, social connectedness, and substance use in a sample of older homeless adolescents: Preliminary findings. *Family & Community Health, 31*(1S), S81–88.

Treno, A. J., Grube, J. W., & Martin, S. E. (2003). Alcohol availability as a predictor of youth drinking and driving: A hierarchical analysis of survey and archival data. *Alcoholism: Clinical and Experimental Research, 27*, 835–840.

Walton, M. A., Chermack, S. T., Shope, J. T., Bingham, C. R., Zimmerman, M. A., Blow, F. C., Cunningham, R. M. (2010). Effects of a brief intervention for reducing violence and alcohol misuse among adolescents: A randomized controlled trial. *Journal of American Medical Association, 304*(5), 527–535.

Warner, L. A., & White, H. R. (2003). Longitudinal effects of age at onset and first drinking situations on problem drinking. *Substance Use & Misuse, 38*(14), 1983–2016.

Weissberg, R. P., Kumpfer, K. L., & Seligman, M. E. (2003). Prevention that works for children and youth. *American Psychologist, 58*(6–7), 425–432.

Chapter 3

Substance Misuse Models and Theories

Models, or frameworks for comprehension, are useful to tie together the theoretical underpinnings, the functional components, and the mechanisms of understanding and intervening on something as complex as adolescent addictions. Historically, those who used too much alcohol or drugs were seen, at best, as weak, and at worst, as evil. The erroneous and outdated moral model suggests that addiction is a choice based on bad values (Wilbanks, 1989). Because the behavior of picking up a drink or a drug appears to be voluntary (i.e., putting the substance into one's body), the assumption has always been that it is a free choice. There are many who still embrace this view regardless of the strong unfolding scientific evidence in the areas of neuroscience, biology, magnetic resonance imagery, and behavioral sciences.

Historically, long before Alcoholics Anonymous (AA) was founded, social worker Mary Richmond (1917/1944) stated that "inebriety is a disease." Several decades later, the rest of the world caught up. In 1951, the World Health Organization came to the same conclusion, finally acknowledging alcoholism as a serious medical problem. In 1956, the American Medical Association declared alcoholism as a treatable illness, and in 1965 the American Psychiatric Association began to use the term disease to describe alcoholism (Straussner, 2001).

Currently, the disease model is not a "theory." Addiction is a brain disease (Erickson, 2007; Volkow, Fowler, Wang, & Swanson,

2007). The brains of people with substance dependence have essentially been hijacked; they may be able to stop for periods of time, but they cannot continue to refrain without a significant shift in their entire world experience, and this powerful psychic change is often a spiritual one. Regardless of its sort, it rarely, if ever, is accomplished by an individual without the help of another. As David Mallett (2013) so eloquently states in his thesis, "The addicted brain's response to these drugs is to induce a craving for more drugs, creating a pathological inability to stop." He cites the definition provided by the American Society of Addiction Medicine (ASAM), which states the following: "Addiction is a primary, chronic disease of brain reward, motivation, memory and related circuitry. Dysfunction in these circuits leads to characteristic biological, psychological, social and spiritual manifestations. This is reflected in an individual pathologically pursuing reward and/or relief by substance use and other behaviors. (ASAM, 2011).

OVERVIEW OF THEORETICAL FRAMES

There are several important theoretical frames that will serve as compasses as you move through the waters of adolescent substance use. First, as has already been discussed, the bio-psycho-social-spiritual model serves as a holistic guide to encompass all aspects of human existence: physiologic, intrapsychic, interpersonal, ecological, and even existential. This model will serve as a reminder of aspects of the problem or illness as well as modes of intervening and areas for growth and strength. For example, biology can include the genetics that may predispose someone for addiction. It also can be an area for focus on physical health and wellness in recovery. And although social isolation and lack of social skills are typical aspects of people with substance disorders prior to and early in treatment, the movement towards intimacy and the ability to be useful through service in recovery provides a powerful sense of purpose.

Next, one should consider a social learning model. Originally denoted by Bandura (1999), the social-cognitive theory of substance use is based in the belief that the exercise of self-regulatory agency plays a central role in intervention. According to Bandura, "perceived self-efficacy is the foundation of human agency" (p. 214). He goes on to explain, "Unless people believe they can produce desired effects by their actions, they have little incentive to act." When people think that they can do what they set out to do, positive changes can occur through cognitive, motivational, and affective processes. This sense of self-efficacy affects every phase of personal change—contemplation of giving up substances, the initiation of efforts to overcome substance use, achievement of desired changes, recovery from relapses, and long-term maintenance of a drug-free life (Bandura, 1999). This model can be used theoretically to guide interventions, or more practically. For example, clinicians can shift their thinking from a client's deficits to strengths by focusing on what the person can do well. Also, literal assessments of perceived efficacy can help identify areas of vulnerability and provide guides for treatment. Bandura would fit his social learning and efficacy paradigm into the bio-psycho-social model by noting that this process is not just a personal one but also a social problem that should be addressed ecologically (see Bronfenbrenner, 1989) from a systems perspective. Such a perspective focuses not only on a micro (individual) level, but on meso (immediate systems such as family, school, and church) and macro (such as agencies, communities, state, and society) levels as well.

Another useful version called the multi-stage social learning model (MSLM) was developed by Simons and colleagues (1988) to specifically delineate adolescent substance use patterns, from initial experimentation to regular use and misuse. The multi-stage social learning model identifies three stages of substance use: (1) the initial experimentation with substance use; (2) a deeper involvement with substance-using peers; and (3) the escalation to more regular use and/or misuse. According to Petraitis, Flay, and Miller (1995), in this first stage, youth experiment with substances if they have observed drug or alcohol use among their peers and/or parents, or if they are raised in a family environment without perceived support, warmth, discipline, or supervision. In the second stage of the MSLM, adolescents are more likely to become involved with delinquent, substance-using peers if they have previously experimented with substances and have poor social skills such as being shy, lacking in empathy, or being uncompromising. In the third stage, adolescents' substance use is more likely to escalate to more frequent use or misuse if they have witnessed excessive use by parents and peers. In addition, this theory notes that substance use behaviors are more likely to escalate when youth are emotionally distressed and have inadequate coping skills. This becomes a mechanism of stress and coping; youth anticipate relief from the effects of the substances, and continued substance use becomes a coping mechanism with which to manage life's problems.

The Transtheoretical Model (TTM), also referred to as Stage of Change, will be utilized as a guiding paradigm for interventions in this text. The Transtheoretical Model is widely recognized as a promising approach to substance use prevention and treatment, and concepts from the model are widely used in community substance use programs. Prochaska and DiClemente (1982) developed this model of change, which contends that it is normal for people to be in varied stages of readiness to make lasting change. This highly influential model in the addictions field has been widely recognized as a promising approach to substance use treatment, both in the U.S. and abroad (Migneault, Adams, & Read, 2005). The most impactful aspect of this model is that it led to a shift in the field of substance use intervention from the highly maintained conviction of counselors that "you have to 'hit bottom' to be in recovery" to the hopeful awareness that there are effective interventions at all stages of readiness for change, even early stages such as precontemplation. In the late 1990s it was typical that psycho-social intake assessments for addictions treatment would ask such questions as, "Are you willing to go to any lengths for your recovery?" If clients answered, in desperation, "Yes!" then they were admitted. Sadly, if they were ambivalent, or balked in any way, they were often sent away, even being encouraged to "go do some more drinking or drugging and come back when you are ready." Not only was this ineffective, it was virtually unethical. But there was no concept of the Transtheoretical Model or Stage of Change Model at that time. Fortunately, with this new lens, clinicians are able to engage with clients who are reaching out for help regardless of the depth of their awareness and working with them to move in positive directions. The "how to's" of this intervention are presented later in this book.

And finally, a theoretical overview of abstinence versus non-abstinence-based models should be considered. Non-abstinence-based prevention models work from a harm reduction perspective (MacMaster, Holleran, & Chaffin, 2005). Harm reduction programs emphasize the identification and reduction of harmful consequences related to the use of alcohol, tobacco, and other drug use rather than only focusing on abstinence. Harm-reduction models are not mutually exclusive of abstinence-based models. Harm-reduction models typically encourage abstinence but acknowledge that some patterns of substance use are more harmful than others.

The most important thing to note about theoretical frames is that all work with clients should be client-centered (or patient-centered if in medical settings); the most effective services are

Figure 3.1: Transtheoretical Model: Stages of Change

Pre-contemplation

"What problem?"

Contemplation

"Okay, so maybe I might have a problem. But then again . . ."

Determination

"I need to do something about this."

Action

"This is what I plan to do . . ."

Maintenance

"I'd like to keep this up."

Relapse

"I'll have to get back on track."

oriented around the needs of that client rather than the bias of the agency and/or clinician. Many counselors in the field of addiction treatment feel, for example, that abstinence-based approaches are the only way to go, fearing that any other mode might be dangerous for a client. However, if one does not work with the process that clients present as their own truth, the likelihood of success is small, or nil. One of the most interesting aspects of this work is that just when helping professionals (or parents, or teachers), feel they know exactly what a client (or child, or student) needs, those professionals are likely in for a surprise. It is so much more important to facilitate growth based on clients' own direction, in partnership; this allows for the self-efficacy that builds the foundation for lasting change. Tatarsky's variation on harm reduction is called integrative harm reduction psychotherapy, an approach that integrates a strategic skills-building focus with an exploration of the multiple meanings of substance use and the importance of the therapeutic alliance (Tatarsky, 2003).

The key to understanding any addiction model is open-mindedness. When one considers how diverse adolescents are, and the wide range of addiction experiences, it is easy to see the importance of being responsive to the unique needs of each person. As noted by the New York Harm Reduction Educators (NYHRE, 2013), "When you judge someone, you don't define them. You define yourself."

KEY TERMS

Moral model of addiction

Disease model of addiction

Bio-psycho-social-spiritual model

Social learning model

Multi-stage social learning model (MSLM)

The Transtheoretical Model (TTM)

Stage of Change Model

Harm reduction

Client-centered

Abstinence-based

Integrative harm reduction psychotherapy

DISCUSSION QUESTIONS

1. Why do you think that the "moral model" continues to persist in the face of cutting edge research to the contrary regarding chemical dependency as a disease?

2. Break into dyads and have one person argue for the abstinence model and the other for the harm-reduction model. When you have exhausted your arguments, switch with someone else and argue the other side.

3. Write a case example of a client in each of the stages of change.

REFERENCES

American Society of Addiction Medicine (ASAM). "Definition of Addiction." ASAM.org. *American Society of Addiction Medicine*, 19 April 2011. Web. 8 May 2013.

Bandura, A. (1999). A sociocognitive analysis of substance abuse: An agentic perspective. *Psychological Science, 10*, 214–217.

Bronfenbrenner, U. (1989). Ecological systems theory. In R. Vasta (Ed.) *Annals of Child Development, 6*, 187–249.

Erickson, C. K. (2007). *The science of addiction: From neurobiology to treatment.* New York: W. W. Norton and Company, Inc.

MacMaster, S. A., Holleran, L., & Chaffin, K. (2005). Empirical and theoretical support for non-abstinence-based prevention services for substance using adolescents. *Journal of Evidence-Based Social Work, 2* (1–2), 91–111.

Migneault, J. P., Adams, T. B., & Read, J. P. (2005). Application of the transtheoretical model to substance abuse: Historical development and future directions. *Drug and Alcohol Review, 24*(5), 437–448.

New York Harm Reduction Educators (2013). Website accessed January, 2014: http://www.nyhre.org/

Petraitis, J., Flay, B. R., & Miller, T. Q. (1995). Reviewing theories of adolescent substance use: Organizing pieces in the puzzle. *Psychological Bulletin, 117*(1), 67–86.

Prochaska, J. O., & DiClemente, C. C. (1982). Transtheoretical therapy: Toward a more integrative model of change. *Psychotherapy: Theory, Research, and Practice, 19*, 276–288.

Simons, R. L, Conger, R. D., & Whitbeck, L. B. (1988). A multistage social learning model of the influences of family and peers upon adolescent substance abuse. *Journal of Drug Issues, 18*(3), 293–315.

Straussner, S. L. (2001). The role of social workers in the treatment of addictions: A brief history. *Journal of Social Work Practice in the Addictions, 1*(1), 3–9.

Retrieved January 27, 2006, from http://alcoholstudies.rutgers.edu/history/html

Tatarsky, A. (2003). Harm reduction psychotherapy: Extending the reach of traditional substance use treatment. *Journal of Substance Use Treatment, 25*(4), 249–256.

Volkow, N. D., Fowler, J. S., Wang, G-J, & Swanson, J. M. (2007). Dopamine in drug use and addiction: Results from imaging studies and treatment implications. *Molecular Psychiatry, 9,* 557–69.

Wilbanks, W. (1989). The danger in viewing addicts as victims: A critique of the disease model of addiction. *Criminal Justice Policy Review, 3*(4), 407–422.

PART II

Prevention and the Family

Now that you have a sense of both the "nature" and the "nurture" aspects that contribute to substance use or misuse in a young person's development, you can focus in on the mechanisms of prevention. Although many evidence-based prevention interventions make up what has come to be known as prevention science, it is important that clinicians recognize that individuals should continually be viewed within their environment. Prevention programs consider school settings, peer interactions, community, and culture in order to be effective.

For children making decisions about substances, the first and perhaps most powerful of these environments is family. Families model behaviors, respond to behaviors, and affect outcomes. Therefore, this section will also explore the family realm as it relates to prevention of substance use.

Chapter 4

Substance Misuse Prevention

OVERVIEW OF SUBSTANCE MISUSE PREVENTION APPROACHES

Those who work in the field of substance use often specialize in one aspect of the continuum of care. Continuum of care is defined by the Center for Substance Use Treatment as "a treatment system in which clients enter treatment at a level appropriate to their needs and then step up to more intense treatment or down to less intense treatment as needed" (CSAT, 2006). It is important to recognize that individuals who engage in drug and alcohol use often will need a spectrum of services that range from prevention to intervention to treatment to relapse prevention. Since "continuum" implies a linear model, some prefer the term "wrap-around services" (used more commonly in mental health realms than substance use). Two metaphors aptly describe this type of comprehensive community of services: a "holding environment" and a "safety net of services."

As noted in an editorial by Pomeroy and Holleran Steiker (2012), historically there has been a palpable schism between "preventionists" and "interventionists" in the field of social work. Despite strides in evidence-based practice pursuits (i.e., rigorous research, replication studies, outcome-based inquiries) in both areas, there is still tremendous room for improvement in communication and collaboration between these realms. Sadly, the two realms are often viewed as being in competition with one another for resources, agency priorities, and funding.

Significant time has been spent developing and implementing various programs at all levels of care, as well as monitoring their effectiveness. Most prevention programs are targeted at children and adolescents, as this is the time when most people initiate use of alcohol and other drugs. When examining trends in drug and alcohol use over the past few decades, it is important to note that age of onset has shifted to younger and younger ages. A survey of U.S. teenagers found that most have used alcohol and drugs by the time they reach adulthood, and researchers said this could be setting many of those kids up for a lifetime of substance use (Swendsen et al., 2012). The survey of more than 10,000 teens, published in the Archives of General Psychiatry, found that almost four out of five teens had tried alcohol and more than 15 percent were abusing it by the time they turned eighteen years old. Some 16 percent were abusing drugs by the age of eighteen. The study is based on interviews with U.S. teens between the ages of thirteen and eighteen surveyed between February 2001 and January 2004. Of the approximately 3,700 teens between the ages of thirteen and fourteen, about 10 percent were drinking alcohol regularly, defined as twelve drinks within a year. That number jumped to about half on the approximately 2,300 surveyed seventeen- to eighteen-year-olds. Almost one in three of the regular users in the oldest age group met the criteria for lifetime alcohol use. The median age of onset for alcohol use, with or without "dependence," was fourteen. Contemplate that for a moment. The median statistically separates the higher half of the sample from the lower half. So imagine that for every fifteen-year-old, there is likely a thirteen-year-old. And for every sixteen-year-old, there is likely a twelve-year-old. And for every seventeen-year-old, there is likely an eleven-year-old.

And so on. . . . As for drugs, about 60 percent of the teens said they had the opportunity to use illicit drugs, such as marijuana, cocaine, tranquilizers, stimulants, and painkillers. About one in ten of the thirteen- and fourteen-year-olds said they used at least one such drug, and that increased to about 40 percent in the oldest age group. Marijuana was the most common type of drug used, followed by prescription drugs. The median age of onset for drug use was fourteen with dependence and fifteen without dependence.

Prevention research has its challenges. Social workers are pressured to focus on measurable outcomes of clinical interventions and, therefore, prevention programs often fall to the wayside, being much harder to prove in terms of efficacy. As noted by Pomeroy and Holleran Steiker (2012), this problem is clearly evidenced by the small number of prevention research publications in the field of social work. Out of 1,951 articles reviewed by the journal of the profession, *Social Work*, only 5.6 percent were categorized as prevention-related (Marshall et al., 2011). However, contrary to current opinion, the literature strongly supports cost effectiveness of prevention efforts (Weissberg, Kumpfer, & Seligman, 2003).

Readily understood is the fact that there is no need to *treat* something that has never *occurred*. However, examining the prevalence of use can help frame the urgency for these strategies. Prevalence data represents the extent of a condition in a population, and this information helps to assess the need for intervention (Friis & Sellers, 1999). Prevalence is not to be confused with incidence, which is the number of new cases in a population over time.

Each year, numerous studies are conducted to determine the prevalence of substance use across the United States. This research helps to determine trends in drug use, and to identify specific prevention targets, particularly in adolescents. The MTF study, conducted by the University of Michigan (Johnston, O'Malley, Bachman, & Schulenberg, 2014) and funded by the National Institute on Drug Abuse (NIDA), has been conducted annually since 1975. Thus, it reveals trends in use over time.

• •

Find trends in data on the Monitoring the Future website: http://www.monitoringthefuture.org/pubs/monographs/mtf-overview2014.pdf

Johnston, L. D., O'Malley, P. M., Miech, R. A., Bachman, J. G., & Schulenberg, J. E. (2014). Monitoring the Future national results on drug use: 1975–2013: Overview, Key Findings on Adolescent Drug Use. Ann Arbor: Institute for Social Research, The University of Michigan.

• •

The MTF data (Johnston et. al., 2014) are useful for understanding the effectiveness of generalized and specific prevention programs. The high rates at which students report using substances, especially alcohol, point to a need for prevention strategies. Prevention programs can be helpful for youth by preventing use altogether, delaying the onset of use, and, among those who are already using substances, reducing the frequency and quantity of use and preventing the use of progressively more harmful and addictive substances.

It has long been recognized that research on age of initiation (i.e., at first use) has shown that later onset can help lessen substance-related consequences (Gonzales, 1983). Gonzales found that students who had their first use of alcohol in high school or college had substantially lower alcohol-related problems than those who began using earlier, such as in elementary or middle school. This finding is not limited solely to alcohol use. Hawkins, Catalano, and Miller (1992) also found that age of first use is a predictor of further drug-related problems encountered by adolescents, regardless of the substance that was used. Many in the substance use treatment field maintain that this is due to the fact that once an adolescent experiences substance use as a coping mechanism, other important social and problem-solving skills are either not learned or fall by the wayside. Although there is agreement about the importance of delaying onset of first use, there is no consensus on the best strategy for prevention. It is also important to note that research has made clear that young people's use of substances is especially dangerous because their brains are still developing and the use of drugs and alcohol can permanently alter and impair brain functioning (Winters & Lee, 2010). As Foster notes, "There's really a type of rewiring that goes on with continued use than can result in an increased interest in using and an inability to stop using."

It has been established by research that one of the most critical goals of prevention interventions is to delay onset of use. Intervening before initiation into drug use can also conceivably prevent dependence.

How can clinicians delay onset?

At young ages, it does make sense to "just say no." In elementary schools, professionals have done a good job, for the most part, creating a culture that sees drug and alcohol use as an anomaly. However, in middle and high schools, the "just say no" mantra is useless, if not comical to the young people.

It may be helpful to take the original DARE curriculum as an example—mind you, the DARE program has worked hard to catch up with the science of prevention and has transformed into a viable program with many of the key elements of a successful prevention program. However, when it first began, DARE was an "information only" program. Police came into the schools, sometimes effectively building relationships with the students, and they showed the students what not to do (in the early DARE days, they even passed around bags of marijuana and had posters with multicolored pills taped to it in order to "show students what not to use). Is it any wonder that early studies of the efficacy of the DARE program showed that it increased student curiosity about and therefore use of substances? Not only have DARE and other information-only programs failed to reduce drug use, but in a number of cases, researchers have noted a subsequent increase in participant substance use (Clayton, Leukefeld, Donohew, Barto, & Harrington, 1996; Harmon, 1993; Lynam, 1999).

Equally ineffective were the "scared straight" brands of prevention and intervention. Although it used to be a common practice to suggest some of the worst negative consequences to clients (e.g., drugs can kill you, amphetamines can give you heart problems, you can die of alcohol poisoning) in the mode of "scare tactics," these techniques have been shown to have little efficacy for drug and alcohol prevention with adolescents and young adults. Scare tactics aim to use fear to motivate changes in behavior. They intend to present a behavior couched in fear, like drug use, that can cause severe physical or emotional injury (overdose, lost relationships, accidents, death), and then they recommend a specific action to prevent the injury (like "don't take drugs". Researchers have studied the effect of scare tactics on young adults and found mixed results; some found that fear influenced behavior; others did not (NIDA, 2012). It depends on whether teens perceive a threat to their safety and how they react to that threat. When faced with scare tactics in drug use prevention messages, some teens feel encouraged to stay away from drugs; others reject the message and either deny that abusing drugs is dangerous or deny that they will suffer the worst effects of drug use ("that won't happen to me"). Many laugh at the attempts that try too hard or are "over the top."

With time, information provision models such as DARE (Clayton, Leukefeld, Bardo, Donohew, & Harrington, 1996; Harmon, 1993; Lynum, 1999) and health belief models (Albert & Simpson, 1985), evolved into more complex social influence models including life skills training (Botvin & Griffin, 2014) and the social competence program (Caplan et. al., 1992) as well as drug resistance strategies training such as Project SMART (Hansen, Anderson, Flay, Graham, & Sobel, 1988), Project ALERT (Ellickson, McCaffrey, Ghosh-Dastidar, & Longshore, 2003), and DRS (Hecht et al, 2003). Although the educational, information-based programs have generally been found to be ineffective, social influence models have been identified as best practice prevention programs by the National Institute on Drug Abuse (NIDA) and the Center for Substance Abuse Prevention (CSAP). Meta-analyses of resistance skills training programs also support their effectiveness (Tobler & Stratten, 1997).

Today, replication and application of evidence-based models are prevalent in the field of substance use prevention and treatment. These attempts tend to be cross-disciplinary, with aspects being explored by social workers, psychologists, nurses, sociologists, and mental health agencies.

The 1920s through the '50s were times of scare tactics and the first media campaigns. "Reefer Madness," a movie about a group of teenagers who use marijuana and go insane, typifies this trend. Nationally the belief was that drugs were a problem of low income areas, used to escape pain and avoid reality. In the 1960s there was a shift in national perspective. Though people still saw drugs as a way to escape pain, there was a new emphasis on the psychedelic experience. In the 1970s, the focus shifted to drugs' usefulness in intensifying experiences, relieving boredom, and giving the illusion of speeding things up. Dramatic prevention attempts such as "Shattered Dreams" (a psycho-dramatic recreation of a fatal DWI accident and its aftermath for high school students) made adults feel good about their efforts to prevent dangerous, high-risk behaviors and outcomes. However, subsequent research has continually found these programs to be ineffective at best and injurious at worst (Ennett, Tobler, Ringwalt, & Flewelling, 1994).

Most of the curricula in these years were based on information dissemination. The 1980s' prevention curricula were focused on communication, decision making, and self-esteem building. A focus on affective education and alternatives to drug use became popular. In these years, Project ALERT (Adolescent Experiences in Resistance Training) began. Also in the 1980s, parent groups such as MADD (Mothers Against Drunk Drivers) began to form in order to combat drug use. Family interventions, such as BSFT (brief strategic family therapy), also became popular. In the late 1980s, a shift in perception became apparent. Society began to view substance use as highly complex, and a new understanding of the disorder became evident. As the 1990s and new millennium approached, research-based curricula became more common and peer-based programs also grew. One strong research-supported program that grew out of these interventions is Karol Kumpfer's Strengthening Families. This evidence-based program has been culturally adapted for unique groups as well (Kumpfer, Molgaard, & Spoth, 1996).

Current trends show the gap between research and application is being bridged. Technology transfer is becoming more important, and evidence-based interventions are becoming standard. Drug resistance strategies training, such as Keepin' It R.E.A.L., is also examining the importance of culturally grounded interventions on effectiveness.

Many substance use counselors, social workers, psychologists, politicians, and other professionals believe the goal of prevention should be solely to promote abstinence. Abstinence refers to general prohibition against use of any drug by an individual. Other professionals believe that the goal should be the reduction of suffering, with a focus on long-term consequences. Clearly, there are settings (such as schools) in which non-abstinence-based prevention messages are not accepted. Parents, teachers, and school administrators often fear that exposure to harm-reduction methods will come across as drug and alcohol promotion (Dodge, Dishion, & Lansford, 2006).

For many youth, a harm-reduction approach to prevention may be more developmentally and culturally appropriate than an abstinence-based curriculum. Youth who have begun to experiment with substances know from experience that drug use does not always result in the dire consequences presented in many abstinence-based prevention programs. These curricula have little credibility for youth who are already using drugs because their experiences are more likely to tell them that drug use improves concentration or relieves anxiety (MacMaster et al., 2005). Literature suggests that some experimentation with drugs is considered normal for the developmental stage of adolescence. For youth who are experimenting with drugs, harm-reduction models are likely to more accurately reflect their goals and life experiences than abstinence-based models (Neighbors, Larimer, Lostutter, & Woods, 2006).

Any discussion of harm reduction must acknowledge the difficulty of implementing such programs. In the United States, harm-reduction models are politically unpopular and are unlikely to be implemented in schools and community-based organizations (Beyers, Toumbourou, Catalano, Arthur, & Hawkins, 2004). Since substance use is illegal, any program that normalizes substance use is likely to be received with strong opposition (Hopson, 2006). It may be necessary to explore new, creative ways of integrating harm reduction and abstinence messages so that a curriculum can emphasize abstinence while acknowledging the extent to which youth experiment with substances (Hopson, 2006; MacMaster & Holleran, 2005).

Some school systems and parents think that drug testing is the answer. There are definitely situations in which drug testing has value and is indicated. There is recent and clear evidence of lower marijuana use in the presence of student drug testing (SDT) in middle and high schools but also evidence of higher use of illicit drugs other than marijuana (Terry-McElrath, O'Malley, & Johnson, 2013). Until further research can clarify the apparent opposing associations, schools should approach SDT with caution.

THE LAW OF PREVENTION IN THE UNITED STATES

In the early twentieth century, alcohol use was common because it was regarded primarily as a benign, joy-invoking substance with health benefits and even preventative powers (Miller, Beckles, Maude, & Carson, 1990). Despite two temperance movements in the 1800s, alcohol-related problems received little significant attention. In 1920 Congress added the 18th Amendment and the Volstead Act in an attempt to outlaw alcohol use definitively. However, this Prohibition led to social unrest and Congress repealed the 18th Amendment in 1933.

In the 1960s, the increase in alcohol consumption coupled with the use of illegal drugs garnered the attention of the public and government officials. New information was available on the nature, magnitude, and incidence of alcohol and other problems, raising public awareness. A decade later, the 1970 Controlled Substances Act noted that drugs are classified according to their medical use, their potential for misuse, and their likelihood of producing dependence. The increase in awareness culminated with the creation of the National Institute on Alcohol Use and Alcoholism (NIAAA) in 1970 and the National Institute on Drug Abuse (NIDA) in 1974. Both of these government agencies introduced prevention components to national programs that, up until that point, primarily concentrated on treatment.

Slowly, prevention came to be recognized as a multi-faceted and viable option in the battle against substance use. The Anti-Drug Use Act of 1986 led to the creation of the United States Office for Substance Use Prevention (OSAP), which consolidated alcohol and other drug prevention activities under the Alcohol, Drug Use, and Mental Health Administration (ADAMHA). The ADAMHA block grant mandated that 20 percent of alcohol and drug funds be utilized for prevention, and the remaining 80 percent be appropriated for treatment services. Six years later in 1992, OSAP transformed into the Center for Substance Abuse Prevention (CSAP), part of the newly founded Substance Use and Mental Health Services Administration (SAMHSA).

CLASSIFICATIONS OF PREVENTION

The Institute of Medicine Classification System

In 1994, the Institute of Medicine (IOM) created a new framework for classifying strategies in prevention. This was based on a pre-existing classification of disease prevention already in use. In this proposal, prevention was divided into three types: universal, selective, and indicated. All prevention strategies can be categorized based on the population they serve.

Universal prevention strategies

These programs address an entire population (country, state, community, school, or neighborhood). The goal is to deter use of

Figure 4.1: IOM Protractor

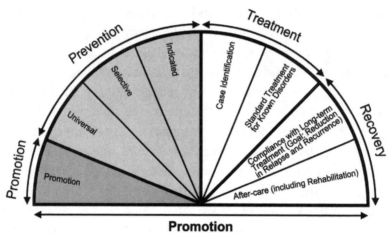

Public Domain: SAMHSA http://captus.samhsa.gov/prevention-practice/
prevention-and-behavioral-health/behavioral-health-lens-prevention/3

substances by providing each member of the community with information and skills to prevent the problem. There is no pre-screening for risk in a universal strategy. The entire population is determined to be at risk, and therefore able to benefit from the program. Although this is the primary mode of intervention in school-based prevention, there is some concern that universal interventions miss the youth that may need it most due to their tendency to be marginal, absent, or already engaged in substance use or misuse.

Selective prevention strategies

These programs are designed to target specific at-risk subsets of the general population. Risk groups may be identified on the basis of biological, psychological, social, or environmental risk factors known to be associated with substance use. Groups that are at higher risk for substance misuse include: students who are doing poorly academically, incarcerated youth, children who are abused, and children of alcoholics and addicts (Hawkins, Catalano, & Miller, 1992).

The selective prevention program is administered to members of the subgroup who are deemed to be at higher risk for substance use than others. A selective prevention program would be appropriate for a neighborhood that has a high incidence of admissions for drug treatment, for example, because youth living in this neighborhood may have a higher risk of drug involvement than those in the general population.

Indicated prevention strategies

These programs are the most specific in their target. They are administered directly to individuals who have shown themselves to be at high risk for substance misuse based on behaviors. An example would be a juvenile who drops out of school or is caught by the police with marijuana. It is important to recognize that non-drug related behaviors also create heightened risk for the individual. The mission of the indicated prevention program is to target individuals who are at a sub-clinical level, but are exhibiting substance misuse-like behavior or are initiating problematic use patterns. Specific family counseling or drug education to a habitually truant teenager are examples of indicated strategies.

Classification by Strategy

The Center for Substance Abuse Prevention (CSAP) and the Substance Use and Mental Health Services Administration (SAMHSA) created another method of classifying prevention strategies.

Table 4.1: Universal, Selective and Indicated Prevention

Universal— Direct & Indirect	Activities targeted to the general public or a whole population group that has not been identified on the basis of individual risk. Direct—Interventions directly serve an identifiable group of participants but who have not been identified on the basis of individual risk. (e.g., school curriculum) Indirect—Interventions support population-based programs and environmental strategies (e.g., establishing ATOD policies).
Selective	Activities targeted to individuals or a subgroup of the population whose risk of developing a disorder is significantly higher than average.
Indicated	Activities targeted to individuals identified as having minimal but detectable signs/symptoms foreshadowing disorder or biological markers indicating predisposition but not yet meeting diagnosis level.

Because any of the following six methods can be utilized in conjunction with universal, selective, or indicated populations, this model is not in conflict with the IOM system.

Information Dissemination

This strategy provides an awareness and understanding of the nature of substance use, misuse, and addiction. It gives information on the effects of misuse on the individual, the family, and the community. It also informs the target of available community resources for prevention and treatment. In this strategy, there is limited communication between the source and the audience. When used alone, information dissemination has not been shown to be effective prevention.

Education

In this strategy, there is communication between the source and the audience. The involvement of the participants is the basis of the intervention. The activities involved are skill building in areas such as decision-making, assertiveness, and critical thinking. Recently, in early prevention interventions, educating youth about their brain chemistry and the potential dangers of drugs to their brains has shown promise (Padgett et al., 2006).

Alternatives

This strategy engages the participant in alternative activities to drugs and alcohol. The belief is that by providing a healthy outlet for activities that are not compatible with the use of substances, a reduction in use will occur. Though this method has not been proven effective alone, it is an important component for the relief of boredom (a common assumption as to the cause of youth substance use).

Problem Identification and Referral

In this strategy, individuals are identified who have already engaged in the use of tobacco, alcohol, or other substances. The goal is to utilize education in order to change the participants' previously held beliefs about substances, therefore changing behavior. This is an important component of any prevention program, especially ones designed for and implemented in community settings with high-risk youth.

Community-based Process

In this strategy, communities are organized in order to more effectively provide prevention services, as well as substance use treatment services for their members. This strategy may encourage community mobilization through coalition building, networking, and interagency agreements among other community-based practices. Participatory Action Research (PAR) is a promising approach for actively collaborating with community members in implementing prevention strategies. This approach is helpful for ensuring that a prevention program incorporates the culture and learning styles of participants (Gosin, Dustman, Drapeau, and Harthun, 2002; Hopson, 2006).

Although PAR has been used as a label for many studies with varying levels of researcher-community member collaboration, the goal of PAR is to achieve active collaboration at every phase of the research including defining goals and methods, gathering and analyzing data, and implementing a change process (Kidd & Kral, 2005). The researcher takes on the role of consultant and lends expertise on methods and theoretical foundations rather than directing the entire research process (Gosin, Dustman, Drapeau, and Harthun, 2002). PAR methods have the advantage of building the capacity among participants to implement and evaluate prevention strategies to meet their own needs (Hughes, 2003).

PAR methods that may be useful in implementing prevention strategies include:

- Interviewing youth about their life experiences, substance use, and strategies for resisting drug use.
- Conducting focus groups with youth and staff in schools or community agencies to explore substances that are problematic in their community, patterns of substance use, and previous attempts to address the problem.
- Engaging youth in creating or adapting a prevention program.
- Collaborating with staff and youth in determining methods for an evaluation of a prevention program.

- Maintaining ongoing communication and consultation between researchers, program implementers, and youth.
- Obtaining feedback from staff and youth about a prevention program (Hopson & Holleran Steiker, 2008; Hopson, 2006).

Environmental

This strategy involves the establishment or changing of policy, written laws, codes, and standards. It also involves the unwritten codes of conduct and attitudes that the community promotes regarding substance use. The goal is to influence the incidence of substance misuse through a change in community attitude. An example may be banning billboards that advertise (and glamorize) the use of cigarettes by young people.

Model of Risk and Resiliency

Although data and statistics can provide trends in substance use and misuse, they do not provide clear explanation for the factors that influence its occurrence. They also do not provide implementation techniques for the previously defined strategies. Social science researchers have worked to provide a better understanding of what factors increase risk (risk factors) and those that encourage resistance (protective factors) to substance use. In this prevention model, the risk factors of each community are assessed, and a prevention intervention is designed to reduce these risks while utilizing and fostering protective factors that are present (Hawkins, et.al., 1992).

Risk and protective factors can be organized by the following domains: individual, peer relational, family, school, or by community influence. Factors can be either a risk *or* protective. For example, intelligence (specifically, the ability to problem solve) is a protective factor to substance use. Conversely, low intelligence (or a low problem solving ability) may result in social disconnectedness, which is a risk factor. Familial influences include abuse, conflict, and substance use history. Alternatively, parental substance resistance role-modeling and positive family communications are protective. The ability to achieve academically and engage with peers in school positively are examples of school protective factors, while poor grades and negative school behaviors such as fighting or learning disabilities may result in risk. Finally, each community holds different beliefs about the use of substances and alcohol, and community bylaws and norms can affect individual decision-making.

Research on risk and protective factors, however, has been hindered by small sample sizes and inadequate validation studies (Ellickson et al., 2003). When studies do have a large enough national sample, background characteristics (e.g., education, family structure, region, etc.) do not account for most of the racial/ethnic or SES differences found in drug use (Wallace & Bachman, 1991).

ETHNICITY, CULTURE, AND PREVENTION

Conceptualizing Culture

The word *culture* implies the established patterns of human behavior that include thoughts, communications, actions, customs, beliefs, values, and institutions of racial, ethnic, religious, or social groups (NASW, 2001). In the United States, culture has mainly been associated with race and ethnicity, but diversity is taking on a more expansive meaning to include the sociocultural experiences of people. This can include differences in gender, social class, religion and spiritual beliefs, sexual orientation, age, and physical and mental ability. This can also include noting the uniqueness of cultural settings such as twelve-step programs (see MacMaster & Holleran, 1995), alternative schools (Hopson, 2006; Hopson and Holleran Steiker, 2008), juvenile justice settings (Garland, 2001), low income housing (MacLeod, 2004), and centers for LGBTQ youth (Welle, 2003).

Most drug prevention programs are created by and for European Americans and tested primarily on this Anglo ethnic group. In addition, most community-based drug prevention programs have focused on primarily white communities or ones that represent primarily one ethnic group (Pentz, Rothspan, Skara, & Voskanian, 1999). It has been suggested that the failure of some prevention programs can be traced to their lack of cultural sensitivity (Hansen, Miller, & Leukefeld, 1995). Current findings indicate that tailoring an intervention to a target population can increase its effectiveness (Hecht et al., 2002; Marsiglia & Booth, 2014). Recently, there has been a shift to ethnically-sensitive programs (Trimble, Bolek, & Niemcryk, 2013), based on the argument that cultural sensitivity enhances prevention efforts and that ethnic matching maximizes program impact (Botvin & Griffin, 2014). However, "culture" and "ethnicity" have been defined in various ways, and at times the constructs are problematic. For example, many studies approach ethnicity in a "glossed" fashion, which denies the heterogeneity within groups and other contextual factors (Trimble, 2007). Definitions have often ignored the issue of acculturation (Berry, 1997).

In addition, although ethnic variables are important considerations, it is also important not to make the assumption that ethnicity equates with risk (Pentz et al., 1999). In most cases, research shows that minority/ethnicity as a risk factor is most likely a proxy for socio-economic status; the Native American population's above-average drug use has been linked directly to this variable (Johnson et al., 1990; Wallace & Bachman, 1991). According to Ellickson and colleagues (2003), African Americans and some Asian groups had significantly lower rates of risky drinking and related problems when family income, education and family structure were held constant, thus supporting SES as a proxy.

It is true, however, that ethnic groups vary widely as to their susceptibility to drugs, their attitudes regarding drugs, and their resistance strategies (Moon, Hecht, Jackson, & Spellers, 1999). Mexican American youth in some parts of the country, for example, have reported receiving drug offers at a significantly higher rate than European Americans or African Americans (Hecht, Trost, Bator, & McKinnon, 1997). Some Latino subgroups and African Americans have lower overall rates of alcohol use than Anglos (Vega, Gil, & Wagner, 1998).

In addition, recent research has found that "more acculturated" Latinos have demonstrated higher rates of drug use than their "less acculturated" peers (Gilbert, 1987; Epstein, Botvin, Dusenbury, Diaz, & Kerner, 1996; Zapata & Katims, 1994). Although Gil, Wagner, and Vega (2000) note that acculturation is a critical factor in examining Latino substance use and "may be an important variable in the planning and implementation of prevention and/or treatment programs" (p. 445), this area has not yet been studied. Acculturative stress is a critical factor in prevention as well (see Marsiglia et al., 2005). It is clear that personal, cultural, and community influences play an important role in an individual's ability to maintain resilience to substance use.

Most prevention research is conducted in school settings with students (Hansen, 1992). However, community settings other than schools often give the opportunity for intervening with the youth that need the prevention messages the most. For example, lifetime rates of alcohol and other drug (AOD) use are higher among homeless and street youth than among sheltered or household youth (Greene, Ennett, & Ringwalt, 1997). Seventy to eighty percent of street youth report daily use of alcohol whereas 35 to 55 percent report weekly or greater use of cocaine, crack, heroin, and/or amphetamines (Greene, et al., 1997; Kipke, Montgomery, Simon, & Iverson, 1997; Koopman, Rosario, & Rotheran-Borus, 1994). Koopman and colleagues (1994) report Hispanic homeless youth are more likely than other ethnic groups (white and black) to continue use of AOD after leaving home. However, a recent study conducted in an urban Texas community did not support this finding (Rew, Taylor-Seehafer, & Fitzgerald, 2001). Although the prevalence of AOD use was similar to that reported in other studies of homeless youth, no significant differences were found between white and Hispanic street youth in AOD use at age of onset or use in the past thirty days (Rew et al., 2001).

Culturally Grounded Substance Prevention

The NIDA funded Drug Resistance Strategies Project (DRS) (1997–2001) in Phoenix, Arizona, implemented with 4,224 youths starting in 1997, involved Caucasian, Latino/a, and African American high school youths from a large city high school in the creation of culturally grounded substance use prevention videos. Previous studies suggest that videos as prevention tools are not only important for engaging African American and Latino youth (Schinke, Botvin, & Orlandi, 1991) but are also an effective mode of intervention with these groups (Hecht, Corman, & Miller-Rassulo, 1993; Polansky, Buki, Horan, Dyche-Ceperich, & Dyer, 1999). The DRS curriculum is based on established social mediators (e.g., cultural norms supporting substances and economic deprivation) and protective factors (e.g., strong role models, educational successes, school bonding, adaptation to stresses, and positive attitudes) (Clayton et al., 1996; Hawkins, Catalano, & Miller, 1992).

The DRS project made the important contribution of combining the core aspects of social influence models with the added integral component of cultural groundedness. The DRS study findings confirm the theoretical rationale for involvement of minority adolescents in the development of substance use prevention projects (Holleran, Reeves, Marsiglia, & Dustman, 2002). The study's experimental design used videos as tools for depicting the "Keepin' it REAL" resistance strategies (Refuse, Explain, Avoid, and Leave). The videos, with protagonists of Anglo, Latino, and African American culture, emphasized values and mores of these cultures. For example, the video depicting Anglo culture portrays individuality, independence from family, and identification with Anglo peers; on the other hand, the Latino video emphasizes familism, ethnic identifications with Latino peers and family, traditional Latino rituals, and language.

Analyses of the DRS project (fourteen months post intervention) indicated that students in the experimental schools had gained greater confidence in the ability to resist drugs, increased use of the strategies taught by the curriculum to resist substance offers (control schools reported a decrease in the use of these resistance strategies), more conservative norms adopted both in school and at home, reduction in the use of alcohol (a decrease of nearly 16 percent in the experimental group and an increase of slightly more than 20 percent in the control group), and less positive attitudes towards drug use. The most poignant implication for this study, however, was that the curricula/videos that integrated elements of minority socio-cultural norms were more successful than the Anglo curricula/videos with significant effects on drug norms, attitudes, and use, particularly alcohol use. These findings support the importance of culturally grounded information in substance use prevention programs. Prevention messages that incorporate cultural elements and are presented within the social context of the participant are more likely to have a positive impact.

The Fidelity versus Adaptation Debate

Although many studies maintain that outcomes of effective prevention interventions do not have differential impact based on ethnicity, it is important to note that research design limitations keep researchers from definitively establishing whether prevention interventions are equally effective with different ethnic groups. The core interventions seem to be effective with multiethnic youth, but some research shows that culturally grounded versions of interventions have increased effects, especially in recruitment and retention (Kumpfer, Alvarado, Smith, & Bellamy, 2002; Holleran et al., 2005; Holleran Steiker, Hopson, Goldbach, & Robinson, 2014). Other adaptations, especially those that compromise "dosage," tend to reduce positive outcomes. Although there has been a dearth of research on fidelity of implementation in the social sciences, research in drug use prevention provides evidence that poor implementation results in a loss of program effectiveness (Dusenbury, Brannigan, Falco, & Hansen, 2003).

In preliminary research, researchers have noted that agencies on the Texas border found some information in the original, universal curriculum irrelevant, outdated, and even, on some occasions, offensive (Holleran Steiker, 2006; Holleran Steiker & Hopson, 2007). In addition, youth felt that curricula needed to reflect their actual language, life events, music, style, and surroundings in order to capture their attention and to resonate with their experiences (Holleran Steiker, 2006).

Much more research is needed in the area of cultural adaptation of drug prevention programming. Clinicians in the field often find themselves adapting the language and activities of a curriculum due to knowledge of the culture of the youth they work with. In fact, findings suggest that a significant number of teachers of substance use prevention curricula did not use a curriculum guide at all, whereas only 15 percent reported they followed one very closely (Ringwalt et al., 2003). Some focus groups found that prevention interventions on the U.S.-Mexico border were tailored by agency staff to fit the culture of the youth in that setting. Controlling for a variety of school and teacher characteristics, teachers in high minority schools adapted curricula particularly in the areas of youth violence, limited English proficiency, and nuances of various racial/ethnic or cultural groups (Ringwalt, Vincus, Ennett, Johnson, & Rohrbach, 2004). Ultimately, it is crucial that preventionists work in close collaboration with agency staff to assure the fit of the program culturally (Botvin & Griffin, 2014).

SUMMARY

In sum, prevention of drug and alcohol misuse is an important piece of the treatment continuum. Most programs are targeted at children and adolescents, as this is the most common onset age. Due to a high incidence of use, especially with alcohol, prevention strategies are necessary. Research has shown that the prevention of onset, or later onset, can help lessen substance-related consequences (Gonzales, 1983).

Historically, substance use has been viewed in many contexts. Despite two temperance movements, alcohol use received little attention until the 1920s, when scare tactics became the primary mode of prevention and campaigning. This continued until the 1960s when the national perspective shifted to educational models, which were not very effective. Interventions have evolved into a more complex social influence model that concentrates on skills training and resistance strategies. Evidence-based (i.e., empirically research-supported) interventions have most recently become the golden standard.

Harm reduction is an alternative approach to substance use prevention that emphasizes the reduction of harmful consequences related to use of substances, rather than focusing only on abstinence. In this model, abstinence is still viewed as ideal, but it is recognized that this may be an unrealistic goal for all individuals. However, because substance use is illegal, any program normalizing the behavior is often received with strong opposition (Hopson, 2006).

In addition to considering abstinence vs. non-abstinence-based models, one must choose the target population for an intervention. There are a variety of interventions that fit varied target groups. Universal prevention programs address an entire population. Selective strategies are designed to target a specific at-risk subset of the general population. Indicated strategies are administered directly to individuals who have shown themselves to be at higher risk for substance use and misuse. One must carefully weigh goals, target population expectations, and agency objectives when deciding on the best model of intervention. It is recommended that decisions about prevention be made, not only by agency administrators, but also by line staff, constituents, and clients receiving services.

Several methods have been identified as appropriate interventions for substance use prevention. Six techniques that are identified by NIDA, and recommended to be used in combination with one another, include: information dissemination, teaching alternatives, problem identification and referral, community-based processes, and environmental strategies.

Figure 4.2: Community-Based Prevention

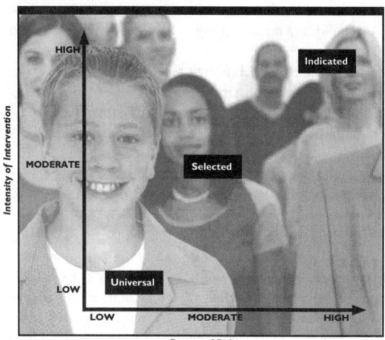

Degree of Risk

● ●

Choosing Evidence-Based Programs

SAMHSA's National Registry of Evidence-Based Programs and Practices (NREPP) www.nrepp.samhsa.gov

● ●

Much of the success of prevention interventions relates to recruitment, engagement, and retention. It has been established that culturally grounded interventions not only accomplish these goals, but also may improve the outcomes, such as reducing alcohol use (Holleran & Hopson, 2007).

It is important to note that ethnicity does not equate with risk (Pentz, et al., 1999) and that protective factors can be found in all cultures. In addition, although culture is generally defined as interchangeable with ethnicity, culture can also include the uniqueness of community, such as the twelve-step program, alternative schools, juvenile justice settings, and centers for alternative youth.

This chapter has emphasized prevention with youth. However, prevention interventions with youth, college students, and adults have much in common. They are all based in risk and protective factors, all should be based in empirically supported research, and all benefit from collaborative input between researchers, recipients, and stakeholders alike. It is recommended that all prevention interventions be based in needs assessment and that they be evaluated proximally (as they unfold) and distally (once they are complete and over time). Although it has been maintained that "an ounce of prevention is worth a pound of cure," prevention scientists might add that if an ounce of prevention works, cure is unnecessary.

KEY TERMS

Continuum of care	Interventionist
Holding environment	Age of onset or initiation
Safety net of services	Prevalence
Preventionist	

DISCUSSION QUESTIONS

1. Discuss what Pomeroy and Holleran Steiker meant when they wrote about the prevention-intervention *continuum* as opposed to *dichotomy*.

2. Imagine that someone you care about (a younger sibling, a cousin, a niece or nephew, a friend) has a serious and escalating problem with drugs. Describe the type of care you would want for this person.

REFERENCES

Albert, W. G., & Simpson, R. I. (1985). Evaluating an educational program for the prevention of impaired driving among grade 11 students. *Journal of Drug Education, 15*(1), 57–71.

Berry, J. W. (1997). Immigration, acculturation, and adaptation. *Applied Psychology, 46*(1), 5–34.

Beyers, J. M., Toumbourou, J. W., Catalano, R. F., Arthur, M. W., & Hawkins, J. D. (2004). A cross-national comparison of risk and protective factors for adolescent substance use: The United States and Australia. *Journal of Adolescent Health, 35*(1), 3–16.

Botvin, G. J., & Griffin, K. W. (2014). Life skills in adolescents. In Thomas P. Gullotta & Martin Bloom (Eds.), *Encyclopedia of primary prevention and health promotion,* pp. 1326–1332. Online publication.

Caplan, M., Weissberg, R. P., Grober, J. S., Sivo, P. J., Grady, K., & Jacoby, C. (1992). Social competence promotion with inner-city and suburban young adolescents: Effects on social adjustment and alcohol use. *Journal of Consulting and Clinical Psychology, 60*(1), 56–63.

Center for Substance Use Treatment (CSAT). *Substance use: Clinical issues in intensive outpatient treatment.* Rockville, MD: Substance Use and Mental Health Services Administration (US) (2006). (Treatment Improvement Protocol (TIP) Series, No. 47.) Chapter 3. Intensive outpatient treatment and the continuum of care. http://www.ncbi.nlm.nih.gov/books/NBK64088/

Clayton, R. R., Leukefeld, C. G., Bardo, M., Donohew, L., & Harrington, N. G. (1996). Risk and protective factors: A brief review. *Drugs and Society, 8*(3/4), 7–14.

Dodge, K. A., Dishion, T. J., & Lansford, J. E. (2006). Deviant peer influences in intervention and public policy for youth. *Social Policy Report,* 1–19.

Dusenbury, L., Brannigan, R., Falco, M., & Hansen, W. B. (2003). A review of research on fidelity of implementation: Implications for drug abuse prevention in school settings. *Health Education Research, 18,* 237–256.

Ellickson, P. L., McCaffrey, D. F., Ghosh-Dastidar, B., & Longshore, D. L. (2003). New inroads in preventing adolescent drug use: Results from a large-scale trial of Project ALERT in middle schools. *American Journal of Public Health, 93*(11), 1830–1836.

Ennett, S. T., Tobler, N. S., Ringwalt, C. L., & Flewelling, R. L (1994). How effective is drug abuse resistance education? A meta-analysis of Project DARE outcome evaluations. *American Journal of Public Health, 84*(9), 1394–1401.

Epstein, J. A., Botvin, G. J., Dusenbury, L., Diaz, T., & Kerner, J. (1996). Validation of an acculturation measure for Hispanic adolescents. *Psychological Reports, 79*(3), 1075–1079.

Friis, R. H., & Sellers, T. A. (1999). *Epidemiology for public health practice (2nd ed.).* Aspen Publishers, Inc.

Garland, D. (2001). *The culture of control: Crime and social order in contemporary society.* Chicago: University of Chicago Press.

Gilbert, M. J. (1987). Programmatic approaches to the alcohol-related needs of Mexican Americans. In M. J. Gilbert & R. C. Cervantes (Eds.) *Mexican Americans and alcohol.* Los Angeles, CA: Spanish Speaking Mental Health Research Center, University of California. pp. 95–107.

Gil, A. G., Wagner, E. F., & Vega, W. A. (2000). Acculturation, familism and alcohol use among Latino adolescent males: Longitudinal relations. *Journal of Community Psychology, 28*(4), 443–458.

Gonzales, G. M. (1983). Time and place of first drinking experience and parental knowledge as predictors of alcohol use and misuse in college. *Journal of Alcohol and Drug Education, 27,* 1–13.

Gosin, M. N., Dustman, P. A., Drapeau, A. E., & Harthun, M. L. (2002). Participatory action research: Creating an effective prevention curriculum for adolescents in the Southwestern US. *Health Education Research, 18*(3), 363–379.

Greene, J. M., Ennett, S. T., & Ringwalt, C. L. (1997). Substance use among runaway and homeless youth in three national samples. *American Journal of Public Health, 87*(2), 229–235.

Hansen, W. B. (1992). School-based substance abuse prevention: A review of the state of the art in curriculum, 1980–1990. *Health Education Research: Theory and Practice, 7*(1), 403–430.

Hansen, W. B., Anderson, J., Flay, B., Graham, J. W., & Sobel, J. (1988). Affective and social influences approaches to the prevention of multiple substance abuse among seventh grade students: Results from Project SMART. *Preventive Medicine, 17,* 135–154.

Hansen, W. B., Miller, T. W., & Leukefeld, C. G. (1995). Prevention research recommendations: Scientific integration for the 90's. *Drugs and Society, 8*(3/4):
161–167.

Harmon, M. A. (1993). Reducing the risk of drug involvement among early
adolescents: An evaluation of drug use resistance education (DARE). *Evaluation Review, 17,* 221–239.

Hawkins, J. D., Catalano, R. E., & Miller, J. Y. (1992). Risk and protective factors
for alcohol and other drug problems in adolescence and early adulthood:
Implications for substance use prevention. *Psychological Bulletin, 112,*
64–105.

Hecht, M., Corman, S., & Miller-Rassulo, M. (1993). An evaluation of the drug
resistance project: A comparison of film versus live performance. *Health
Communication, 5,* 75–88.

Hecht, M., Trost, M. R., Bator, R. J., & McKinnon, D. (1997). Ethnicity and sex
similarities and differences in drug resistance. *Journal of Applied Communication Research, 25*(2), 75–97.

Holleran, L. K., Castro, F., Coard, S., Kumpfer, K., Nyborg, V., & Stephenson, H.
(2005). *Moving towards state of the art, culturally relevant prevention interventions for minority youth.* Presented at the Society for Prevention
Research annual meeting, May 27.

Holleran, L. K., Reeves, L., Marsiglia, F. F., & Dustman, P. (2002). Creating
culturally grounded videos for substance abuse prevention: A dual
perspective on process. *Journal of Social Work Practice in the Addictions,
2*(1), 55–78.

Holleran Steiker, L. K. (2006). Consulting with the experts: Utilizing adolescent
input in substance use prevention efforts. *Social Perspectives/Perspectivas
Sociales, 8,* 53–66.

Holleran Steiker, L. K., & Hopson, L. M. (2007, February). *Evaluation of culturally
adapted, evidence-based substance use prevention programs for older
adolescents in diverse community settings.* Advancing Adolescent Health
Conference. The University of Texas at Austin, Center for Health Promotion
Research. February 28.

Holleran Steiker, L. K., Hopson, L. M., Goldbach, J. T., & Robinson, C. (2014)
Evidence for site-specific, systematic adaptation of substance prevention
curriculum with high-risk youths in community and alternative school
settings. *Journal of Child & Adolescent Substance Abuse, 23*(5), 307–317.

Hopson, L.M. (2006, November). *Effectiveness of culturally grounded adaptations of an evidence-based substance use prevention program with alternative school students*. Unpublished dissertation. University of Texas at Austin School of Social Work.

Hopson, L. M. & Holleran Steiker, L. K. (2008). Methodology for Evaluating an Adaptation of Evidence-based Drug Abuse Prevention in Alternative Schools. *Children in Schools*, 30 (2), 116–127.

Hughes, J. N. (2003). Commentary: Participatory action research leads to sustainable school and community improvement. *School Psychology Review, 32*(1), 38–43

Johnson, C. A., Pentz, M. A., Weber, M. D., Dwyer, J. H., MacKinnon, D. P., Flay, B. R., et al. (1990). The relative effectiveness of comprehensive community programming for drug use prevention with risk and low risk adolescents. *Journal of Consulting and Clinical Psychology, 58*, 4047–4056.

Johnston, L. D., O'Malley, P. M., Bachman, J. G., & Schulenberg, J. E. (2014). *Monitoring the Future national results on drug use: 2012 overview, key findings on adolescent drug use*. Ann Arbor: Institute for Social Research, The University of Michigan.

Kidd, S. A, & Kral, M. J. (2005). Practicing participatory research. *Journal of Counseling Psychology, 52*(1), 187–195.

Kipke, M. D., Montgomery, S. B., Simon, T. R., & Iverson, E. F. (1997). "Substance abuse" disorders among runaway and homeless youth. *Substance Use and Misuse, 32*(7–8), 969–986.

Koopman, C., Rosario, M., & Rotheram-Borus, M. J. (1994). Alcohol and drug use and sexual behaviors placing runaways at risk for HIV infection. *Addictive Behaviors, 19*(1), 95–103.

Kumpfer, K. L., Alvarado, R., Smith, P., & Bellamy, N. (2002). Cultural sensitivity and adaptation in family-based prevention interventions. *Journal Prevention Science, 3*, 241–246.

Kumpfer, K. L., Molgaard, V., & Spoth, R. (1996). The strengthening families program for prevention of delinquency and drug use in special populations. In R. Peters & R. J. McMahon (Eds.) *Childhood Disorders, Substance Use, and Delinquency: Prevention and Early Intervention Approaches*. Newbury Park, CA: Sage Publications.

Lynam, D. R. (1999). Project DARE: No effects at 10-year follow-up. *Journal of Consulting and Clinical Psychology, 67*, 590.

MacLeod, J. (2004). *Ain't no makin' it: Aspirations and attainment in a low-income neighborhood*. Oxford: Westview Press.

MacMaster, S. A., & Holleran, L. K. (2005). Incorporating 12-step group attendance in addictions courses: A cross-cultural experience. *Journal of Teaching in the Addictions, 4,* 79–91.

MacMaster, S. A., Holleran, L., & Chaffin, K. (2005). Empirical and theoretical support for non-abstinence-based prevention services for substance using adolescents. *Journal of Evidence-Based Social Work, 2,* 91–111.

Marshall, J. W., Ruth, B. J., Sisco, S., Bethke, C., Piper, T. M., Cohen, M., & Bachman, S. (2011). Social work interest in prevention: A content analysis of the professional literature. *Social Work, 56*(3), 201–211.

Marsiglia, F. F., & Booth, J. M. (2014). Cultural adaptation of interventions in real practice settings. *Research on Social Work Practice.* Online publication accessed 5/17/15. http://rsw.sagepub.com/content/early/2014/05/21/1049731514535989.full.pdf+html

Marsiglia, F. F., Kulis, S., Wagstaff, D. A., Elek, E., & Dran, D. (2005). Acculturation status and substance use prevention with Mexican and Mexican American youth. *Journal of Social Work Practice in the Addictions, 5*(1), 85–111.

Miller, G. J., Beckles, G. L. A., Maude, G. H., & Carson, D. C. (1990). Alcohol consumption: Protection against coronary heart disease and risks to health. *International Journal of Epidemiology, 19,* 923–930.

Moon, D. G., Hecht, M. L., Jackson, K. M., & Spellers, R. E. (1999). Ethnic and gender differences and similarities in adolescent drug use and refusals of drug offers. *Substance Use & Misuse, 34,* 1059–83.

National Association of Clinicians (2001). *NASW standards for cultural competence in social work practice.* Retrieved February 6, 2007 from http://www.socialworkers.org/sections/credentials/cultural_comp.asp

Neighbors, C., Larimer, M. E., Lostutter, T. W., & Woods, B. A. (2006). Harm reduction and individually focused alcohol prevention. *International Journal of Drug Policy, 17*(4): 304–309.

Padget, A., Bell, M. L., Shamblen, S. R., & Ringwalt, C. L. (2006). Does learning about the effects of alcohol on the developing brain affect children's alcohol use? *Journal Prevention Science, 7,* 293–302.

Pentz, M. A., Rothspan, G. T., Skara, S., & Voskanian, S. (1999). Multi-ethnic considerations in community-based drug use prevention research. In S. B. Kar, (Ed.) *Substance Use Prevention: A Multicultural Perspective.* Amityville, N.Y.: Baywood Publishing Company, Inc.

Polansky, J. M., Buki, L. P., Horan, J. J., Dyche-Ceperich, S., & Dyer, D. (1999). The effectiveness of substance abuse prevention videotapes with Mexican American adolescents. *Hispanic Journal of Behavioral Sciences, 21*(2), 186–198.

Pomeroy, E. C., & Holleran Steiker, L. K. (2012). Prevention and intervention on the care continuum. *Social Work, 57*(2).

Rew, L., Taylor-Seehafer, M., & Fitzgerald, M. L. (2001). Sexual abuse, alcohol and other drug use, and suicidal behaviors in homeless adolescents. *Issues in Comprehensive Pediatric Nursing, 24*(1), 225–240.

Ringwalt, C. L., Ennett, S., Johnson, R., Rohrbach, L. A., Simons-Rudolph, A., Vincus, A., & Thorne, J. (2003). Factors associated with fidelity to substance use prevention curriculum guides in the nation's middle schools. *Health Education & Behavior, 3*, 75–391.

Ringwalt, C. L., Vincus, A., Ennett, S., Johnson, R., & Rohrbach, L. A. (2004). Reasons for teachers' adaptation of substance use prevention curricula in schools with non-white student populations. *Journal Prevention Science, 5*, 61–67.

Schinke, S. P., Botvin, G. J., & Orlandi, M. A. (1991). *Substance abuse in children and adolescents: Evaluation and intervention*. Newbury Park, CA: Sage Publishers.

Swendsen, J., Burstein, M., Case, B., Conway, K. P., Dierker, L., He, J., & Merikangas, K. R. (2012). Use and abuse of alcohol and illicit drugs in US adolescents: Results of the National Comorbidity Survey–Adolescent Supplement. *Archives of General Psychiatry, 69*(4), 390–398.

Terry-McElrath, Y. M.; O'Malley, P. M., & Johnson, L. D. (2013). Middle and high school drug testing and student illicit drug use: A national study 1998–2011. *Journal of Adolescent Health, 52*(6): 707–715.

Tobler, N. S, & Stratton, H. H. (1997). Effectiveness of school-based drug prevention programs: A meta-analysis of the research. *Journal of Primary Prevention. 18*, 71–128.

Trimble, J. E. (2007). Prolegomena for the connotation of construct use in the measurement of ethnic and racial identity. *Journal of Counseling Psychology, 54*(3), 247–258.

Trimble, J., Bolek, C. S., & Niemcryk, S. J. (2013). *Ethnic and multicultural drug abuse: Perspectives on current research*. Birmingham, NY: Haworth Press.

Vega, W. A., Gil, A. G., Wagner, E. (1998). Cultural adjustments and Hispanic adolescent drug use. In W. A. Vega & A. Gil (Eds) *Drug use and ethnicity in early adolescents*. New York, NY: Plenum Press, pp. 125–48.

Wallace, J. M., & Bachman, J. G. (1991). Explaining racial/ethnic differences in adolescent drug use: The impact of background and lifestyle. *Social Problems, 38*, 333–357.

Weir, E. (2000). Raves: a review of the culture, the drugs and the prevention of harm. *Canadian Medical Association Journal, 162* (13), 1843–50.

Weissberg, R. P., Kumpfer, K. L., & Seligman, M. E. P. (2003). Prevention that works for children and youth: An introduction. *American Psychologist, 58*, 425– 432.

Welle, D. L. (2003). LGBTQ youth: Research on developmental complexity. *Society for Research on Adolescence Newsletter, Fall, 1*:7–8.

Winters, K. C., & Lee, J. (2010). *Drugs and the developing brain: The science behind young people's substance use.* Center City, MN: Hazelden.

Zapata, J. T., & Katims, D. S. (1994). Antecedents of substance use among Mexican-American school age children. *Journal of Drug Education, 24*(1), 233–251.

Chapter 5

Family and Parental Interventions and Attitudes

FAMILY DYNAMICS

There is almost no way around heartbreak when a parent realizes a child is entering the world of drugs and alcohol. Yes, denial (a psychological defense mechanism characterized by an unconscious inability to see a difficult reality) may be a distinct part of the picture due to how hard it is to imagine those we love in the depths of pain and suffering, but on some level, parents often know that young people who experiment with substances, and most do or will, enter an exponentially riskier world than they existed in before they used substances. They may or may not know that this is potentially life threatening.

In order to enter the world of an addicted family, one must have a sense of the family dynamics that emerge when a youth has a problem with drugs/alcohol. If one peruses the literature or facilitates a group for parents of teen drug and alcohol users, the following family (especially parental) responses become apparent:

- begging
- pleading
- bargaining
- negotiating

- manipulating
- bribing
- praising
- screaming
- snooping
- arguing
- defending
- denying
- emoting, emoting, emoting . . .

Ironically, the more parents of teens emote, the farther the teen wants to be away from them. In treatment, it is not uncommon to hear teens saying that the reason they used was that their parents were "always on them" or "constantly crying (or yelling and screaming) about something or other."

In desperation, some parents think "tough love" may be the answer, but it is illegal to kick a child out of the house unless you have declared them legally incorrigible. A better strategy for parents is to gather facts and record them. Think about that term, "legally incorrigible." It means legally *incapable of correction.* Think back to the values written about early in this book. Can you imagine parents reaching the point where they give up and formally declare their child "broken and unfixable"? It is the work of trained helping professionals that can shift the gears in the downward slide. Through the facilitation of a talented clinician, instead of giving up, parents can be empowered. Much like the tradition modeled in formal interventions, lists of truths can be read as bottom lines to set ultimatums when families are ready to insist an adolescent pursue treatment. The Johnson model intervention method is one way in which family, friends, and loved ones can show their full support. This method was founded by Vernon Johnson in the late 1960s in an effort to address psychological disorders and serious personal problems. In popular culture, many have witnessed this model through the TV show "Intervention" (which unfortunately spends more time focusing on the "car wreck" of the addict/alcoholic's and their family's life than the intervention and recovery process itself). The Johnson model intervention method uses a lovingly confrontational approach, in which a close friend or family member sets up a meeting with the addict, helps him or her realize the damage addiction has done, and encourages him or her to get help and enter a treatment center immediately. Of course, all interventions must be supervised by a professional interventionist to ensure that proper procedure is followed and that everything goes according to plan. The Johnson model intervention method is widely used and accepted as effective, but is also shunned by some due to its potentially confrontational nature. This model may result in conflict that may complicate the intervention process. There are elements that are not captured in the televised version. For example, the trained interventionist meets with the family six to eight times prior to the meeting with the addict/alcoholic in order to be sure that they are prepared. The preparation involves getting their emotions out so that the intervention with the person with substance use problems will be focused on facts, lists, and solutions. Research shows that formal interventions have a very high success rate because, if done well, families and friends are all "on the same page," and the person being confronted becomes aware that they will lose their entire support network if they do not follow through with the prescribed treatment. In the end, the family and friends all say, "I will support you if you go to treatment. If you do not, I will not be in your life." They do this out of their awareness that "enabling" the person to continue with their addiction is, essentially, contributing to their suicide (conscious or unconscious) by substances. A bag is packed and waiting, as is a bed in a treatment facility. Many surrender to the truth, break down their defenses, and give up fighting. Some fight on into what twelve-step programs refer to as the "gates of insanity or death."

More recently, evidence has been found to support another model for families, entitled Community Reinforcement and Family Training (CRAFT). This intervention, supported by the American Psychological Association, is designed to increase family compliance with an intervention for persons with substance misuse in order to increase the rate of engagement of those addicted individuals in treatment. The specific procedures involved in CRAFT include motivation building, functional analysis, contingency management training, communication skills training, treatment entry training, immediate treatment entry, life enrichment, and safety training.

The research support for CRAFT is as follows. Sisson and Azrin (1986) recruited twelve adult women with an alcoholic husband, brother, or father and randomly assigned them either to an early version of CRAFT or to a traditional Al-Anon intervention. Results indicated that CRAFT was considerably more successful in getting the persons with substance misuse into treatment and reducing their alcohol consumption in comparison to the Al-Anon group. Miller, Meyers & Tonigan (1999) conducted a controlled comparison of CRAFT, the Johnson Intervention, and Al-Anon facilitation (TSF) that randomized 130 caregivers of problem drinkers to receive twelve hours of contact in one of the three conditions. CRAFT and TSF had better retention than the Johnson Intervention. Consistent with previous studies, participants tended to drop out of the Johnson intervention in order to avoid the family confrontation with the drinker. The CRAFT intervention also engaged substantially more drinkers into treatment (64 percent CRAFT vs. 23 percent Johnson and 13 percent TSF).

Kirby, Marlowe, Festinger, Garvey, and LaMonaca (1999) randomly assigned thirty-two caregivers of drug users to CRAFT or a twelve-step self-help group. Findings showed that caregivers who were assigned to CRAFT attended more sessions than those in twelve-step groups and were more likely to complete a full course of counseling during which the persons abusing drugs were far more likely to enter treatment (64 percent vs. 17 percent). Reductions in drug use occurred during the study, but there was no group x time interaction. Similarly positive outcomes were found with drug users and engagement of the drug-misusing family members in treatment (Smith & Meyers, 2004).

Parents of adolescents with substance use problems struggle with a profound dilemma. They know that they cannot manage their child's problem, and often the more they try, the worse it gets for everyone. However, if and when they "let go," they are plagued by terror of losing their child to the horrors of the drug world, or worse. This is why parents need support from others in similar situations to remain healthy, to get the support they need, and to make sane and solid decisions while caring for an addicted child. David Sheff, author of *Beautiful Boy*, describes the experience thusly: "I became addicted to my child's addiction. When it preoccupied me, even at the expense of my responsibilities to my wife and other children, I justified it. I thought, 'How can a parent not be consumed by his child's life-or-death struggle?' " (2008: p. 15).

One person in a "Young People and Drugs Class" in recovery tells this poignant story:

I was coming home at 2 and 3 in the morning, night after night one summer, drunk and high after hanging with a bunch of serious alcoholics and addicts at a bar ironically called "Good Times" (we had ceased having good times quite a while back). Every night I would come home and my father would be waiting for me on the steps. Some nights he would hug me, tell me he loved me, remind me I was worth so much more than this, and put me to bed gently, while he cried. Other nights he would yell and scream, "How could you do this to yourself and to us?" Other nights he would beg and plead for me to stop and promise me all kinds of things I wanted if I would change my ways. One night I came home and he wasn't on the steps. I fumbled with my key, drunk and high, and tripped up the stairs to my parents' bedroom and I woke him up to tell him I was home safe. He looked me in the eye and without any emotion at all he said, "The behavior will stop or you will not live in my house." I got clean and sober within months of that night. I have never forgotten it. He was done. It was time.

The concept of "family disease" is a critical piece in understanding the nature of the impact of drugs and alcohol on individuals and systems. Families work to maintain homeostasis (Dayton, 2012) or balance, and many of the major and minor adjustments made to strike the balance are not conscious but automatic. Other changes are purposeful and well thought out. Perhaps the best metaphor for homeostasis is a mobile; picture a delicate mobile with family members gently dangling and bobbing in the air. Now grab one member (the one that is consumed by drugs or alcohol) and yank it dramatically downward. Watch all the other members violently bob up and down and fly through the air until they readjust to new positions when the drug using member is in a new place. If one member dramatically is tugged again, the whole system flies around until it settles, and this happens over and over again. Families are constantly doing these adjustments even in families without illness. In families with the disease, the adjustments are profound and can be exhausting and system-threatening.

Because the disease is progressive, family members seamlessly slip into patterns of relating that become increasingly more problematic and chaotic. The children are often left to fend for themselves and anyone bold enough to confront the obvious disease may be branded as a family traitor. Family members may withdraw into their own private worlds or compete for the little love and attention that is available. In the absence of reliable adults, siblings may become "parentified" and try to provide the care and comfort that is missing for each other.

Alcoholic or addicted families may become characterized by a kind of emotional and psychological constriction, where family members do not feel free to express their authentic selves for fear of triggering disaster (often described anecdotally by such families as "walking on eggshells"); their genuine feelings are often hidden under strategies for keeping safe, like pleasing or withdrawing. The family becomes organized around trying to manage the unmanageable disease of addiction. They may yell, withdraw, cajole, harangue, empathize, criticize. . . . They become remarkably inventive in trying everything they can come up with to contain the problem and keep the family from blowing up. As Dayton (2012) so powerfully puts it, "The alarm bells in this system are constantly on a low hum, causing everyone to feel hyper-vigilant, ready to run for emotional (or physical) shelter or to erect their defenses at the first sign of trouble."

Because family members avoid sharing subjects that might lead to more pain, they often wind up avoiding genuine connection with each other. Then when painful feelings build up, those feelings may rise to the surface in emotional eruptions or get acted out through impulsive behaviors. Thus, these families become systems for manufacturing and perpetuating trauma. Trauma affects the internal world of each person, their relationships, and their ability to communicate and be together in a balanced, relaxed, and trusting manner. As the "elephant in the living room" increases in size and power, the family has to become ever more cautious in keeping its internal structures from weakening and becoming overwhelmed. But family members are often caught in a losing battle. As described by expert Tian Dayton (2012), "The guilt and shame that family members feel at the erratic behavior within their walls, along with the psychological defenses against seeing the truth, all too often keep this family from getting help." Thus, the development of the individuals within the family, and the family unit itself, become compromised. They lose their capacity to adjust to "life on life's terms" as the twelve-step programs call it. They need to gain insight and relearn (or learn if they never knew in the first place) healthy ways to rise to the changes inherent in living a full and satisfying life.

A word about the term "dysfunctional family." Some people joke, to keep this light-hearted, "We put the "fun" in dysFUNctional." Be cautious about joking in this minefield. The term "dysfunctional family" is a punitive and judgmental label that has little utility. If anything, it discourages and disheartens. Also, as anyone who has witnessed addicted and recovering families for a while realizes, it simply isn't accurate. There are aspects that are dysfunctional in all families, just as there are strengths in all families. In addition, families that are surviving drug and alcohol use or addiction are often "hyper-functional" in the sense that everyone is working overtime to try to keep the family together, keep the addict alive, and figure out solutions to the crisis. The term "hyper-functional" is more accurate, positive, and encouraging, and it honors those involved.

David Sheff notes, "Someone who heard my story expressed bafflement that [my son] Nic would become addicted saying, 'But your family doesn't seem dysfunctional.' We *are* dysfunctional—as dysfunctional as every other family I know. Sometimes more so, sometimes less so. I'm not sure if I know any 'functional' families, if functional means a family without difficult times and members who don't have a full range of problems." (Sheff, 2008). Sheff notes that more than half of all children will experiment with drugs and although some will have no major negative consequences, others will have outcomes that are "catastrophic." What often happens to family members of adolescents with drug and alcohol problems is that they become what is commonly referred to as "codependent." Sheff encapsulates the challenge of recovery to any parent of an addicted child, thusly: "I learned that my preoccupation with [my son] Nic didn't help him and may have harmed him. Or maybe it was irrelevant to him. However, it surely harmed the rest of my family—and me." (2008, p. 15).

According to Tian Dayton (2012), families where addiction is present are, at best, painful to live in, and, at worst, traumatizing or potentially fatal in varying degrees. The addicted family system is often characterized by broad swings, from one end of the emotional, psychological, and behavioral spectrum to the other. Dayton's work highlights the fact that family members are inundated with stress, fear, illusion, and lies. She notes that the family system is often warping reality to try to maintain a family order that they experience as gradually slipping away.

In their youth, children of alcoholics or drug-addicted parents (COAs or CODA) may feel overwhelmed with powerful emotions that they lack the developmental sophistication and family support to process and understand. As a result, they may resort to intense defenses, such as shutting down their own feelings, denying there is a problem, rationalizing, intellectualizing, over-controlling, withdrawing, acting out, or self-medicating, as a way to control their inner experience of chaos.

When alcohol or drugs are introduced into a family system, the family's ability to regulate its emotional and behavioral functioning is severely challenged. The family will generally reach as a unit to balance itself. In alcoholic homes, this may become a precarious sort of balance. Family members can become subsumed by the disease to such an extent they lose their sense of normal. Their life becomes about hiding the truth from themselves, their children, and their relational world. Trust and faith in an orderly and predictable world are challenged as one's family life becomes chaotic. Children and adults in the family may lose their sense of who they are and what they can depend upon. Promises are broken and those they depend on for support and stability betray and deceive them.

It is no wonder that children who grow up in such systems experience problems both in the present and later in life. Children from these families may find themselves moving into adult roles carrying baggage that they don't know exactly what to do with and that get them into trouble in their relationships and/or work lives. Most of the time, they don't even know that they are carrying heavy loads that no longer serve them.

When what is going on within the family is never talked about, children are left to make sense of it on their own. Dayton (2012) notes that avoiding talking often leads to confusion and disconnection. Talking about and processing pain is a necessary deterrent to developing post-traumatic symptoms that show up later in life. Intense emotions such as sadness, that are an inevitable part of processing pain, can make family members feel like they're "falling apart" and consequently they may resist experiencing the pain they are in. Intense emotions become associated with the sense that things are potentially insecure or even life threatening. If addiction remains untreated, maladjusted coping strategies become deeply entrenched. Dayton's work illustrates that when highly stressful relational environments persist over time, they can produce cumulative trauma (2012). Stress and trauma affect both the mind and the body and can lead to deregulation in the body's limbic system—the system that helps regulate emotions and bodily functions. Because the limbic system governs such fundamental functions as mood, emotional tone, appetite, and sleep cycles, when it becomes deregulated it can manifest as an impaired ability to regulate levels of emotion, especially fear, anger, and sadness. This lack of ability to regulate mood may lead to chronic anxiety or depression. For many, it emerges as substance or behavioral disorders—for example, problems in regulating alcohol, eating, sexual, or spending habits (Dayton, 2012).

One powerful dynamic in families with alcohol/drug related communication patterns is denial. This coping mechanism protects family members from having to face truths that they simply cannot integrate into their realities. For example, one mother told the following story. She said that her son wanted her to walk the periphery of her back yard each evening before bed with a flashlight. As strange as the request seemed, she welcomed the opportunity to connect with her son, to meet a need, to do something that brought him comfort. She simply couldn't consciously see that he was paranoid from drug use or insanity.

Even an addiction counselor's daughter, when she told her mother that she was going to try AA in her sophomore year of college, received the response, "Oh, that isn't your problem. Don't over react. I'm sure it is because you are the child of an alcoholic." Even knowing all that this family knew of alcoholism, its genetic aspects, and its potentially life threatening consequences, this mother couldn't wrap her mind around the truth.

One mother came to her family support group one evening and excitedly reported that her marijuana-smoking son had "found God." When her fellow group members asked how she knew this, she said that he had asked where the tiny Bible was so he could carry it with him. Suddenly, the counselor's face went very serious. The counselor had put the pieces together. She had heard the story before. The tiny Bibles, with the thin pages, were often used for rolling papers for marijuana joints. The mother refused to believe this explanation, even when she went home and found whole sections torn from the book.

WARNING SIGNS AND RED FLAGS

In the world of child and adolescent drug and alcohol use and dependence, family members are often the first to note concerns about the young person who is using substances. This section explores things that family members often notice (or fail to notice, depending on the case) as "red flags" for a problem with drugs and/or alcohol. The list has been enhanced by CPS (Child Protective Services) social workers who participated in drug and alcohol trainings. In home visits, they became very astute at noticing the "clues" that can help families and workers intervene quickly, sometimes saving families from years of crisis, or even tragedy.

Paraphernalia

The term drug "paraphernalia" refers to any equipment that is used to produce, conceal, and/or consume illicit drugs. Under federal law, the term drug paraphernalia means "any equipment, product, or material of any kind which is primarily intended or designed for use in manufacturing, compounding, converting, concealing, producing, processing, preparing, injecting, ingesting, inhaling, or otherwise introducing into the human body a controlled substance." This list was compiled and enhanced during workshops with addictions counselors and CPS workers who did home visits. This aspect of assessment extends the concept of "detective work" because many everyday, common household items can be used as drug paraphernalia and as drugs themselves.

- pipes (metal, wooden, acrylic, glass, stone, plastic, or ceramic), often mistaken by parents as "miniature collections"
- roach clips and other home-made clips for holding small marijuana "roaches" (for example, if boys have bobby-pins and short hair, this is an anomaly)
- miniature spoons
- chillums (cone-shaped marijuana/hash pipes)
- bongs
- home-made pipes and bongs (these can look like anything from Lego creations, to art sculptures, to hollowed-out potatoes)
- cigarette papers (youth are creative, and one parent noted that she thought her son had "found Jesus" but he was actually using Bible paper to roll marijuana joints)
- cocaine freebase kits or "fix kits"
- aluminum foil with burnt sections
- shoebox tops (used to sort seeds and stems from marijuana buds)
- lighters, matches, or ashtrays

- straws, especially cut to shorter sizes for snorting
- whipped cream dispensers turned huffing devices
- pills of any sort (even in vitamin or over-the-counter bottles)— parents often overlook aspirin bottles or allergy medicine containers and youth learn that these are good disguises for other pills
- clothing or purses with secret pockets such as "stash hats" (hats with pockets inside, literally sold to hide drugs)

In addition to items that can give clues into the substance use of youth, it is important to note young people's health and physical signs which might indicate drug or alcohol use:

- integumentary lesions (i.e., marks on the skin from needles)
- burnt finger tips
- rotten teeth
- noticeable weight loss or gain
- for girls, drastic or messy make-up
- unhealthy hair
- unhealthy nails
- sores or picked scabs (often associated with amphetamine use)

Also, youth who are using or abusing substances often display behavioral changes. Note that none of the following in and of themselves are purely diagnostic, but combinations of these should lead to concern and consideration of screening and even assessment.

- giving up old friends
- dropping hobbies and activities that used to bring joy

- hanging out in odd locations
- isolation
- self-injury: cutting, eating disorders
- drastic appearance changes (e.g., piercing self, tattoos, unusual clothing)
- becoming a "chameleon" (blending into peer groups without a sense of own identity)
- grades dropping
- truancy
- legal issues
- running away
- sexual issues
- family conflicts
- personality changes
- fear-based decision making or paranoia
- negativity, nihilism, or loss of belief in good things
- risk-taking behaviors and poor judgment, especially sensation seeking

But even with this list in mind, it is important to note that youth are diverse and complex. Some cope by working harder in school, or by spending hours on the Internet, or by channeling pain through art or music. Young addicted people sometimes seek comfort in relationships or sex. Others seek comfort with food. The bottom line is that the most solid indicator of substance use or dependence is simply this: an inability to stop using. This does not necessarily mean daily or even regular use. Many describe it thusly: "I didn't have problems every time I used, but every time I had problems, I was using."

FAMILIES, RESILIENCE, AND RECOVERY

Resilience

Too many texts catalogue the traumas of children who grow up in drug and alcohol dependent families. It is, however, possible to see the "silver lining" of growing up in such families. A new and growing literature on post-traumatic growth captures the powerful strengths that can come from adversity.

In treating Adult Children of Alcoholics (ACOAs) it is important to identify the qualities of strength and resilience that they possess. ACOAs can be marvelously adaptive and resourceful. As the Italian proverb goes, "What doesn't kill you makes you stronger." Many COAs and ACOAs develop unusual personal strengths. One of the most important things that resilient children share in common, according to Wolin and Wolin (2010), is a strong, bonded relationship with at least one other person, usually within the extended family network, often a grandmother, aunt, or uncle.

Wolin and Wolin have created what they call a resilience mandala, representing those qualities that are resilience enhancing. Each circle of the diagram represents a stage of development. At the center of the circle is the self. The ring closest to the center holds the name of the childhood phases of all the resiliencies. Moving outward, the next ring holds the adolescent stages, and the one after that, the adult stages. The outermost ring gives the general, overall name of each resiliency.

They are:

- independence

- creativity

- relationships

- insight
- humor
- morality
- initiative

Some of the risk factors for children that can lead to psychological and emotional problems later in life are:

- poverty
- overcrowding
- neighborhood and school violence
- parental absence
- unemployment or instability

These can be the children who are likely to wind up in the health care or penal system. However, some children grow up in the middle of all this and still come to have productive lives and relationships. Wolin and Wolin (2010) studied these children and their growth into adulthood in order to identify the attitudes and qualities that resilient children and adults seemed to possess and what factors might have contributed to building them. They discovered that resilient children tend to fit the following profile:

- They have likable personalities from birth that attract parents, surrogates, and mentors to want to care for them. They are naturally adept recruiters of support and interest from others and drink up attention, care, and support from wherever they can get it.
- They tend to be of at least average intelligence, reading on or above grade level.

- Few have another child born within two years of their birth.
- Virtually all of the children have at least one person with whom they have developed a strong relationship, often from the extended family or close community.
- Often they report having an inborn feeling that their lives are going to work out.
- They can identify the illness in their family and are able to find ways to distance themselves from it; they don't let the family dysfunction destroy them.
- They work through their problems but don't tend to make that a lifestyle.
- They take active responsibility for creating their own successful lives.
- They tend to have constructive attitudes toward themselves and their lives.
- They tend not to fall into self-destructive lives.

Wolin and Wolin (2010), in studying resilient adults, found that the following tended to be true:

- They found and built on their own strengths.
- They improved deliberately and methodically on their parents' lifestyles.
- They married consciously into happy, healthy, strong families.
- They fought off memories of horrible family get-togethers in order create their own rituals.
- There tended to be what Wolin and Wolin refer to as the "magic two hundred mile" radius between them and their families of origin, enabling them to stay somewhat apart from the daily conflicts of potential family difficulties.

KEY TERMS

Denial

Johnson model of formal
  intervention

Confrontational approach

Family disease

Homeostasis

Parentified child

Emotional and psychological
  constriction

Hyper-vigilant

Dysfunctional family

Hyper-functional family

Codependent

Children of alcoholics or drug
  addicted parents (COAs or
  CODA)

"Red flags"

Paraphernalia

Resilience

DISCUSSION QUESTIONS

1. Give an anecdotal example of each of the dynamics illustrated in the section titled "Family Dynamics."

2. Watch an episode of "Intervention" and critically evaluate what is effective in the show and what is not. Where is it Hollywood sensationalism and where good science?

3. Make a list of the "red flags" for substance misuse, broken down into bio-psycho-social-spiritual categories.

4. Think of ways to use the resiliency mandala.

5. Make a list of the payoffs and the downsides of being a child of an addict/alcoholic.

REFERENCES

Dayton, T. (2012). *The ACOA trauma syndrome: The impact of childhood pain on adult relationships.* Deerfield Beach, FL: Health Communications, Inc.

Hawkins, D. J., Catalano, R. F., & Miller, J. Y. (1992). Risk and protective factors for alcohol and other substance problems in adolescence and early adulthood: Implications for substance abuse prevention. *Psychological Bulletin, 112*(1), 64–105.

Kirby, K. C., Marlowe, D. B., Festinger, D. S., Garvey, K. A., & LaMonaca, V. (1999). Community reinforcement training for family and significant others of drug abusers: A unilateral intervention to increase treatment entry of drug users. *Drug and Alcohol Dependence, 56*(1), 85–96.

Miller, W. R., Meyers, R. J., & Tonigan, J. (1999). Engaging the unmotivated in treatment for alcohol problems: A comparison of three strategies for intervention through family members. *Journal of Consulting & Clinical Psychology, 67*(5), 688–697.

Sheff, D. (2008). *Beautiful boy: A father's journey through his son's addiction.* Boston, MA: Houghton Mifflin Company.

Smith, J. E., & Meyers, R. J. (2004). *Motivating substance abusers to enter treatment: Working with family members.* New York, NY: Guilford Press.

Wolin, S. J., & Wolin, S. (2010). *The resilient self: How survivors of troubled families rise above adversity.* New York, NY: Villard Books.

PART III

Empirically Supported
Screening and Assessment

Previous chapters have examined the problem of substance misuse, modes of prevention, and the environments that surround and affect youth. This section considers those who are already misusing substances. It begins with an overview of the *Diagnostic Statistical Manual* (DSM) changes; these are important because the new DSM-5 changes the entire conceptual view of youth and substances. Although clinicians used to be concerned with the dichotomy between substance misuse and dependence, the frame has shifted dramatically to considering substance use disorders along a spectrum from mild to severe. Subsequently, assessment tools and techniques have shifted with this paradigm (Straussner, 2013). This section addresses this frame as well as tools and techniques. As you will see, screening and assessment are as much of an art as they are a science. One cannot mechanically ascertain such a complex and intricate issue. So in approaching a young person to gather information about substance use, you must become more like a clever detective than a medical diagnostician. There are reliable and valid instruments you can use to help determine the problem and its many aspects, but you must use all of your connecting skills and talents to get the true story and to take it to the next place—intervention.

Chapter 6

Youth and Adolescent Substance Misuse Screening, Assessment, and Diagnosis

OVERVIEW OF THE DSM-5 AND SUBSTANCE USE DISORDERS

The Diagnostic and Statistical Manual of Mental Disorders (DSM), the primary publication of the American Psychiatric Association, presents diagnostic criteria, descriptions, and other information to guide the classification and diagnosis of mental disorders. The DSM is considered the standard classification of mental disorders used by mental health professionals in the United States. The edition published in 2000 (DSM-IV) was replaced in May of 2013 by the DSM-5. Practitioners who work with children and adolescents with substance use disorders have heard and repeated the humorous recovery phrase, "All you have to change is your entire life." Well, when it comes to the diagnosis of substance use disorders and the changes from the DSM-IV to the DSM-5, "all you have to change is your entire understanding." Now, before you panic, there are some excellent reasons for the changes and it is likely that, by the end of this chapter, you will be glad for the changes for your clients' sake. First and foremost, please focus on this frame: The DSM-5 revisions aim to capture children's, adolescents' and emerging adults' experiences and symptoms more accurately than the DSM-IV.

The most recent version of *The Diagnostic and Statistical Manual* embraces a perspective considering mental health across the lifespan. Rather than isolating childhood conditions, the new manual underscores how psychiatric disorders can manifest throughout a client's lifespan, embracing what the American Psychiatric Association (2013) refers to as a "new lifespan approach to mental health." Each disorder is now set within a framework that recognizes age-related aspects, chronologically listing diagnoses that are most applicable to infancy and childhood first, followed by diagnoses that are more common to adolescence and early adulthood, and ending with those that are often diagnosed later in life. Thus, disorders previously addressed in a single "infancy, childhood, and adolescence" chapter are now integrated throughout the book. Systems-oriented social workers will be relieved to know that families and consumer advocacy groups gave feedback and in many cases met with the DSM-5 workgroups.

Changes in Terminology and Symptom Specificity

For adolescents, emerging adults, and adults, historically, the diagnosis of dependence has caused much confusion. Many people have confused the term "substance dependence" with the variably defined and unclear term "addiction." In actuality, substance dependence can be a normal physiological response to a substance and does not necessarily imply the complexities attributed (or erroneously misattributed) to the term addiction. This overview will provide you with a logic model for conceiving and integrating the DSM changes into your practice. So breathe, and take a look.

The fifth edition of the *Diagnostic and Statistical Manual of Mental Disorders* (DSM-5) includes a significantly revised chapter

116

entitled "Substance-Related and Addictive Disorders." The new chapter includes fundamental alterations to (1) the disorders grouped therein and (2) changes to the criteria of certain disorders (American Psychiatric Association, 2013). First, consider the terminology:

• •

Substance use disorder now combines the previous categories of "substance abuse" and "substance dependence" into a single category entitled "substance use disorder," measured on a continuum from mild to severe.

• •

Each specific substance (other than caffeine, which cannot be diagnosed as a substance use disorder) is addressed as a separate use disorder (e.g., alcohol use disorder, marijuana use disorder, etc.). In the new DSM-5, substances are diagnosed based on the same all-encompassing criteria. The experts who redesigned the new DSM paradigm for substance use disorders aimed to strengthen the criteria though this combination. The list of symptoms has been expanded. For example, whereas the DSM-IV diagnosis of substance abuse required only one symptom, mild substance use disorder in DSM-5 requires two to three symptoms from a list of eleven.

Here is the most exciting part. The changes were made with practice in mind! In the DSM-IV, the distinction between abuse and dependence was constructed on the conceptualization of abuse as a mild or early phase and dependence as the more severe manifestation. In practice, however, as many of you may have experienced, the abuse criteria were quite severe for some clients, especially adolescents. The revised, single diagnosis of substance use disorder will undoubtedly match the symptoms that patients experience more accurately. Here are a few examples:

- Drug craving has been added to the list. Many of you will realize that this was a glaring omission in the previous symptomology.
- Problems with law enforcement are eliminated. True to social work values and knowledge, cultural considerations make that criterion difficult to apply both nationally and internationally. Also, this recognizes that legal consequences for children and adolescents have typically fallen on parents and guardians.

Consideration of Other Behavioral Addictions and Related Compulsive Behaviors

The other substantive change worth noting in this overview is that the DSM-5 has added gambling disorder as the sole condition in a new category called behavioral addictions. Previously, DSM-IV listed this process as pathological gambling (PG) under the section called "Impulse Control Disorders Not Elsewhere Classified," along with compulsive hair pulling (trichotillomania), intermittent explosive disorder, kleptomania, and pyromania. The DSM-5 officially renames "pathological gambling" as "gambling disorder." Researchers and clinicians alike celebrate this change due to the concern that the label "pathological" is a derogatory term that reinforces the social stigma of being a problem gambler. The category is now found under the heading "Substance-Related and Addictive Disorders." The rationale for this change is that the growing evidence reveals common elements with substance use disorders not only from the external consequences (e.g., financial and relationship difficulties) but also in terms of their biological and psychosocial symptoms. According to Charles O'Brien, chair of the Substance-Related Disorders Work Group for DSM-5, brain imaging studies and neurochemical tests have powerfully supported the fact that gambling activates the reward system in much the same way that substances do. Neuroscience and genetics research have played a key role in establishing that gambling addicts report cravings and highs in response to their stimulus of choice and that this disorder runs in families, often alongside other addictions. The movement of gambling disorder to the substance use section of the DSM-5 will likely enhance screening and intervention efforts in specialty settings such as substance use disorder settings (Petry, Blanco, Stinchfield, & Volberg, 2013).

Particularly relevant to adolescents currently are the related topics of "Internet addiction," "sex addiction," and non-suicidal self-injury (i.e., self-harm without the intention of suicide). All of these conditions were reportedly considered for related diagnostic categories, but work group members decided there was insufficient research data for them to be included as of yet. Instead, Internet gaming disorder is included in Section III of the manual, entitled "Emerging Measures and Models." Disorders listed here require further research before their consideration as formal disorders. Social workers should continue to engage in and endorse research in these areas.

Although there has been discussion of the relationship between eating disorders and substance use disorders, they remain separate in the DSM-5. Eating disorders, previously listed among "Disorders Usually First Diagnosed in Infancy, Childhood, or Adolescence," are now listed in the "Feeding and Eating Disorders" chapter.

Shifts to Reduce Stigma and Increase Focus on Person in Environment

The DSM-5 work groups clearly have had reduction of stigma, accuracy of symptomology, and cultural considerations in mind as they designed the new guiding text. Clearly, part of removing stigma is about choosing the right words. Replacing the term "drug abuser," for example, with "a person with a substance use disorder" creates powerful shifts which have been supported with recent research (Kelly, Dow, & Westerhoff, 2010), as does replacing "pathological gambler" with "someone with a behavioral addiction." Although substance use and gambling are deemed "disorders" (related to the research on the brain and disrupted pleasure pathways), other attempts have been made to clarify such distinctions. For example, replacing "disorder" with "dysphoria" in the diagnostic label related to gender identity is not only more appropriate and consistent with respectful clinical sexology terminology; it also removes the connotation that the patient is disordered.

How will your practices change to accommodate the new DSM? Well, you will have to break your habit of using the terms "abuse" and "dependence" and get used to all substance use disorders (designated by substance) being characterized in terms of mild to severe. You will be able to emphasize the aspects of substance use disorders that are related to brain chemistry and thus affect the client's and family's acceptance and understanding of the diagnoses. And you must consider how to navigate the difficult terrain of dual and multiple diagnoses, some of which are made clearer in the DSM-5 and others that are still relegated to the mysteries of Section III. It is clearly a learning curve for all, but with positive directions for youth in the area of mental health.

ENGAGING YOUTH IN THE DIAGNOSTIC PROCESS

Picture this: An adolescent has been caught by his (or her) parent, high. The parent is in a total panic. The youth is defensive, angry, self-righteous (after all, "My friends all do it!" and "How dare they accuse me without knowing for sure?" and "It's not a *really* serious drug like shooting heroin" and, and, and . . .). The adolescent is fearful of losing freedom and privileges, and embarrassed (having sworn that only stupid kids get caught, the youth is feeling pretty dumb). Most of all, perhaps consciously, perhaps not, such young people are terrified that something will get in the way of their drug and alcohol use. Remember that their brain chemistry, if they are dependent, will give them the message that they *need* the substance(s) and everything else revolves around that primary maladaptive instinct to use.

They come into your office. If you launch into questions off of a clipboard, this young person's fear is going to expand; their defensiveness will be augmented; their anger, self-righteousness, and instinct for self-protection will grow. However, if you are somehow able to connect with this young person and really, honestly convey that you care about them and what happens here, they may actually relax, tell the truth, and work with you instead of against you.

So how do you do this? One professor likes to use sports metaphors. He states that if you try to catch a hard ball by reaching your hands forward, you'll find yourself with a broken finger. However, if you watch the ball, start moving your hands in its direction before it even reaches you, gently bring it close, and allow its momentum to move your hands beyond where you might think you need to stop, you will not only catch the ball without getting hurt, but you will have added momentum to throw the ball back with power and accuracy. This is what that looks like in words:

> Clinician: Hey, glad you are here. Bet you aren't so glad, huh?
> Busted Teen: Right.
> Clinician: I know it sucks to be caught. I want you to know that
> I am not here to nail you or punish you. I'm here to help

you and your family figure out what's going on and what needs to happen, if anything.

Busted Teen: Look. I just tried pot once or twice. Everyone does it. I don't do drugs. I don't know why my parents are being such idiots.

Clinician: I hear you. Parents sometimes *way* overreact. It seems to you that it is no big deal, but to your parents, it is scary because it means that the door to the world of drugs and alcohol for their kid is open and for a parent, that's scary even if it is just pot.

(NOTE: It is okay to reflect teens' belief that it is "just pot" at this point even if you know its dangers and feel strongly that clients are in deeper than they realize. They need to know you aren't judging them and that you are open to the possibility that they have tried it and will decide it isn't for them and move on.)

Before we talk about what happened, I'd love to know more about who you are.

What are you into? (Prompts can help if you know from the parents that the kid is a star football wide receiver or a dancer or guitarist.)

Busted Teen: Yeah, I will probably get a football scholarship and I get all A's and B's and my parents are still all over me like I'm some kind of drug addict or something.

Clinician: Look. That's what I'm here for. I promise you that after I do a full assessment, if it turns out that you do not have a problem with drugs or alcohol, I will do all that I can to get your parents to back off some. However, I cannot do this unless you commit to being really honest and thorough with me in this assessment. You have to tell me every related thing that comes to your mind because, otherwise, you make me into a liar and that isn't okay. Deal?

(Now you are baffled, right? How can a clinician make a promise like this? Well, it is true. If a client is thorough and the assessment does not show that the adolescent has a problem with drugs and alcohol, it *is* the clinician's responsibility to get the parents to relax and lay back. The irony is that the more thorough the client is, the greater the chance that the assessment tools will pick up on a problem if there is one.)

It is readily known in the field that some counselors and social work practitioners are more effective than others (Najavits & Weiss, 1994). These clinicians tend to engage and maintain clients for longer periods. In addition, they elicit client strengths, leading to higher client satisfaction and ongoing post-treatment recovery (Saleeby, 1996). Despite years of research on the success or failure of substance use treatment programs, the role of the clinician in this realm has received little attention (NIAAA, 2001). The existing studies focus primarily on treatment modes, techniques, and patient variables. Substance use clinicians show disparate effectiveness rates, surprisingly independent of the clinician's professional background and of patient characteristics at treatment onset (Najavits & Weiss, 1994). In the literature of general psychotherapy, abundant research exists examining the efficacy of counseling. However, there is a noteworthy absence of studies examining the differential effects regarding the quality of therapy. This is especially poignant when one considers that the substance use clinician is often recognized as the primary clinician in addiction treatment. The few studies that have been done to explore this variable suggest that the clinician may in fact be one of the most crucial factors in successful addictions treatment (Imhof, 1991; Flores, 1988).

Competencies of Effective Clinicians

Over the past several years the Addiction Technology Transfer Center (ATTC) program has developed and studied a set of 121 competencies thought to be essential to effective clinical practice with substance users and addicts (Adams & Gallon, 1997). The competencies include knowledge, skill, and attitude statements. The fundamental elements include understanding addiction, treatment knowledge, application to practice, and professional readiness. The ATTC conducted a seventeen-state survey of supervisors and counselors from 563 agencies in addiction treatment settings (n = 1227). Responses showed a high degree of internal consistency (r = .99) related to the above clinical competencies as essential to effective practice. Thus, it is clear that although these variables are important factors, they are not being studied from the perspective of treatment outcomes.

Qualities of Effective Clinicians

Despite the stereotypical impression of substance use clinicians who work with adolescents as aggressive confrontationalists, data support an empathic and supportive style as most effective (Miller & Rollnick, 2013; Valle, 1981; McNeece & DiNitto, 1994). In addition, successful case outcomes are more related to a clinician's skill than his/her theoretical orientation (Najavits & Weiss, 1994).

Existing studies that do address the role of the clinician tend to examine characteristics of the clinician rather than the process of therapy. Characteristics include such dichotomies as professional versus paraprofessional or recovering addict versus non-recovering. After more than fifty studies of this type, no significant differences among such categories of clinicians have been discovered (McClellan, Woody, Luborsky, & Goehl, 1988).

The research on clinician effectiveness in the field can be characterized as (1) clinician skills, behavior, and style during treatment and (2) the pre-existing characteristics of the clinician (e.g., personality, socio-demographics, and ethnicity). With regard to clinical skills and style, the most frequently studied and clearly established characteristics associated with clinician effectiveness is interpersonal functioning (Valle, 1981). More recently, Miller and Rollnick (1991) recommend social work skills such as accurate empathy, genuineness, and establishing good rapport as essential ingredients to motivating clients towards successful recovery.

The historical study conducted by Milmoe, Rosenthal, and Blane (1967) addressed the issue of negative affects conveyed by clinicians. This study used rated audiotapes of nine clinicians, finding that the level of anger and anxiety in clinicians' voices during an initial interview was inversely proportional to a client's likelihood of pursuit of alcoholism treatment. This supports findings that show that rapport is crucial to engagement in treatment (Miller & Rollnick, 2013). Rapport has been defined as "the relative harmony and smoothness of relations between people" (Spencer-Oatey, 2005, p. 96).

Studies of pre-existing clinician qualities utilize varied measures and conceptual definitions; therefore, it is currently impossible to draw conclusions about this variable in client treatment. Interesting inferences have historically been drawn. One study concludes that clinicians with higher retention rates were female, older, and more introverted (Rosenberg, Gerrein, & Manohar, 1976). Another study researched counselors who gave the MMPI (Minnesota Multiphasic Personality Inventory) personality test to heroin-addicted clients. The researchers found that the most effective counselors tended to be more "hypochondriacal, paranoid, manic" and "lower in ego strength" (Snowden & Cotler, 1974). Thus, certain characteristics usually regarded as problematic or even pathological may promote success in counseling certain drug addicts.

On the other hand, it seems that open-mindedness and humility may be important characteristics of clinicians. Najavits and Weiss (1994) found that less effective clinicians provided more positive self-ratings than more effective clinicians. More refined and established measures of clinician characteristics are needed.

Clinicians must be culturally aware and sensitive to individual, family, and group dynamics. They must not misuse their power. Toseland and Rivas (2012) note that different group facilitation styles match different types of groups. It is up to the leader to assess and meet the particular needs of each group.

Confrontation is a delicate area in group work. This intervention technique should be used only when necessary to facilitate individual growth and group process (Toseland & Rivas, 2012). If used incorrectly, confrontation can result in client passivity, attrition, anger, or hostility. Especially when working with adolescents, clinicians must also be adept at addressing and resolving conflicts. Though necessary for emergence and growth, conflict must be carefully managed to maintain the atmosphere of trust in the group. Therefore, it is important to examine clinician characteristics and skills in order to determine the effectiveness of the group.

Many clinicians inquire whether to self-disclose if they have had personal experiences that resonate with those of their client or client system. In order to build a real relationship with an adolescent, you have to be genuine. That doesn't mean you have to share everything that runs through your mind. For example, it is not helpful to articulate your perception that they cannot change or get well. However, it is fine to share honestly when you are frustrated in the relationship, when you are confused, and when you are excited, proud, or hopeful.

Sense of humor can be a useful tool. There is one caveat: Use it only if you have one. An attempt to be funny if you don't have a sense or rhythm for humor can undoubtedly do damage. Be careful; some people think that they are funny and others do not think so. There has been research that supports the therapeutic effects of humor through the mechanisms of distancing from negative situations (Martin, Kuiper, Olinger, & Dance, 1993), regulating negative emotions (Fredrickson, Mancuso, Branigan, & Tugade, 2000), and cognitive distraction (Strick, Holland, van Baaren, & van Knippenberg, 2009). Individuals with a "sharp" or "dry" sense of humor (i.e., those who utilize sarcasm readily) should be especially cautious. The late Beverly Koenigsberg, MSW, LCDC, an addictions therapist for over thirty years, pointed out that the etiology of the word "sarcasm" is from the Latin word *sarcasmos*, and from Greek *sarkasmos*, which translate to "tear flesh." She noted that humor should not be utilized when it has the explicit or even subtle intention to injure. In work with adolescents, this is especially important; the clinician models appropriate use of humor for young adults who may not know when it is helpful and when hurtful.

Balancing Creative Inquiry with Valid Screening and Assessment

Working with adolescents demands creativity. Not only does assessment work with adolescents necessitate thinking "outside the box," it often requires getting rid of the box altogether. In many ways, being an addictions specialist is more like being a detective than a doctor. If you ask an adolescent a direct question about symptoms or behavior such as, "Do you have a drug or alcohol problem?" the unequivocal and predictable answer will be "No." If, however, you ask them a series of questions that lead to clues, you will have the information it takes to connect the adolescent with a skilled assessment expert to confirm your suspicions. The relationship you build with the person in front of you and how you ask the questions are critical to the outcome of the assessment.

TOOLS AND TECHNIQUES FOR SCREENING AND ASSESSMENT

There are a multitude of screening mnemonics used to assess basic concerns about adolescent alcohol and substance use problems. The most common tools are as follows: CAGE, TWEAK, CRAFFT, RAPS, and RUFT-Cut (each being an acronym for screening inquiry prompts) (Clark, Chung, & Martin, 2011).

For example, consider the screening tool, the TWEAK. *T* stands for "tolerance." Although you could ask directly, "Do you drink or drug more than other people?" this will likely elicit a defensive answer rather than a true one. Instead, you can reframe the question slightly and ask, "Are you able to drink or use without getting seriously drunk or high?" or "Can you drink/use more than others and still feel in control?" Although these answers seem to the adolescent to be telling you that they do not have a problem, they are actually red flags for substance use and possibly even dependence.

W stands for "worried." You can ask, "Do other people worry about your use of drugs or alcohol?" You can frame the question empathically as concern for the clients' desire to have their parents, siblings, relatives, boyfriends/girlfriends, and so on "off their back." Again, the client feels supported, and you are also able to gather the important information that others are concerned about the individual's substance use. You will be amazed at how much detail a client will share if you take a non-judgmental stance.

E stands for "eye opener." Do not actually use this term, as it is quite outdated. You might word your question thus: "Have you ever, upon wakening, used something to either get you going or calm you down?" The beauty of this question is that it has an inherent stigma protection because anyone who has ever had a cup of coffee would have to answer "yes" to this question. Originally, the question was designed to read, "Have you used before noon?" Anyone who has lived or worked with adolescents knows that many teens are nocturnal creatures and, especially in summer, rarely if ever consciously experience the noon hour. It would be all too easy for them to use the justification that they cannot possibly be alcoholic or addicted because they never use before noon. This would be a ridiculous point if they are never up before noon.

A stands for "amnesia" and gives the clinician a prompt to ask about potential blackouts or brownouts. Yes, brownouts. Remember that substance users are master rationalizers. If you ask them if they have had blackouts (defined as chunks of time lost to memory because of substance use), they may think, "Well, I remember most of that evening, so that wouldn't really be a blackout, right?" Therefore, it is helpful to explain that short memory losses, or small pieces of the drinking or drugging episode lost to memory, would be characterized as "brownouts."

K stands, well, symbolically, for "kut down." Yes, TWEAK is a silly mnemonic, but it works well for memory purposes (you know "tweak" is the word for when a cocaine user is craving cocaine). This is another tricky question; when you ask, "Have you ever tried to or successfully cut down your use of alcohol or drugs?" many young people will puff up and proudly report, "Yes, I used to use a lot more and now I have it all under control." This is another red flag. Most social drinkers or recreational users never have any reason to cut down. Cutting down means that the use resulted in some kind of consequences. The answer to this question may lead into a wonderful opportunity for you to follow up with a non-judgmental probe, such as, "Interesting. Congrats for being able to cut down. What were your reasons for cutting down?"

Some research has shown that the most effective standardized screening instrument for adolescents is the CRAFFT. The CRAFFT is a behavioral health screening tool for use with those under the age of twenty-one and is recommended by the American Academy of Pediatrics' Committee on Substance Use for use with adolescents. It consists of a series of six questions developed to screen adolescents for high-risk alcohol and other drug use disorders simultaneously. It is a short, effective screening tool meant to assess whether a longer conversation about the context of use, frequency, and other risks and consequences of alcohol and other drug use is warranted.

Screening using the CRAFFT begins by asking the adolescent, "Please answer these next questions honestly," telling him or her, "Your answers will be kept confidential," and then asking three opening questions. If the adolescent answers "No" to all three opening questions, the provider only needs to ask the adolescent the first question (the CAR question). If the adolescent answers "Yes" to one or more of the three opening questions, the provider asks all six CRAFFT questions. (See "The CRAFFT Screening Test" box.) CRAFFT is a mnemonic acronym of key words in the six screening questions. According to the directions for the standardized, evidence-based screening, the questions should be asked exactly as written. The more of a relationship you have with the individual, the greater the likelihood that the person will be honest in the discussion. Therefore, it is valuable to lead up to the screening with an affirmation, reflective listening, and non-judgmental inquiry about what brought the person to where they are now.

● ●

The CRAFFT Screening Test

C   Have you ever ridden in a CAR driven by someone (including yourself) who was high or had been using alcohol or drugs?

R   Do you ever use alcohol or drugs to RELAX, feel better about yourself, or fit in?

A   Do you ever use alcohol or drugs when you are by yourself, ALONE?

F   Do you ever FORGET things you did while using alcohol or drugs?

F   Do your family or FRIENDS ever tell you that you should cut down on your drinking or drug use?

T   Have you ever gotten into TROUBLE while you were using alcohol or drugs?

● ●

As noted earlier, adolescents with substance use issues tend to be very guarded and defensive when it comes to inquiries about their use. Direct questions or judgment will cause clients to shut down immediately. Creative facilitation and inquiry have been useful to clinicians. Following are six examples of such inquiries:

Question 1: Of the drugs you have experimented with, which is/are your favorite(s) and why? If you have already built a safe and healthy rapport with the adolescent, they will start to tell you and essentially "give themselves away." You can watch their eyes widen, their heart race, and the excitement grow. It has been the experience of many an addictions counselor, social worker, and substance use researcher that once you get drug-using adolescents talking about their use, they often talk freely and animatedly about the subject. It is probably their favorite topic of discussion. Their guardedness about the subject is usually directly proportional to the clinician's own fear, hesitation, and stigma placed on the subject.

• •

The Sara Bellum Blog is written by a team of National Institute on Drug Abuse (NIDA) scientists, science writers, educators, and teens. They connect you with the latest scientific research and news so you can use that information to make healthy, smart decisions. NIDA has thousands of researchers around the world who study drug addiction and come up with ways to help people recover and live healthy lives.

http://teens.drugabuse.gov/blog/category/about-sara-bellum

• •

Question 2: Does anyone in your family have any compulsive behaviors? Note that the question does not say "addiction," "drug problem," or "alcoholism." These words, although more accurate perhaps, are often too charged to elicit affirmative responses. Sometimes it is useful to suggest the litany of compulsive behaviors that tend to run in families with drug and alcohol dependence, such as obesity, gambling, cigarette smoking, compulsive shopping or spending, and love or sex addiction. It is important to note that although the mechanisms of these "process disorders" are very different from the brain disease of drug and alcohol use and dependence, they are similar and can serve as further clues when compiling a full and comprehensive psychosocial assessment and drug and alcohol screening. There is a fast-developing science exploring potentially addictive behaviors that do not involve the ingestion of a drug; some researchers argue that all addictions consist of a number of distinct common components (salience, mood modification, tolerance, withdrawal, conflict, and relapse) and that these compulsive behaviors are a part of a similar bio-psycho-social-spiritual process (Griffins, 2005).

Question 3: What are the payoffs and downsides to your drug or alcohol use? This question is related to motivational interviewing. The National Institute on Drug Abuse iterates the important fact that young adults recognize when they are being manipulated to think or behave a certain way (NIDA, 2012). It is much more effective to ask youth what their experiences and negative consequences have been and highlight these as part of the assessment and intervention process. The instances that scare tactics are relevant and effective are when they are genuinely part of a young person's reality; when a youth says, "My cousin is in prison for drugs," this is a fact that can deeply impact the young person's decisions with regard to their own drug and alcohol use. One youth, when asked why he gave up marijuana, told the story of a friend who smoked a "doobie" which turned out to be laced with PCP. The friend proceeded to punch a mirror, picked up a piece of glass, and began shaving his facial skin off while looking in the mirror. The boy was so terrified by his friend's experience that he knew he was "done with weed." The research shows some interesting findings with regard to children of alcoholics who have witnessed a parent's alcoholism. Apparently, almost a third of these youth have made a decision not to drink alcohol because of what they have witnessed in their parent(s).

Now, you may be thinking, "Why would you ask a youth to illuminate the payoffs for their drug or alcohol use?" There is a good reason to do so. Preventionists have missed the boat for years in ignoring the truth that most youth experiment and use

substances with impunity. Society has opted to tell young people, "Drugs and alcohol are bad/They will hurt you or even kill
you." This message, although well-meaning, is not fully truthful.
Adults use alcohol to celebrate; media messages are inundated
with alcohol as sexy and fun; and this is a society of medications,
excesses to feel good, and fixes. Society models the idea that
drugs and alcohol are good and will help you, and youth have
their own positive experiences of substances. The number one
reason why youth use drugs is "it feels good." In research focus
groups, middle and high school aged youth reported the following "payoffs" to drug and alcohol use:

- It helps me sleep.
- It helps me get going in the morning.
- It helps me focus at school.
- It helps me feel comfortable around other people, especially
  peers.
- It helps me relax during sex.
- It helps me get better grades in school.
- It makes me funnier.
- It makes me feel prettier or cooler or better looking.
- It makes me more creative, artistic, musical. . . .
- The first time I used was the first time I got a break from flash-
  blacks from my sexual/physical abuse.
- The first time I used was the first time I was able to tolerate
  my parents' fights.
- The first time I used was the first time that I didn't hate myself
  so much.

These experiences are real. Clinicians who discuss these truths
with clients have far greater credibility and rapport than those
who deny the facts.

Question 4: Might you be willing to cut down on the substance(s) that are giving you the most problems? This may seem counter-intuitive to some who believe strongly in abstinence-based-only models. This question grows from the harm-reduction model, which posits that it is better to have adolescents reduce risk even if they continue engaging in risky behavior than to have them make no change at all. When abstinence-based-only models were the norm, some counselors refused to treat clients who weren't ready for abstinence. Many of those clients spiraled into much more serious situations and many of them died. Fortunately, today we are aware of the Stage of Change Model, which replaces this previous paradigm with one that allows for intervention with individuals at any level of readiness for change. (See Chapter 7.)

Question 5: What do you like to do besides do drugs and alcohol? What are you good at? This area of exploration sometimes eludes clinicians who focus on the problem rather than the person, forgetting the importance and value of strengths-based interventions (Saleeby, 1996). This line of questioning accomplishes a dual role: First, it allows you to build the relationship with the client and praise what they do well. Many adolescents are so unaccustomed to this that they become uncomfortable and you may have to use humor or change the subject in order to maintain the safe milieu. Second, it gives you a sense of things that a client might lean on as coping mechanisms and alternatives to substances. It is worth exploring artistic abilities, musical talent, affinity for sports, sense of humor, communication skills, writing abilities, and other areas of interest.

In introductory social work courses, students are taught to "start with a strength." With drug using/abusing adolescents this may be easier said than done. Young substance users often embrace offensive personas in order to keep people at arm's length. Essentially, if you cannot get close, you cannot get between them and their beloved partner, alcohol or drugs. For example, imagine a young client coming in to your office for an assessment. He wears camouflage pants, a tight sleeveless undershirt revealing his scarred arms and wrists, hair in a Mohawk style, bare feet, and a strong stench that conveys a lack of affinity for hygiene. The young man's face is self-pierced, with safety pins all over it, in various stages of healing, some old and some new. Take a minute to think about how you might "start with a strength" with this client.

You might make the choice, as one clinician did, to say, "My, aren't you bold!" The instinct was good. The young man went around telling his peers that his counselor said he was bold.

Question 6: Are you up for meeting some really cool young people who you have a ton in common with and who sat where you sit now? Let's face it. Adolescents would much rather hang with peers than adults; doing so is developmentally appropriate and pre-scripted. Although it was once difficult to find communities of young people in recovery, such communities are much more common and accessible today. Recovery communities are another aspect of the substance use field that have transformed dramatically. Gone are the days of punitive therapeutic communities (TCs) in which teens would have their heads shaved and be given toothbrushes to clean bathroom floors. The old philosophy that inflated egos needed to be smashed and rebuilt has been let go in lieu of the belief that people with drug and alcohol problems have a brain disease and deserve the dignity and grace afforded medical clients. Innovative programs for adolescents have undergone almost a pendulum swing of a change from the prison-like programs with counselors screaming confrontations to "enthusiastic recovery" (Meehan, 2000). Instead of being beaten into recovery, these young people are being loved into recovery. Perhaps "love" is a dangerous word to use, as it might be misconstrued. "Tough love" and other programs of the seventies, eighties, and nineties made clear that parents and programs "enabling" injurious behaviors were doing more harm than good (Donahue, & Azrin, 2012) and although this is still true, somewhere along the line, clinicians recognized that the inflated egos of adolescent addicts were also symptoms of a profoundly deeper impairment—a warped sense of self so insidious that shame was the primary motivating factor in these kids' lives (Rosenkranz, Henderson, Muller, & Goodman, 2012). Inflicting more shame might get them to comply in the short term but in the long term would likely contribute to their self-loathing. The present-day, evidence-based models take into consideration the challenges and the strengths, the fears and the courage it takes to move forward, the gravity of the situation and the humor necessary to get through some days. A balance is needed for young people to get well.

Complexities and Comorbidities

Depression is often part and parcel of adolescent substance use. One psychiatrist likes to ask, "What percentage of adolescent addicts are depressed?" He waits until his audience guesses, usually between 30 and 50 percent. Then he smiles and responds, "No, 100 percent. There is no way to be an addicted adolescent without symptoms of depression." He goes on to explain that not all teens who are drug or alcohol dependent are dually diagnosed with a pre-existing clinical depression, but teens who are far enough along to make it to in-patient treatment will have at least some reactive symptoms of depression.

How do doctors discern clinical depression for which teens may be "self-medicating" from teens who are seriously abusing substances and subsequently show signs of depression (which, ironically, they may then use as an excuse for further drug and alcohol use)? Research suggests a connection between depression and adolescent substance use (Kaplow, Curran, Angold, & Costello., 2001; Stice, Burton, & Shaw, 2004; Windle & Windle, 2001). However, not all studies have found this relationship significant (e.g., Hussong & Hicks, 2003). Unfortunately, as illuminated by Ohannessian and Hesselbrock (2009), in the majority of studies in which a significant relationship has been observed, clinical measures were used to assess depression. They note that measures usually include items relating to aspects of depression (e.g., irritability, anxiety, and academic problems), not necessarily including sadness, making the findings relating to depression muddy at best.

What of this self-medication hypothesis? This premise maintains that used substances relieve "human psychological suffering in susceptible individuals and that there is a considerable degree of psychopharmacologic specificity in an individual's preferred drug" (Khantzian, 2003, p. 47). The key to this hypothesis is that specific substances are being chosen to alleviate mental, emotional, or psychological distress. Therefore, this does not just mean substance use concurrent with mental illness (or dual diagnoses). Although it is intriguing to imagine that addicts may be self-medicating, it has not yet been supported sufficiently to be iterated beyond its hypothetical status. Lagoni, Crawford, & Huss (2011) studied 700 mentally ill chemical users and did not find support for the hypothesis.

Sometimes, co-occurring complexities are more a function of environmental factors, trauma, and socio-economic status (SES) than psychology. With regard to violence and adolescent substance use, the effects of exposure to school violence, community violence, child abuse, and parental intimate partner violence

(IPV) on youths' subsequent alcohol and marijuana use are undeniable (Wright, Fagan, & Pinchevsky, 2013). Researchers have found that exposure to violence in a one-year period increased the frequency of substance use three years later. The specific relationships between victimization and use varied for alcohol and marijuana use, with alcohol use not having a statistically significant relationship. Community violence and child abuse (but not school violence or exposure to IPV) have been established as predictive of future marijuana use (Wright, Fagan, & Pinchevsky, 2013). However, the accumulation of exposure to violence across "life domains" was detrimental to both future alcohol and marijuana use.

KEY TERMS

Empathic Style	Strengths-based interventions
Interpersonal functioning	Recovery communities
TWEAK	Therapeutic communities
CRAFFT	Enthusiastic recovery
Compulsive behaviors	Warped sense of self
Motivational interviewing (MI)	Comorbidity
Scare tactics	Trauma
Payoffs of substance use	Socio-economic status (SES)

DISCUSSION QUESTIONS

1. Read the scenario again and brainstorm other ways to respond to the input in the session.
2. Practice using the TWEAK and the CRAFFT and note the strengths and weaknesses of these screens for adolescents and emerging adults.

139

3. Discuss the "self-medication" premise. How does this premise affect how clinicians work, how clients connect with help, and how substance abusing adolescents might characterize their substance use or dependence?

4. How does violence intersect with adolescent substance misuse?

REFERENCES

Adams, R. J., & Gallon, S. L. (1997). *Entry-level addiction counselor competency survey national results.* Portland, OR: Northwest Regional Educational Laboratory.

American Psychiatric Association (2013). *Diagnostic and statistical manual of mental disorders (5th ed.).* Arlington, VA: American Psychiatric Publishing.

Clark, D. B., Chung, T., & Martin, C. (2011). Alcohol use frequency as a screen for alcohol use disorders in adolescents. *Int. Journal of Adolescent Medicine and Health, 18*(1), 181–188.

Donahue, B., & Azrin, N. H. (2012). *Treating adolescent substance use using family behavior therapy: A step-by-step approach.* Hoboken, NJ: Wiley & Sons.

Egan, G. (1998). *The skilled helper (6th ed).* Pacific Grove, CA: Brooks/Cole.

Flores, P. (1988). *Group psychotherapy with addicted populations.* New York: Haworth.

Fredrickson, B. L., Mancuso, R. A., Branigan, C., & Tugade, M. M (2000). The undoing effect of positive emotions. *Motivation and Emotion, 24*(4), 237–258.

Griffins, M. (2005). A components model of addiction within a biopsychosocial framework. *Journal of Substance Use, 10*(4), 191–197.

Hussong, A. M., & Hicks, R. E. (2003). Affect and peer context interactively impact adolescent substance use. *Journal of Abnormal Child Psychology, 31,* 413–426.

Imhof, J. (1991) Countertransference issues in alcoholism and drug addiction. *Psychiatric Annals, 21,* 292–306.

Kaplow, J. B., Curran P. J., Angold A., & Costello E. J. (2001). The prospective relation between dimensions of anxiety and the initiation of adolescent alcohol use. *Journal of Clinical Child Psychology, 30,* 316–326.

Kelly, J. F., Dow, S., & Westerhoff, C. (2010). Does our choice of substance-related terms influence perceptions of treatment need? An empirical investigation with two commonly used terms. *Journal of Drug Issues, 40,* 805–818.

Khantzian, E. J. (2003). Understanding addictive vulnerability: An evolving psychodynamic perspective. *Neuropsychoanalysis, 5*, 5–21.

Kleinman, P., Woody, G., & Todd, T. (1990). Crack and cocaine abusers in and outpatient psychotherapy. *National Institute on Drug Abuse Research Monograph, 104*, 24–38.

Lagoni, L., Crawford, E., & Huss, M. T. (2011). An examination of the self-medication hypothesis via treatment completion. *Addiction Research and Theory, 19*(5), 416–426.

Lofland, J., & Lofland, L. (1995). *Analyzing social settings: A guide to qualitative observation and analysis.* Belmont, CA: Wadsworth, Inc.

Martin, R. A., Kuiper, N. A., Olinger, L. J., & Dance, K. A. (1993). Humor: Coping with stress, self-concept, and psychological well-being. *Humor: International Journal of Humor Research, 6*, 89–104.

McCaul, M., & Svikis, D. (1991). Improving client compliance in outpatient treatment: Counselor-targeted interventions. *National Institute on Drug Abuse Research Monograph, 106*, 204–217.

McClellan, A., Woody, G., Luborsky, L., & Goehl, L. (1988). Is the counselor an "active ingredient" in substance abuse rehabilitation? An examination of treatment success among four counselors. *Journal of Nervous and Mental Disorders, 176*, 432–440.

McNeece, C.A., & DiNitto, D.M. (1994). Chemical dependency: A systems approach. Englewood Cliffs, NJ: Prentice Hall.

Meehan, B. (2000). *Beyond the yellow brick road: Revised.* Kersey, CO: Meek Publishers.

Miller, W. R., & Rollnick, S. (1991). *Motivational interviewing: Preparing people to change addictive behavior.* New York, NY: Guilford Press.

Miller, W. R., & Rollnick, S. (2013). *Motivational interviewing (3rd ed.): Helping people change.* New York, NY: Guilford Press.

Milmoe, S., Rosenthal, R., & Blane, H. (1967). The doctor's voice: postdictor of successful referral of alcoholic patients. *Journal of Abnormal Psychology, 72*, 78–84.

Najavits, L. M., & Weiss, R. D. (1994). Variations in therapist effectiveness in the treatment of patients with substance use disorders: An empirical review. *Addiction, 89*, 679–688.

NIAAA (2001). 8hhttp://www.niaaa.nih.gov

NIDA (2012). *Scare tactics: Does fear influence your opinion about drug use? NIDA for Teens: Science behind Drug Use.* 9http://teens.drugabuse.gov/blog/category/about-sara-bellum

141

Ohannessian, C. Mc., & Hesselbrock, V. M. (2009). A finer examination of the role that negative affect plays in the relationship between paternal alcoholism and the onset of alcohol and marijuana use. *Journal of Studies on Alcohol & Drugs, 70*(3), 400–408.

Petry, N. M., Blanco, C., Stinchfield, R., & Volberg, R. (2013). An empirical evaluation of proposed changes for gambling diagnosis in the DSM-5. *Addiction, 108*, 575–81.

Rosenberg, C., Gerrein, J., & Manohar, V. (1976). Evaluation of training in alcoholism counselors. *Journal of Studies on Alcohol, 37*, 1236–1246.

Rosenkranz, S. E., Henderson, J. L., Muller, R. T., & Goodman, I. R. (2012). Motivation and maltreatment history among youth entering substance abuse treatment. *Psychology of Addictive Behaviors, 26*(1), 171–177.

Rubin, A., & Babbie, E. (1999). *Research methods for social work (4th ed.).* Pacific Grove, CA: Brooks Cole.

Saleeby, D. (1996). The strengths perspective in social work practice: Extensions and cautions. *Social Work, 41*(3), 296–305.

Snowden, L., & Cotler, S. (1974). The effectiveness of paraprofessional ex-addict counselors in a methadone treatment program. *Psychotherapy: Theory, Research and Practice, 4*, 331–338.

Spencer-Oatey, H. (2005). (Im)politeness, face and perceptions of rapport: Unpackaging their bases and interrelationships. *Journal of Politeness Research, 1*(1), 95–119.

Stice, E., Burton, E. M., & Shaw, H. (2004). Prospective relations between bulimic pathology, depression, and substance abuse: Unpacking comorbidity in adolescent girls. *Journal of Consulting Clinical Psychology, 72*, 62–71.

Strauss, A. L. (1987). *Qualitative analysis for social scientists.* Cambridge, MA: Cambridge University Press.

Straussner, S. L. (Ed.) (2013). *Clinical work with substance-abusing clients (3rd ed.).* New York, NY: Guilford Press.

Strick, M., Holland, R. W., van Baaren, R. B., & van Knippenberg, A. (2009) Finding comfort in a joke: Consolatory effects of humor through cognitive distraction. *Emotion, 9*(4), 574–578.

Toseland, R. W., & Rivas, R. F. (2001). *An introduction to group work practice.* Boston, London, Toronto: Allyn and Bacon.

Valle, S. K. (1981). Interpersonal functioning of alcoholism counselors and treatment outcome. *Journal of Studies on Alcohol, 42*, 783–790.

Windle, M., & Windle, R. C. (2001). Depressive symptoms and cigarette smoking among middle adolescents: Prospective associations and intrapersonal and interpersonal influences. *Journal of Consulting Clinical Psychology, 69,* 215–226.

Wright, E. M., Fagan, A. A., & Pinchevsky, G. M. (2013 in press). The effects of exposure to violence and victimization across life domains on adolescent substance use. *Child Use & Neglect.*

PART IV

Evidence-Based Treatment Interventions

Now the moment you've all been waiting for . . . (drumroll please). How to help! There are a variety of research-supported interventions that are being utilized successfully with adolescents. Although years ago the adolescent treatment picture looked grim, today there are promising methods and programs. Be prepared to experience acronyms which, at first, may seem confusing. You will learn about MET and CBT. You will also learn techniques related to family systems and family therapy interventions. Ultimately, this section will introduce and piece together the puzzle of effective youth substance use disorder interventions.

The most important aspect of this section is, as noted earlier, a focus on the complexities of intervention. For this reason, case studies are used to show how the techniques look in real life (all case studies are based on real clients and therapeutic experiences of the author). Remember that there are numerous ways to intervene successfully with every client—and each person that is trying to help must recognize that they are the instrument of change and must be authentic and true. Consequently, all interventions will look a bit different. The basics are clearly outlined, but you will have to embrace the intervention in ways that are genuine. Ultimately, your empathic and real connection with the young person will allow for the powerful changes to occur.

Chapter 7

Different Approaches to Evidence-Based Treatment

When an adolescent is assessed and intervention is deemed necessary, it is important for teens to be linked with the appropriate treatment services. Treatment for adolescents is complicated by the complex needs of teens and their families; the spectrum of problems; levels of willingness to change; and knowledge of, availability of, and access to resources. Ideally, a treatment will be holistic, addressing all aspects of the bio-psycho-social-spiritual model.

Although youth have unique needs, stories, and access to care, research heartily supports the provision of multiple services (i.e., individual, group, family, twelve-step). As in the field of mental health, it is valuable for there to be a variety of services that surround the youth and their family system with support, direction, and resources; this has been referred to as "wraparound services" for obvious reasons (Bruns et al., 2010). It might also be called a "holding environment" because it elicits an image of youth being surrounded by care. The model highlights the importance of resources and attachment to others as curative. As noted earlier in this book, the guiding framework is the social-ecological model, so that no one is ever assumed to live in a vacuum. Complex personal, environmental, social, and societal factors are always at play.

Group work is very effective with adolescents because of the strong peer group influences (Winters, Botzet, & Fahnhorst,

2011). Personal decision making is a critical piece in adolescent treatment and recovery. Therapeutic group work is the predominant mode of intervention for evidence-supported reasons. Groups provide feedback from others to gain communication skills, accurate perceptions of self and others, and new coping mechanisms involving intimacy and honesty.

There is no denying that, ultimately, an individual's personal choice does come into play with regard to using drugs or alcohol. This can be a confusing "stuck point" for teens and families in early treatment because they often hear mantras such as "Alcoholics and addicts can't control their use once they have started using" and "The 3 C's" for families ("You didn't *cause* it, you can't *control* it, and you can't *cure* it.") Addiction is a chronic, but treatable, brain disorder. Adolescents who are actively using and addicted cannot control their need for alcohol or other drugs, even in the face of negative health, social, or legal consequences. This lack of control is the result of alcohol- or drug-induced changes in the brain. Those changes, in turn, cause behavioral changes. The brains of addicted people "have been modified by the drug in such a way that absence of the drug makes a signal to their brain that is equivalent to the signal of when you are starving," says National Institute on Drug Abuse Director Nora Volkow. As she notes, it is "as if the individual was in a state of deprivation, where taking the drug is indispensable for survival. It's as powerful as that." She adds, "To appreciate the grips of addiction, imagine a person that wants to stop doing something and they cannot, despite catastrophic consequences. We're not speaking of little consequences. These are catastrophic. And yet they cannot control their behavior" (HBO/NIDA, 2014).

However, once adolescents become aware of their addictions, begin the work of healing their brain chemistry, and find ways to feel good without artificial chemically induced states, they get a great deal of control over their choices and behaviors. They get a chance to choose who they hang with, how they spend their time, and what suggestions they will follow. Addictions professionals often say that 100 percent of addictions treatment clients would recover if they would follow 100 percent of the suggestions. The difficulty is that clients, especially adolescents (not to mention those with comorbid mental illness or personality disorders), pick and choose what directions they will follow. Also, in some cases, adolescents are unable to follow the directions they are given. It is only rarely that adolescents are truly "constitutionally incapable" of being honest and working the program laid in front of them. Most are simply at early stages of readiness for change. Perhaps they are in "precontemplation" because of extensive justifications, rationalizations, and other defense mechanisms protecting their substance use as a means of coping with pain. Or they may be ill equipped to deal with the challenges of daily life and the complexities of intimate relationships. They often rebel, choosing the opposite of what is in their best interest. Or they underestimate what recovery will take or overestimate the power of their own self-will with regard to drugs and alcohol. The truth is that no matter how deep the pain of the consequences are that spur movement into treatment and recovery realms, the pain often cannot compete with the power of euphoric recall (i.e., retention of the positive memories of use rather than the negative consequences) and the brain's capacity to retain the memory of a high (especially in the midst of stressful situations) (Nestler & Malenka, 2004).

The key is this: Until adolescents embrace a program of recovery of some sort (or something viable to take the place of using), they will continue to use. Change is hard. It is clear that in order to make a significant change, an individual must deeply concede that the payoffs outweigh the downsides of the change.

This concept of decisional balance (Janus & Mann, 1977) is a useful mechanism in working with adolescents.

The wave and push for evidence-based treatment and prevention is definitely a positive direction for clinicians in the sense that they are no longer "shooting from the hip" and they can now: (1) incorporate interventions that have proven efficacy with populations they serve, (2) recognize when interventions are useful even when they are counter-intuitive, and (3) no longer need to guess what works.

One note of caution, which has been stated before and has been repeated purposefully in this text: There is no one-size-fits-all intervention that works for all individuals. It is critical that relationship skills, listening, and being present are foundations of all interventions. Clinicians have known this since the beginning of helping professions (Smalley, 1967) and it is not to be forgotten or ignored.

MOTIVATION ENHANCEMENT THERAPY

The concept of motivational interviewing (MI) evolved from experience in the treatment of problem drinkers and was first described by Miller (1983) in an article published in *Behavioral & Cognitive Psychotherapy*. Miller and Rollnick (2001) later elaborated on the concept in a more detailed description of clinical procedures. Their definition is this: Motivational interviewing is a directive, client-centered counseling style for eliciting behavior change by helping clients to explore and resolve ambivalence. Compared with non-directive counseling, it is more focused and goal-directed. The primary goal is the exploration and resolution of a client's ambivalence (mixture of perceived payoffs and downsides) about a problematic behavior. Miller and Rollnick differentiate between the "spirit" and the "techniques" of MI and emphasize that the following elements of spirit are as important as the skills:

- Motivation to change is elicited from the client and not imposed from without. (i.e., identifying and mobilizing the client's intrinsic values and goals to stimulate behavior change).

- It is the clients' task, not the counselor's, to articulate and resolve their ambivalence. Ambivalence takes the form of a conflict between two courses of action, each of which has perceived benefits and costs associated with it.

- Direct persuasion is not an effective method for resolving ambivalence. It is tempting to try to be "helpful" by persuading the client of the urgency of the problem and the benefits of change. It is fairly clear, however, that these tactics generally increase client resistance and diminish the probability of change (Miller, Benefield, & Tonigan, 1993; Miller & Rollnick, 2001).

- The counseling style is generally a quiet and eliciting one.

- Motivational interviewing involves no training of clients in behavioral coping skills, although the two approaches are not incompatible.

- Readiness to change is not a client trait but a fluctuating product of interpersonal interaction. The therapist is therefore highly attentive and responsive to the client's motivational signs.

- The therapeutic relationship is more like a respectful partnership or companionship than expert/recipient roles; the clinician allows for freedom of choice (and consequences) regarding the client's own behavior.

● ●

Warning: If motivational interviewing becomes a trick or a manipulative technique, its essence has been lost.

Miller & Rollnick, 2009

● ●

The following are the specific skills a clinician utilizes to engage in a motivational partnership:

- Seek to understand the person's frame of reference, particularly via reflective listening.
- Express acceptance and affirmation.
- Elicit and selectively reinforce the client's own self-motivational statements, expressions of problem recognition, concern, desire and intention to change, and ability to change.
- Monitor the client's degree of readiness to change and ensure that resistance is not generated by jumping ahead of the client.
- Affirm the client's freedom of choice and self-direction.

MET is a four-session adaptation of the check-up intervention (Miller & Rollnick, 2009). It was developed specifically as one of three interventions tested in Project MATCH (1993), a multisite clinical trial of treatments for alcohol use and dependence. Two follow-up sessions (at weeks 6 and 12) were added to the traditional two-session check-up format to parallel the twelve-week (and twelve session) format of two more intensive treatments in the trial. Motivational interviewing is the predominant style used by counsellors throughout MET.

Brief Motivational Interviewing

A menu of concrete strategies form the basis for "brief motivational interviewing," which was developed for use in a single session (around forty minutes) in primary care settings with non-help-seeking excessive drinkers (Rollnick, Heather, & Bell, 1992). The originators found that it was not immediately apparent to primary care workers how to apply the generic style of motivational interviewing during brief contacts. Therefore Rollnick,

Heather, and Bell designed this set of quick, concrete techniques meant to manifest the spirit and practice of motivational interviewing in brief contact settings. An unresolved issue is whether the spirit of motivational interviewing can be captured in still briefer encounters of as little as five to ten minutes. Numerous attempts to do this are under way, although only one method has been published to date (Stott, Rollnick, Rees, & Pill, 1995).

BRIEF INTERVENTION

Brief intervention has often been confused with motivational interviewing, prompted perhaps by the introduction of more generic terms such as "brief motivational counseling." Such brief interventions, focused on drinking, have been offered to two broad client groups: heavy drinkers in general medical settings who have not asked for help, and help-seeking problem drinkers in specialist settings (Bien, Miller, & Tonigan, 1993).

Attempts to understand the generally demonstrated effectiveness of brief intervention have pointed to common underlying ingredients, one expression of which is found in the acronym FRAMES, originally devised by Miller and Sanchez (1994). The letters of FRAMES refer to the use of *Feedback*, *Responsibility* for change lying with the individual, *Advice*-giving, providing a *Menu* of change option, an *Empathetic* counseling style, and the enhancement of *Self*-efficacy (see Bien et al., 1993; Miller & Rollnick, 2001). Although many of these ingredients are clearly congruent with a motivational interviewing style, some applications (e.g., of advice-giving) are not (Rollnick, Kinnersley, & Stott, 1993). Therefore, motivational interviewing ought not be confused with brief interventions in general. Miller and Rollnick have suggested that the word "motivational" be used only when there is a primary intentional focus on increasing readiness for change. Further, "motivational interviewing" should be used only when careful attention has been paid to the definition and characteristic spirit described previously.

Differences from More Confrontational Approaches

Although motivational interviewing does, in one sense, seek to "confront" clients with reality, this method differs substantially from more aggressive styles of confrontation. More specifically, Miller and Rollnick regard motivational interviewing as not being offered when a therapist:

- argues that the person has a problem and needs to change
- offers direct advice or prescribes solutions to the problem without the person's permission or without actively encouraging clients to make their own choices
- uses an authoritative/expert stance, leaving the client in a passive role
- does most of the talking, or functions as a unidirectional information delivery system
- imposes a diagnostic label
- behaves in a punitive or coercive manner

Motivational interviewing is based in the collaboration or partnership between client and facilitator, shaped by an understanding of what it takes for individuals to change behaviors that are not working for them. If it becomes manipulation, its essence has been lost (Rollnick & Miller, 1995).

Motivational Interviewing Strategies

The following are the motivational interviewing strategies (Miller and Rollnick, 1995) for helping professionals (which clearly can be learned and practiced). The order is a general progression, but clinicians should follow the client's lead and utilize the most natural skill possible to allow for increasing trust and openness on the part of the client. Warmth, empathy, and reflective listening should be utilized in conjunction with each of these skills.

- Listen carefully so that you can share the client's frame of reference.
- Be accepting and affirming.
- Question purposefully about clients' feelings, ideas, concerns, and plans, affirming their freedom of choice and self-direction.
- Provide structured feedback, preferably tangible reports with screening scores, and the like.
- Elicit and selectively reinforce the client's own self-motivational statements, expressions of problem recognition, concern, desire and intention to change, and ability to change.
- Monitor the client's degree of readiness to change, and ensure that the client sets this pace, not the clinician.
- Let adolescents argue for change and elaborate about their ambivalence rather than doing this for them.
- Monitor and "roll with resistance." Try to keep it low. Avoid argumentation.
- Summarize and reframe perceptions in new light and reorganized forms, motivating client to acknowledge problems, consequences, and changes whenever possible.
- Shift when ready from *reasons* to change to a *plan* for change. Consider a change plan worksheet with such sections as: the changes I want to make, the most important reasons to make these changes, the steps I plan to take in changing, the ways others can help me, I will know the plan is working if . . . , and some things that could interfere with my plans.

Miller (1998) concurs with the scientific determination that the term "addiction" implies some reduction in volitional control of a behavior. Besides diminished volitional control, what qualifies a behavior as addicting is that it persists despite harmful consequences. In other words, "Motivation for the behavior has become more attractive than alternative rewards" (Miller, 1998). The goal of the collaboration between client and clinician is to find motivations that outweigh the motivations of the problematic behavior (Miller, 1998). The competing motivations may be multiple, and suffering associated with an addictive behavior tends to increase over time, shifting the weight of payoffs and downsides. Miller describes the subsequent transformation as follows:

> For a brief time in motivational interviewing, we lend clients another perspective, a mirror, a chance to step safely outside of their own frame of reference and to see themselves with new eyes. This is not done by saying, "Listen to me. Here is how I see you," which places the person in the role of a passive listener. It is done by a temporary kind of merging. From the perspective of the therapist we call it empathy, seeking to see the world through the eyes of the client. In a metaphoric sense, we temporarily step inside the client, or better—become one with the client. Naturally, this improves the therapist's understanding of the client, but I think that it also changes the client's perspective. It is as if the client, too, can step into this empathic frame of reference and look back upon himself or herself. From the merged perspective of empathy, the person sees that something is possible, and the seeing begins to make it possible. It was Fritz Perls' definition of teaching: to show a person that something is possible. We refer to it as supporting self-efficacy, but I think it's more than telling a client, "you can do it." It is somehow helping the client see that he or she can do it. (Miller, 1998)

What are some hypothesized motivational issues for the adolescent population?

- *Hypothesized motivational principles that may apply to youth as well as to adults:* It's better if young people argue for change than if the therapist does this. It is important to monitor resistance and keep it low.
- *Hypothesized motivational principles that may differ for youth vs. adults:* Youth tend to rebel against prescriptive authorities (parents teachers, etc.) who may foist misinformation on them in order to change their behavior. It is for this reason that experts in the area of MI tend to feel that verbal interactions and connections are even more important for adolescents than adults and that written feedback may have less impact on youth than on adults.

How does MI fit into the range of typical treatments for youth and high-risk behaviors? Usual treatments seem to be providing information (education) and skill-building. MI fits nicely here because it can prepare youth to accept typical treatments or act as a stand-alone treatment for risky behaviors.

How might one do MI or something consistent with MI with this population? Miller and Rollnick have used MI in an ER setting, with youth presenting for and currently being treated for injuries. They either intervene with the youth right in the ER or, if the young people are hospitalized, see them in their hospital beds after they go through the ER. These brief interventions last an average of twenty minutes, are performed face-to-face under only semi-private conditions (e.g. behind drawn curtains in the ER), and are loosely structured: opening (rapport building, stage-setting), open discussion about how youth view the behavior in question, informal feedback using limited normative information about other youth, a brief negotiation of what the youth is ready/ willing to do differently, and a closing on good terms. This single contact is the extent of the intervention, except for telephone calls to collect data on self-reported behavior change at three and six months after the injury/intervention.

● ●

Review of MI Techniques

- Listen reflectively and with empathy.
- Show acceptance and affirmation whenever genuinely possible.
- Question purposely about clients' feelings, ideas, concerns, and plans, affirming their freedom of choice and self-direction.
- Provide structured feedback, preferably tangible reports.
- Elicit and selectively reinforce the client's own self-motivational statements, expressions of problem recognition, and intention to change.
- Ensure that clients set the pace in regard to their readiness to change.
- Specifically for adolescents, remember that it is best if youth argue for change and elaborate about their ambivalence.
- Monitor resistance. Roll with it. Keep resistance as low as possible.
- Summarize and reframe perceptions in a new light and in reorganized forms, motivating clients to acknowledge problems, consequences, and changes whenever possible.
- When clients are ready, shift their focus from *reasons* to change to a *plan* for change.

● ●

CASE STUDIES

In order to understand and practice motivational interviewing with adolescents with substance issues, it is helpful to witness specific scenarios. The following are based on true client experiences, protecting their anonymity and confidentiality. They can be used by professors as role plays. They purposefully outline various stages in the Stage of Change continuum so that discussion can occur about variations regarding intervention and potential responses at each stage.

• •

Questions for Patients in the Precontemplation and Contemplation Stages

Precontemplation Stage (Goal: Patient will begin thinking about change.)

"What would have to happen for you to know that this is a problem?"

"What warning signs would let you know that this is a problem?"

"Have you tried to change in the past?"

Contemplation Stage (Goal: Patient will examine benefits and barriers to change.)

"Why do you want to change at this time?"

"What were the reasons for not changing?"

"What would keep you from changing at this time?"

"What are the barriers today that keep you from change?"

"What might help you with that aspect?"

"What things (people, programs, and behaviors) have helped in the past?"

"What would help you at this time?"

"What do you think you need to learn about changing?"

Information from Miller, W. R., & Rollnick, S. (2001). *Motivational interviewing: Preparing people to change addictive behavior*. New York, NY: Guilford Press, pp. 191–202

• •

Case Study: Alcohol

Initiation

Rose is 15. She is pretty and, by all present-day standards, "cool" and well-liked in school. She has always had to try hard to get decent grades (which she must get for her parents to let her stay on the cheerleading squad) and although she has friends, she is an introvert and feels safer and more comfortable alone. She has really bad asthma and her inhaler hasn't been working lately. Her mom has started giving her a spoonful of rum before bed to help her sleep and keep her from coughing. For whatever reason, the crazy remedy has actually worked. Rose is sleeping like a baby for the first time in years.

Precontemplation

Rose wondered if it was the "medicine" or just having her mom be so sweet, giving it to her and stroking her hair while she tried to fall asleep, that made her feel so good. But after a few weeks, she woke up gasping for air again. She walked downstairs, thinking, "I'll just take a gulp of the rum," and she did. And it worked. Before she knew it, she was sneaking a cupful to her room every night—and filling the rum bottle with water when it got low. And getting kids to steal rum from their parents to replace the rum at her house so her parents wouldn't notice how much rum was disappearing. When that got too crazy, she tried other stuff in the liquor cabinet—and to her relief, it worked too. She even liked the taste of some of the other liquor even better than the rum. She knew she could get in trouble, but she also neatly rationalized that it was medicinal.

Contemplation

Rose started to worry that something might be wrong. She wrote in her diary, "I don't know myself anymore." She found herself passing more and more on invites to hang with friends at night, especially for sleepover parties. She found she had a serious crush on Hunter, a kid who had a reputation for being a "heavy hitter," binge drinking every weekend. She also found that some mornings, she couldn't get up and out on time and had a horrible headache. Those mornings, she discovered that if she took a sip of the left-over drink, she felt better and could go to school and be okay. She figured out that she could add some vodka to her water bottle for lunch. The thing that amazed Rose the most was that when she went to parties and had something to drink there, she felt totally at home. She didn't feel shy or scared or self- conscious! She finally felt comfortable in her skin. At times, when she had to hide the bottles or get more, she hoped no one would figure out how much she was drinking. On some level, she was absolutely aware that she was hiding a problem from her family and friends.

One night, she got up the nerve to start talking with Hunter at a party. They were playing quarters and she was surprisingly good at it. She was delighted when he had his arm around her and they were leaving the party. But the next thing she remembered was him dropping her off at home, kissing her, and saying, "Fun time—let's do it again soon." When her mom saw that Rose had come in drunk and gotten sick on her clothing, she called for help.

Conversation with clinician

Clinician: So glad you are here, Rose. I know you said on the phone that you really are just doing this to get your mom to stop "worrying and bugging you," right?

Rose: That's right. She worries all the time about stupid stuff. All the kids in my grade use drugs and alcohol and I could give it up any time I want. I just like to do it sometimes, but it certainly isn't a serious thing or anything.

Clinician: Cool—you just do it sometimes. Do you mind telling me about your drug and alcohol use?

Rose: Oh, other than my inhaler for my asthma, I only drink every once in a while.

Clinician: Nothing else?

Rose: Nope.

Clinician: What do you like to drink?

Rose: Oh, I don't have a favorite drink or anything like that. I just have some if it is around, you know?

Clinician: Mmm-hmmm.

Rose: And sometimes a little bit helps me fall asleep.

Clinician: So it helps you.

Rose: Yeah.

Clinician: Does it help you any other ways?

Rose: Well, my mom used to give me a little rum when I had a really bad asthma attack and it would calm the coughing down.

Clinician: Like cough medicine.

Rose: Yeah, only better, 'cause it really worked and I fell asleep and it lasted through the night.

Clinician: So how often do you use it for asthma or sleep?

Rose: Not too often. (awkward pause) I guess that sounds pretty bad, huh?

Clinician: It's understandable—bet those asthma attacks are pretty scary . . .

Rose: You have no idea.

Clinician: Are there other things you like about alcohol?

Rose: I like that it makes me feel less shy at parties, but that's about it.

Clinician: Makes you less shy?

Rose: Yeah, like I feel like I have more to say, and I'm funnier. And I don't worry as much what people think of me.

Clinician: And you talk with people you might not usually feel comfortable talking with . . .

Rose: Yeah! That's right! How did you know? I got my nerve up to talk with this really cool guy the other night and we hung out. I never would have done that if I hadn't had a few beers.

Clinician: So it was a fun night?

Rose: Yeah, well, mostly, I guess. I sort of, well, parts of it I don't totally, well, you know.

Clinician: Your mom said you came home pretty drunk and that you had gotten sick.

Rose: I guess that's right, but I don't really remember that part. I remember hangin' out and having his arm around me and him dropping me at home.

How might you elicit self-motivational statements? Here's one possibility: "So you really like the way alcohol helps you sleep, and deal with your asthma, and be more outgoing, but it sounds like there are some things that you might not like so much about it, right?"

Case Study: Pills

Initiation

Tim is the football quarterback for the freshman team, a popular kid among boys and girls, and the life of the party. He has a sense of humor that is a bit raucous but sharp, and he can be charming and charismatic. Although he is only sixteen, friends of his father are already trying to get him to commit to working for their companies after high school. Everyone knows he will be a success.

163

Tim loves risk. He fell in love with skateboarding when it was in vogue when he was in sixth grade. He loved the toughest jumps and grinds and thought helmets were stupid. He loved to snowboard too. He often is heard saying, "If it isn't a rush, why bother?" One day, he was just doing a simple ollie and he landed wrong and twisted his ankle and heard a pop. It hurt like hell and he knew it was broken. The doctor put a cast on and gave him Tylenol with Codeine pills.

Precontemplation

The pain was so bad that Tim took twice the dose on the first night just to sleep. He got the prescription refilled a few times and even after he was healed, he liked to take a few of the pain pills every once in a while just "to take the edge off life" and to "spice things up." His friends jokingly called him a "stimulus junkie."

Contemplation

One weekend when his parents are out of town, Tim has an idea. He wants to throw a rave at the house and tells each friend to bring one unused bottle of pills from the medicine cabinet at home. When his friends arrive, Tim pours all the pills into a bowl. He then announces that everyone should take a few and wash 'em down with their beer and start dancing and see what happens. Tim wakes up in the hospital the next morning and is told that they had to pump his stomach. His mom is sitting by his bed and her eyes are red and sore, obviously from crying hysterically. Tim realizes he needs to figure out where he crossed the line so he can get things back under control.

Determine how you might shift Tim from contemplation to determination and action steps.

Case Study: Marijuana

Initiation

Joe started smoking cigarettes at his best friend Carl's house when his mom and dad weren't home. They knew where Carl's mom kept her carton of Marlboros and she'd never miss one pack. They liked the way they felt grown up when they smoked. They promised they'd never get hooked liked some kids do. How stupid to spend the money and take on the health risks of that ugly habit! But once in a while, during a movie, on the weekend with a beer or two, it just felt, well, it felt right. They didn't smoke anywhere else.

Precontemplation

Carl convinced Joe to try a marijuana joint instead of the cigarette one weekend and Joe thought, "What the heck." He liked it and they laughed and raided the kitchen for munchies and he didn't have any negative consequences—no paranoia, no coughing, nothing. He felt relieved—marijuana was natural and less dangerous than cigarettes, he told himself, and Carl agreed.

Contemplation:

A teacher caught Joe outside his school smoking a marijuana joint with friends. Later, Joe told his mom and dad that he wasn't smoking it; the teacher just assumed he was because he was with the group. But his mom insisted on giving him a drug test (he didn't know she had bought one at the CVS) and it showed marijuana without a doubt. Now he wasn't just busted but a liar so his parents wouldn't believe a word he had to say. Here's the thing. He liked pot. He didn't smoke it every day and he didn't even smoke it every time it was offered to him. He did find it relaxed him when he was stressed. He liked that it made him laugh a lot. He felt more comfortable around girls when he was high. But now he had gotten caught and it was a big deal—at school, at home, everywhere.

Determination/Action

His parents made Joe meet with a drug counselor. Mike wasn't anything like what Joe had imagined. He had thought Mike would be really confronting and mean, but the guy was actually really nice, cool, funny, and laid-back! In fact, the guy didn't even try to convince him he was an addict or that he had to stop! What Mike did was say that only Joe could decide if the payoffs outweighed the downsides. Mike invited Joe to hang with some other kids "in recovery" and assured him it was voluntary and he could leave at any time. He even joked that there were "cute gals" and winked. Joe thought, well, it was worth it to get his parents off his back. He went to the young people's meeting and couldn't believe how cool the kids were. They were attractive, bright, hilarious, and really deep. They seemed to really make sense and have a sense of purpose in the world. They seemed to know who they were and were comfortable with themselves. He decided he'd try this for a while. He committed to Mike to go without pot or other substances for thirty days and then talk again.

Relapse

Joe went for fourteen days without marijuana. He was very proud of himself. In fact, he decided he deserved to celebrate his two-week mark with a blunt. He figured no one would know. But when he met with Mike, he found himself telling him as he walked in the door.

166

What motivational interviewing strategies might Mike use to engage Joe in the recovery process? How might the relapse become a productive part of his recovery rather than a point of shame or an excuse to give up?

Case Study: Heroin

Initiation

Lizzie was finally dating the boy she had wanted to date for over a year. She was so excited, nervous, and determined to be who he wanted her to be so they would last. So when he took her to a really wild party down the shore, at a really modern house with strobe lights and tons of people she didn't know, she just went with it. Before she knew it, they were putting lines out on the tables. She had tried cocaine before, so it didn't totally freak her out. She thought, "Okay, I'll do a line or two and that will be that." But someone said, "Sweetheart, this ain't cocaine. Wait 'til you try this!" Her boyfriend, Ed, whispered, "Time for some bipping, Sweetheart. Buckle your seatbelt!" Lizzie's heart was pounding—partly from having Ed whisper in her ear, partly from the pounding music of the party, partly from fear of not knowing what she was getting into. She reached for the straw and snorted and immediately knew this was like nothing she had ever known and her life would never be the same. She was in love.

Precontemplation

Within days she was willing to have Eddie tie a tourniquet on her arm and shoot the heroin into her arm. She couldn't imagine anything was more important than sharing this high with this man. Anyone who wouldn't want her to do this simply didn't know what it was to have this heavenly experience. If they tried it, they would understand.

Contemplation

She came to consciousness in a place that looked like a basement. It was cold and dirty. The windows were broken. She realized she didn't know if it was day or night. She looked at her cell phone and saw that she only had a little charge left. Her mother and father had left her messages and texts for the past three days. The final text said, "We've called 911 and the police are searching for you. Please call! We love you." She felt sick and leaned over and vomited, realizing that it wasn't the first time she had done so in this place. She thought, "Maybe this isn't going to work." But she saw Ed next to her, holding her hand, and she figured she could do it better next time.

Action

Lizzie was so sick, tired, achy, and alone. She had never known this feeling before. The thought popped into her head that it might be better if she were dead. She wondered where Eddie was and had a vague memory of him leaving. She saw others around and someone came up to her, desperately asking her if she had any stuff for him to use. She was embarrassed, ashamed, fearful, angry, defensive, and craving a high like nothing she had ever known. She knew that if someone offered her some, she'd use. Instead, in a moment of clarity and sheer desperation, she called her mom and said, "Mom, please help me."

Imagine you are the clinician that Lizzie's mom takes her to see. Write or role play your MI conversation with Lizzie.

MEASURING STAGE OF CHANGE

Adolescents who enter treatment for substance use disorders must be ready to change their behavior in order for treatment to work. Unlike adults, many adolescents are sent to treatment against their will and do not desire to make the changes necessary to overcome their problems with alcohol or other drugs. Measuring the motivation level of the adolescents, and determining what stage of readiness they are in, is a critical component to ensuring a positive treatment outcome. The three primary measures used to assess readiness to change in the adult population are the Stages of Change and Treatment Eagerness Scale (SOCRATES), the Readiness Ruler (RR), and the Staging Algorithm. The SOCRATES measures readiness to change through scaling, the RR is a ten-question scale, and the algorithm bases its evaluation of readiness on a five-point scale.

Stephen A. Maisto of the Department of Psychology at Syracuse University wanted to determine which scale would be the most effective at assessing adolescents' readiness and measuring drinks per drinking day (DDD). For his study, his research team administered all three measures to 161 adolescents who were undergoing treatment for substance use and found that the Readiness Ruler (see box, below) was the most effective tool. Maisto and his team note that the Readiness Ruler is the simplest, easiest readiness measure because it is a brief Likert scale self-administered by respondents (Maisto, Krenek, Chung, Martin, Clark, & Cornelius, 2011).

COGNITIVE BEHAVIORAL THERAPY

As the name so elegantly suggests, cognitive behavioral therapy (CBT) is a blend of two therapies: cognitive therapy (CT) and behavioral therapy. CT was developed by psychotherapist Aaron Beck, M.D., in the 1960s. CT focuses on a person's thoughts and beliefs and how they influence a person's mood and actions, and aims to change a person's thinking to be more adaptive and healthy. Behavioral therapy focuses on a person's actions and aims to change unhealthy behavior patterns.

CBT helps a person focus on current problems and how to solve them. Both patient and therapist need to be actively involved in this process. The therapist helps the patient learn how to identify distorted or unhelpful thinking patterns, recognize and change inaccurate beliefs, relate to others in more positive ways, and change behaviors accordingly.

CBT is especially useful for dual diagnoses and can be applied and adapted to treat many specific mental disorders. Many studies have shown that CBT is a particularly effective treatment for substance use disorders. It has also had significant impact on depression, especially minor or moderate depression. This is especially important for adolescents with substance use disorders because of the extremely high correlation between depression and drug and alcohol use. Some people with substance use disorders (with or without depressive symptoms) may be successfully treated with CBT only. Others may need both CBT and medication. CBT helps people restructure negative thought patterns. Doing so helps people interpret their environment and interactions with others in a positive and realistic way. It may also help people recognize things that may be contributing to their substance use and help them change behaviors that may be making their life situation and subsequent feelings and maladaptive responses worse.

In addition, CBT has been shown to be effective for anxiety disorders, which are also concurrent with substance use in high numbers of adolescents (Wu et al., 2010). With such clients, CBT aims to help a person develop a more adaptive response to a fear. A CBT therapist may use exposure therapy to treat certain anxiety disorders, such as a specific phobia, post-traumatic stress disorder (PTSD), or obsessive compulsive disorder. Exposure therapy has been found to be effective in treating anxiety-related disorders. It works by helping a person confront a specific fear or memory while in a safe and supportive environment. The main goals of exposure therapy are to help the patient learn that anxiety can lessen over time and give that person the tools to cope with fear or traumatic memories.

A recent study sponsored by the Centers for Disease Control and Prevention concluded that CBT is effective in treating trauma-related disorders in children and teens. People with bipolar disorder usually need to take medication, such as a mood stabilizer. But CBT is often used as an added treatment. The medication can help stabilize people's moods so that they are receptive to psychotherapy and can get the most out of it. CBT can help a person cope with bipolar symptoms and learn to recognize when a mood shift is about to occur. CBT also helps a person with bipolar disorder stick with a treatment plan to reduce the chances of relapse (e.g., when symptoms return).

Eating disorders can be very difficult to treat, and when they occur co-morbidly with substance use or dependence, the picture can be very challenging. However, some small studies have found that CBT can help reduce the risk of relapse in individuals with anorexia who have restored their weight. CBT may also reduce some symptoms of bulimia, and it may also help some people reduce binge-eating behavior.

For drug and alcohol use, CBT focuses on recognizing erroneous thinking related to using substances. Cognitive restructuring involved in cognitive behavioral work originated with Aaron Beck (1976) and Albert Ellis (1962). It uses Socratic questioning and rational disputation to modify maladaptive (or "distorted") thoughts. This intervention can be adapted to maintain developmental and systems perspectives (age, context, risk and protective factors, language, social skills, and problem solving abilities).

171

The following are common thought errors which can be recognized and corrected with CBT:

- Mindreading
- Fortune telling
- Catastrophizing
- All or nothing thinking
- Labeling
- Value judgments
- Over-generalizing
- Selective focus

More specifically for adolescent substance users, these are ways that the above listed errors manifest:

- black and white thinking: all good or bad
- *This* time, I will be able to stop
- I am only hurting myself
- I can stop any time I want to
- I won't use my substance of choice anymore and I'll be fine if I switch to . . .
- I don't really have a problem because so-and-so is so much worse, or because x, y, or z hasn't happened to me
- I have to use because of my life situations
- substances are the glue that hold me together (when in fact it is the solvent making everything come apart)
- I am a bad or broken person and therefore deserve to hurt myself
- I have sacrificed enough for others and now deserve to "enjoy myself"

- I need these meds for _____ (e.g., pain, anxiety, loss, stress, energy, etc.)
- I am an addict; I have to use. I am an alcoholic; I have to drink.

• •

Outline of Standard Course of Cognitive-Behavioral Therapy (CBT)

1. Elicit information regarding symptom development and contributing factors (objective, subjective, multiple information when feasible).
2. Develop goal list with youth and caregivers along with cognitive-behavioral plan.
3. Identify underlying beliefs, attitudes, assumptions, expectations, goals, self-statements, and automatic thoughts. Teach how to monitor negative or maladaptive thoughts/feelings. Reward self-monitoring.
4. Identify specific behavioral and interpersonal skill deficits (and strengths).
5. Investigate contributing medical, social, and environmental factors (including stressful life events).
6. Select and introduce cognitive and behavioral interventions.
7. Assign homework to practice what is learned during the session.
8. Evaluate effectiveness of intervention (objective ratings, observations, and subjective reports).
9. Introduce relapse prevention interventions, and schedule booster sessions.

• •

RELAPSE PREVENTION

There are things individuals can do to help prevent relapse once they have established a foundation for their abstinence. Old relapse prevention models utilized in the 1980s and '90s, created by Ernie Larson (1999), Terrance Gorski (1989), and others, made the important point that getting sober in the acute stage is not enough for ongoing wellness. Larson's (1999) coined phrase "stage II recovery," forced everyone in the field to look beyond the initial establishment of abstinence and towards successful and full lives as a critical aspect in the process of bio-psycho-social-spiritual reparation. Ernie died of cancer in January, 2010, and has left behind a legacy of awareness about steps towards a lifetime of joy and serene living for addicts and alcoholics.

Critical Considerations for Relapse Prevention Planning

1. Recognize and avoid "triggers." These are not just associations but chemically "hard wired" precipitants to craving phenomena. Triggers can be people, places, and things that are integral in the addiction.

2. Stress can prompt a relapse. A person's brain retains a memory of the relief of the high long into recovery (perhaps permanently) and accesses this memory when under stress.

3. Accountability to an individual, counselor, sponsor, or group can make all the difference between maintaining abstinence and relapsing. For adolescents, the best possible mode of accountability is an alternative peer group (to be discussed in detail later in the book).

4. "Plan your own relapse" is a term indicating that individuals know what their relapse would likely look like and, therefore, it is helpful to articulate this to others and use it as a sort of "map of the minefield."

5. "Clean house," a common expression in twelve-step programs, has two meanings. In its literal sense, it means making sure that one's living space is free of any mood and mind

altering substances, including unnecessary medications, alcohol, alcohol-based products, and any other substance that might cause a relapse. People in early recovery do best if they aim at being too careful; it is better to err on the side of being cautious than taking any unnecessary risks. For example, although most people are confident that wine cooks out of most dishes, the taste of the wine and knowing it is there may be problematic for some drug-dependent individuals in terms of relapse. The more figurative interpretation of "clean house" has more to do with addressing faulty thinking, character defects, resentments, and other aspects of self that might prompt a relapse and get in the way of recovery. Many people address such aspects via the twelve steps, but others utilize therapeutic and/or spiritual settings.

6. Attend to physical health. The body and mind both need to heal from drug and alcohol use. Eating well, exercising, reducing stress, meditating, and laughing all help the systems of the body recalibrate for recovery and well-being.

7. Have fun. The word "sober" can be misleading. It is not likely that someone will maintain abstinence if they are miserable, bored, angry, or depressed. Many addicts and alcoholics have spent so much time and energy revolving around substances that they have little idea what they like to do and what they are good at. It is for this reason that it is so important for young people in recovery to explore fun activities, preferably with recovery communities.

8. It has been noted that nothing protects against relapse like helping others. Young people who choose recovery are in a unique position to be useful to others. They can speak to school counselors, students, parents, and other community groups. They can sponsor other young people in twelve-step programs. Service accomplishes two powerful and critical objectives. First, it gives a sense of meaning and purpose to

the young person's recovery efforts. Second, it diverts the individual from the almost inevitable self-absorption that comes along with addiction and early recovery.

FAMILY SYSTEMS APPROACH

As noted in the discussion of the ecological model, adolescents never exist in a vacuum (although if you speak with them and their parents, they will often tell you that they wish that they did). It is critical that both prevention and treatment interventions and recovery foundations are holistic, encapsulating the need for awareness of "person in environment" at all times. Context is everything, especially for adolescents, because they are so hyper-aware and super-conscious of their role and identity in the midst of their peer groups and others around them. This is also true with regard to their identity in juxtaposition or opposition to others, such as parents, especially in the midst of the appropriate developmental process of individuation.

As mentioned earlier, the teenager's quest to become independent (i.e., individuation) is a normal part of development. The parent should not see it as a rejection or loss of control. Parents should aim at consistency and be available as a sounding board for the youth's ideas, without dominating the child's newly independent identity. Although adolescents typically challenge authority figures, they need or want limits, which provide a safe boundary for them to grow and function. Power struggles should be avoided, if possible. One of the parties (typically the teen) will be overpowered, causing the youth to lose face. This can cause the adolescent to feel embarrassed, inadequate, resentful, and bitter. Keeping open lines of communication and clear, yet negotiable, limits or boundaries may help reduce major conflicts.

Family work (i.e., therapy, facilitation, counseling, or whatever guidance you are providing depending on your role or discipline) is a delicate endeavor. Families with addicted youth are often raw with emotions, driven by a thousand versions of fear, and packed with deeply engrained behaviors that are often counter-productive and hard to unlearn. Although it may seem as if clinicians are there to work with families with "problem" children, one of their most important tasks must be to de-label identified patients (IPs). A child who is acting out may be doing so as a conscious or unconscious "cry for help" for their family or self. In family systems work, the entire family is the client, and there is value in exploring the role of the symptoms but not in singling out the "sick" one and blaming and shaming.

Parents of adolescents with substance issues often feel like they are handcuffed into a seat of a Mack truck being driven on and off the road by their impaired adolescent. They are trying to survive, save their families, and save their child. Even if they are in profound denial, on some level they know that drugs and alcohol can kill their child. That is why they go to such lengths to try to make their child happy. It is recommended that, as their clinician, you see the parents alone first to coach, support, plan, establish rapport, and assess bonds/conflicts. Refer to Chapter 5 for more details about how to interact with parents and about their dynamics in relation to their child. Most important, remember that your goal should be to help them move to establish a healthier form of homeostasis (i.e., balance) than they have had. Be flexible with resistant members; consider inviting someone rather than painting the meeting as an obligation. Individual and family goals flow from exploration of the complex interplay of needs and wants. Modify the status quo in these families by utilizing the following techniques:

- Explore metacommunication (a process that identifies and modifies aspects of communication that are not verbal and explicit such as inconsistencies, dissonance, disconfirming beliefs, incongruencies, nonverbal messages, double-binds, etc.).

- Identify patterns and work towards changing rigid or unhealthy family rules (while illuminating how rules can undermine growth).

- Assess level of willingness to change.

- Enhance communication and relationship skills such as utilizing "I statements," helping family members see and affirm strengths, educating on the value of amends, resolving resentments, modifying complementary interactions, and so on.

- Disengage from conflict (arresting unproductive dramatic escalations which often occur when feelings are hurt), and focus more on patience, tolerance, and working together.

- Focus away from the past and more onto the here and now and on plans for the future (with clear expectations, goals, rewards, and consequences). In the midst of this work, reduce blame.

- Teach how to make requests and to turn down requests respectfully.

- Adjust distorted perceptions.

- Assess alignments (e.g., using advanced therapeutic techniques at your disposal such as family sculpting, diagrams, genograms; see fig. 7.1) and modify problematic alignments.

- Strengthen marital/partner coalitions.

- Mark generational boundaries.

- Address various groupings of members.

- Formulate tasks to strengthen relationships.

Figure 7.1: Genograms

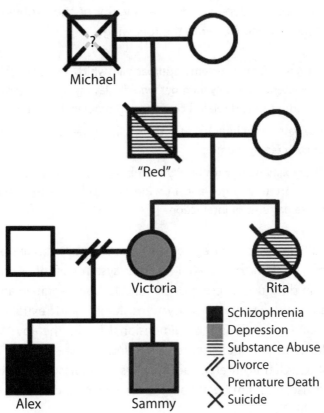

Michael

"Red"

Victoria

Rita

Schizophrenia
Depression
Substance Abuse
Divorce
Premature Death
Suicide

Alex

Sammy

VARIOUS MODES OF EVIDENCE-BASED
FAMILY THERAPY

Strong family systems models for adolescent drug users, such as brief strategic family therapy (BSFT) (Szapoczink & Kurtines, 1989) have their roots in structural family therapy (Minuchin, 1974) and strategic family therapy (Haley, 1976). BSFT typically involves twelve to twenty-four sessions, lasting about ninety minutes, for four months, plus up to eight "booster" sessions. The number of sessions needed depends on the severity of the problem. The basic tenets of BSFT include the following:

- BSFT is a family systems approach in which the drug-using adolescent is a family member who displays symptoms, including drug use and related co-occurring problem behaviors.
- The patterns of interaction in the family influence the behavior of each family member.
- Therapists work with family members to plan interventions that carefully target and provide practical ways to change those patterns of interaction.

Multiple systems or ecologically based family models aim to change family factors as well as other systems of influence that maintain drug use. These models tend to be integrative and target drug use directly in subsystems, family, and "extrafamilial" work. One example is multidimensional family therapy (MDFT) (Liddle, 2002) for adolescents. Regardless of the particular theoretical basis, family therapy approaches for adolescents with substance use problems generally have similar fundamental goals (Rowe, 2012):

- Utilize the support and leverage of the family to address the reality and consequences of the individual's drug use and implement other important lifestyle changes.
- Alter problematic aspects of the family environment to maintain positive changes in the individual and other family members and promote long-term recovery.

Solution-focused family therapy (DeShazier et al., 2007) is a method of family work that is brief, strengths-based, and change-oriented. The following key concepts and definitions are related to brief strategic family therapy and have excellent utility with adolescents with substance use and their families:

- Complaint: This is the issue on which the selective attention of the family is focused. It is not necessary to know the cause of or very much about the problem itself in order to resolve it. No extensive diagnoses are involved. This school of thought does *not* believe that the problem serves a function in the family system.

- Exceptions: These are times when the problem does *not* occur. Gather as many as possible with the question, "What other times . . . ?" Be patient, use prompts, and reinforce with positive responses.

- Scaling techniques: The clinician helps the client and family members affix problem descriptions and solutions at both ends of a Likert scale and then asks where they are on the scale.

- Miracle questions: This is an intervention strategy intended to help the client/system envision a new way of behaving. The clinician asks the client to imagine what will be different when a miracle occurs and the problem that brought them to therapy has disappeared.

- Coping questions: These are variations on scaling questions. "On a scale of 1 to 10, with 10 being you would do anything to solve this problem and 1 being that you do not care so much for solving it, where would you say you are right now?"

- Customer: The client is seen as a consumer of services rather than a "patient."

- "Think break": This is time (towards the end of the session, with or without a team of experts) to reflect on compliments that can be made to the family and tasks for follow-up.

- Joining: This is the task of building rapport, which the therapist does by chatting, mirroring, depathologizing/normalizing, focusing on strengths, and noting that the family already has the solutions to their problems.

- Presuppositional language: This is language framed in such a way, either by choosing a specific verb tense, or implying the occurrence of a particular event, that it leads the family to believe that a solution will be achieved. Such language helps the client restructure cognitive meanings about self and problems (e.g., saying *"when* you start doing better" instead of *if* and changing *"I don't know"* to *"If you did know, what would you say?"*)

- Externalizing language: Such language separates problems from the client and increases the client's self-control over behaviors (e.g., "When your disease of alcoholism tries to get you in trouble with your wife, what does it make you do?" and "Are there times you stand up to your disease and not let it push you around?")

- Homework: Most sessions culminate in compliments and a task to work on prior to the next session. Such homework can include recording behaviors, reflections, and activities and is usually co-constructed with the client(s).

- First formula task: Ask family members to take note of what is happening when the problem is not occurring.

- Betting: The therapist challenges the family with a small monetary or "gentleman's" bet relating to the continuation of the identified change. Be careful; you must convey that you have confidence they can win the bet. This approach works even better if a third party (family member, teacher, etc.) makes the challenge and the therapist can ally with the client.

- A new context: "What needs to occur for [the desired behavior] to happen again or more often?"

- Reversal questions: The therapist asks if someone has any advice for anyone else in the family in terms of helping that person. For example, "What advice can you give your mother about how she can get you to go to school in the morning?"

- Flagging the minefield: The therapist asks the client to identify factors that could result in the "old" pattern. This serves to clearly differentiate between the past and present and also warns the client of the possibility of relapse.

- Relationship questions: These questions are used for meta-perspective. "What does [name of significant person] think of your problem?" Ask clients such questions regarding a variety of people in the clients' system. The questions can also help you see how the client constructs the problem (e.g., "Who makes it worse?" "Who makes it better?").

De Shazer and Molnar's (1984) Paradigm

- "formula first session task"
- "do something different" (left vague for family to figure out)
- "pay attention to what you do when you overcome the urge to [the problem behavior or complaint]
- "a lot of people in your situation would have" (suggesting negative alternatives and framing stability as the most difficult course of action, demanding the most change)

KEY TERMS

Holistic approach

Wraparound services

Therapeutic group work

The three "C's"

Stages of readiness for change

Precontemplation

Defense mechanisms

Euphoric recall

Decisional balance
Relationship
Motivational interviewing (MI)
Ambivalence
Reflective listening
Affirmation
Motivational Enhancement
  Therapy (MET)
Brief Motivational Interviewing
  (BMI)
Brief intervention
FRAMES
SOCRATES
Readiness Ruler
Staging Algorithm
Cognitive behavioral therapy
Exposure therapy
Cognitive restructuring
Thought errors
Stage II recovery

Triggers
Stress
Solution-focused family
  therapy
Complaint
Exceptions
Scaling techniques
Miracle questions
Coping questions
Think break
Joining
Presuppositional language
Externalizing language
First formula task
Betting
Reversal questions
Flagging the minefield
Relationship questions
Sponsor

DISCUSSION QUESTIONS

1. Think critically about the potential strengths and limitations of research-supported evidence-based practice with adolescents who misuse substances.

2. Discuss the benefits of the wraparound model and the various components of the care continuum—in patient care, outpatient care, individual, group work, family intervention, recovery support settings, mutual aid groups, and so on.

3. Would you think it more appropriate and accurate to refer to a motivational interviewer as a counselor, advisor, or facilitator? Why? (Hint: Review the spirit of MI list.)

4. Discuss the commonalities and differences between motivational interviewing and brief interventions.

5. Have a conversation in a dyad. As you have the conversation, jot down notes about meta-communications witnessed during the conversation. Then discuss and see how accurate your perceptions were and where you misinterpreted based on your own beliefs, style, and life experience.

REFERENCES

Bien, T. H., Miller, W. R., & Tonigan, J. S. (1993). Brief interventions for alcohol problems: A review. *Addiction, 88*(3), 315–336.

Bruns, E. J., Walker, J. S., Zabel, M., Matarese, M., Estep, K., Harburger, D., & Mosby, M. (2010). Intervening in the lives of youth with complex behavioral health challenges and their families: The role of the wraparound process. *American Journal of Community Psychology, 46*, 314–331.

De Shazer, S., & Molnar, A. (1984). Four useful interventions in brief family therapy. *Journal of Marital and Family Therapy, 10*(3), 297–304.

Haley, J. (1976). *Problem-solving therapy.* San Francisco, CA: Jossey-Bass. http://www.hbo.com/addiction/understanding_addiction/18_what_is_addiction.html

Gorski, T. (1989). *Passages through recovery: An action plan for preventing relapse.* Center City, MN: Hazelden.

Liddle, H. A. (2002). Multidimensional family therapy for adolescent cannabis users. *Cannabis Youth Treatment (CYT) Series,* Volume 5. Rockville, MD: Center for Substance Abuse Treatment, Substance Abuse and Mental Health Services Administration.

Maisto, S. A., Krenek, M., Chung, T. A., Martin, C. S., Clark, D., & Cornelius, J. R. (2011). A comparison of the concurrent and predictive validity of three measures of readiness to change alcohol use in a clinical sample of adolescents. *Psychological Assessment, 23*(4), 983–994.

Miller, W. R. (1998). Toward a motivational definition and understanding of addiction. *Motivational Interviewing Newsletter for Trainers, 5*(3), 2–6.

Miller, W. R., & Rollnick, S. (2001). *Motivational interviewing: Preparing people to change addictive behavior.* New York, NY: Guilford Press.

Miller, W. R., & Rollnick (2002). *Motivational interviewing: Preparing people for change (2nd ed.).* New York, NY: Guilford Press.

Miller, W. R., & Rollnick, S. (2009). Ten things that motivational interviewing is not. *Behavioral and Cognitive Psychotherapy, 37*(2), 129–140.

Miller, W. R., & Rollnick, S. (2013). *Motivational interviewing: Helping people change (3rd ed.).* New York, NY: Guilford Press.

Miller, W. R., & Rose, G. S. (2010). Motivational interviewing in relational context. *American Psychologist, 65*(4), 298–299. doi: 10.1037/a0019487.

Miller, W. R., & Sanchez, V. C. (1994). Motivating young adults for treatment and lifestyle change. In G. S. Howard & P. E. Nathan (Eds.) *Alcohol use and misuse by young adults* (pp. 55–81). Notre Dame, IN: University of Notre Dame Press.

Nestler, E. J., & Malenka, R. C. (2004). The addicted brain. *Scientific American, 290*, 78–85.

Rollnick, S., & Miller, W. R. (1995). What is motivational interviewing? *Behavioral and Cognitive Psychotherapy, 23*, 325–334.

Rollnick, S., Heather, N., & Bell, A. (1992). Negotiating behavior change in medical settings: The development of brief motivational interviewing. *Journal of Mental Health, 1*(1), 25–37.

Rollnick, S., Kinnersley, P., & Stott, N. (1993). Methods of helping patients with behavior change. *Behavioral Medicine Journal, 307*, 188–190.

Rowe, C. L. (2012). Family therapy for drug abuse: Review and updates 2003–2010. *Journal of Marital and Family Therapy, 38*(1), 221–243.

Smalley, R. E. (1967). *Theory for social work practice.* New York, NY: Columbia University Press.

Stott, N., Rollnick, S., Rees, M., & Pill, R. (1995). Innovation in clinical method: Diabetes care and negotiation skills. *Family Practice, 12*, 413–418.

Szapoczink, J., Kurtines, W. M., & Contributors. (1989). *Breakthroughs in family therapy with drug-abusing and problem youth.* New York, NY: Springer.

Winters, K. C., Botzet, A. M., & Fahnhorst, T. (2011). Advances in adolescent substance abuse treatment. *Current Psychiatry Reports, 13*(5), 416–421.

Wu, P., Goodwin, R. D., Fuller, C., Liu, X., Comer, J. S., Cohen, P., & Hoven, C. W. (2010). The relationship between anxiety disorders and substance use among adolescents in the community. *Journal of Youth and Adolescence, 39*(2), 177–188.

Chapter 8

Support Groups, Twelve-Step, and Other Paths to Recovery

As noted in the discussion of bio-psycho-social-spiritual aspects of drug use and dependence, one of the most insidious and difficult to remedy aspects of the manifestations of the disease is the isolation of the user. This sense of utter aloneness coupled with a bizarre sense of grandiosity in spite of horrible low sense of self and lack of self-efficacy often leads drug and alcohol users and individuals with a substance use disorder to the gates of insanity, suicidality, or death.

Therefore, one of the critical pieces in any form of recovery is a real and intimate, honest connection with at least one other person. It is sad and important to note that there are some people, in the experience of twelve-step programs, who are "constitutionally incapable of being honest." The program goes on to note that many of those people cannot recover, although some do and many do.

Although many addictions counselors who find sobriety as a pathway of recovery in Alcoholics Anonymous, Narcotics Anonymous, or other twelve-step programs think that anyone who is capable of being honest can get well in "the rooms," it is clear that there are many roads to recovery, for there are so many complex versions of substance use and dependence. For example, the concept of "instantly addicting" drugs like heroin is erroneous. Pharmacologist Carlton Erickson notes that there are those who can use drugs such as heroin without becoming dependent in the scientific sense of the word. Such people may be able to stop on their own without ongoing attendance at twelve-step meetings for a lifetime. Other people, however, who have disrupted brain chemistries, may find that even after ten, twenty, or even more years of regular AA or NA attendance, they still "crave" a substance when in stressful situations. It may be tempting to judge such individuals as "weak" or to assume that perhaps they are not "working the program" hard or well enough. Those that have found twelve-step programs to be the ideal "blueprints for living" often find it impossible to imagine that any other path could work for someone. It is also important to note that there are those that may not have the brain disease and instead have problematic drinking or drugging, which falls somewhat lower on the spectrum of substance use disorders. These individuals might adjust their use with such positive life changes as diet, exercise, yoga, meditation, individual or group therapy, biofeedback, increased sleep, and so on.

It is important to clarify that "self-help" and drug and alcohol dependence are in many ways oxymorons. Many have observed that it is only through recognition and a "giving up" (or "surrender") of the self that one can truly find recovery. This in and of itself is a tricky concept. Clearly, although recovery cannot be achieved on self-will alone, there is a certain amount of self-will necessary for movement in positive directions. As some have been known to say, "God won't drive the car to the meeting." In the field of working with individuals who are in the clutches of the devastating disease, many trained in the traditional twelve-step modality use the term "self will run riot" (i.e., substance users can wind up with people and in places they otherwise could avoid (Kurtz & Chambon, 1987). It is not reasonable for substance users to rely on their brains until they heal and the neuro-chemistry readjusts. Comedian John Larroquette jokes in his routine, "When I got sober the first thing I had to do was fire my brain." His joke captures how people with alcoholism or addiction often cannot trust their own thinking in the throes of active addiction.

Many note that people cannot possibly think their way out of addiction. So how do individuals navigate their way when drugs and alcohol have assumed power over their lives and selves? It is here that the concept of spirituality becomes of paramount importance to those seeking a life of recovery. It is important to distinguish the difference between religion and spirituality. Perhaps the most important aspect for young adults who have been misusing drugs or alcohol is the experience of a shift from total self-reliance to connectedness with at least one other person. This concept is challenging for young addicts for several reasons:

- They are developmentally striving for independence and it pains them to rely on anyone other than themselves (even more than adult addicts/alcoholics).
- Young people who have used and misused substances have often lied, cheated, and manipulated to keep substances available and at the center of their world—thus, they often assume that others operate this way and therefore trust is a concept that is very hard to grasp, much less achieve. This is seen anecdotally by increased perception of peer use discussed earlier in this text.
- Young drug and alcohol users keep people at arm's length out of shame and fear. They believe that people truly are better off without them due to their low self-worth. They live in shame. Rather than being aware of their mistakes, they believe they *are* a mistake, that they are bad rather than ill.

189

- Intimacy takes years of practice, self-knowledge, trust, the ability to love self and others, and honesty. These are skills and qualities that newly recovering people have not yet developed.

Spirituality means believing in something other than self. And it boils down to shifting into hope by virtue of recognizing that others can and are willing to help.

It should be noted that twelve-step programs are still clearly one of the most successful modes of recovery for those with the disease of addiction (Kelly, Myers , & Brown, 2002); over 9 percent of the U.S population has attended an AA meeting. It is common for those who come to meetings such as AA, NA, and CA to think that they do not need to go to the lengths recommended in the program. They hear recommendations that sound daunting. For instance, they hear the suggestion that they go to a meeting a day for ninety days, which is not in the *Big Book* (the book Alcoholics Anonymous considers its "text" but which does increase chances of recovery for newcomers who need a complete shift in community as well as those with low-recovery capital in their environments). They're also told to get a sponsor (a mentor to walk them through the steps), which may sound strange to someone who has not worked a twelve-step program. People tell them not to form any romantic relationships in the first year (again, not in the *Big Book*, but a recommendation based on the experiences of many who have found such relationships to be a path to relapse). They hear the advice to avoid "people, places, and things" they associate with their use, which sounds like a very tall order. They may even hear recovering people joke, "All you have to change is your entire life." Until people have some time and history behind them, they won't find this the least bit funny.

Although much of the literature explains the twelve steps, the culture of twelve-step programs often goes without description (MacMaster & Holleran, 2005). Adolescents may have a particularly hard time acclimating to twelve-step culture if they are not connected or guided to meeting with young people who are in similar situations. In studies of whether adolescents affiliate with twelve-step programs, the researchers make sure to highlight the importance of distinguishing between mere attendance and affiliation, or true active engagement in the suggested recovery processes (Room & Greenfield, 1993; Kelly, Myers, & Brown, 2002).

PEER-TO-PEER MUTUAL AID GROUPS

Although for many years recovery was defined as complete abstinence from substances and/or related behaviors, there is growing awareness that individuals have varied experiences, chemistries, and paths to wellness. There are some young people who determine, either due to internal or external consequences, that abstinence is their solution. Of these youth, some need programs of support and others, perhaps those with less severe substance use disorders or less disrupted brain pleasure pathways, are able to shift gears in their life and achieve abstinence without rigorous therapeutic work, twelve-step programs or other mutual aid peer groups. Still others determine that abstinence is not their pathway to recovery and that reducing use, or limiting use to certain substances or amounts, is their own solution. There are many different versions of substance use disorders, as there are varieties of cancer, or types of diabetes. The different stories warrant different directions. It is important to value each person's pathway—after all, each person is the expert in his or her own life experience.

191

In addition to twelve-step fellowships (Alcoholics Anonymous), there are a number of "roads to recovery," a phrase coined by two pioneering researchers in the addiction recovery realm, John Kelly and William White (2012). These are also touted as "pathways to recovery" in the emerging recovery movement in the United States. The following peer-to-peer mutual aid groups have noteworthy membership, attendance, and reported efficacy rates; this variety of settings broadens the support options for young people who desire a change related to their substance use or misuse:

- Twelve-step programs
- SMART recovery
- LifeRing
- Moderation Management
- SOS (Secular Organizations for Sobriety)
- Celebrate Recovery and JACS
- Women for Sobriety

The most prominent alternatives to twelve-step spiritually based programs are the cognitively based groups: SOS, SMART Recovery, LifeRing, and Moderation Management. Religiously based peer-to-peer recovery support groups include JACS (for Jewish people in recovery) and Celebrate Recovery (for Christians in recovery) (Kelly & White, 2012).

Secular Organizations for Sobriety (SOS) was started in 1986 by an unhappy AA member, Jim Christopher, for atheists/agnostics. SOS is an alternative recovery method for persons with addiction who are uncomfortable with the spiritual content of widely available twelve-step programs. SOS maintains that sobriety is a separate issue from religion or spirituality. This program does not utilize steps; it is based on an emphasis on the "sobriety priority." SOS credits the individual for achieving and maintaining his or her own sobriety, without reliance on any "Higher Power." The following are the general principles of SOS:

- All those who sincerely seek sobriety are welcome as members in any SOS group.
- SOS is not a spin-off of any religious or secular group. There is no hidden agenda, as SOS is concerned with achieving and maintaining sobriety (abstinence).
- SOS seeks only to promote sobriety amongst those who suffer from addictions.
- As a group, SOS has no opinion on outside matters and does not wish to become entangled in outside controversy.
- Although sobriety is an individual responsibility, life does not have to be faced alone. The support of other alcoholics and addicts is a vital adjunct to recovery.
- In SOS, members share experiences, insights, information, strength, and encouragement in friendly, honest, anonymous, and supportive group meetings.
- To avoid unnecessary entanglements, each SOS group is self-supporting through contributions from its members and refuses outside support.
- Sobriety is the number one priority in a recovering person's life. As such, he or she must abstain from all drugs or alcohol.
- Honest, clear, and direct communication of feelings, thoughts, and knowledge aids in recovery and in choosing nondestructive, non-delusional, and rational approaches to living sober and rewarding lives.
- As knowledge of addiction might cause a person harm or embarrassment in the outside world, SOS guards the anonymity of its membership and the contents of its discussions from those not within the group.

- SOS encourages the scientific study of addiction in all its aspects. SOS does not limit its outlook to one area of knowledge or theory of addiction.

http://www.sossobriety.org/MeetingInfo/SOS_Principles.pdf

The main difference between SMART (Self Management and Recovery Training) and a twelve-step program is that a spiritual belief is not required and is not a focus of SMART recovery. The program does not prohibit members of a spiritual or religious background, though the concepts are not focal points for success. The underlying principle of abstinence, though, is present in both twelve-step groups and SMART recovery, a lesser-known fact that is important to note. There are approximately 650 SMART groups worldwide. SMART started in 1994 as Rational Recovery, based in rational emotive therapy (RET), conceived by Albert Ellis. Reason and scientific knowledge are the authorities for SMART. Using rational emotive therapy, SMART participants are not required to label themselves as "alcoholics" or "addicts" but instead create within themselves self-responsibility, self-motivation, and self-discipline as the primary means of stopping substance use. The program leaves to each individual such decisions as whether to label oneself and whether to consider addiction a disease or a matter of self-reflection and exploration. Effectiveness research has its limitations, but it is clear that this model works best as a supplement to a twelve-step group, in combination with intensive personal counseling, and for those who have not crossed into clinical addiction on the substance use disorder spectrum. SMART recovery is based in RET's problem-solving tools:

- ABC model: a process to identify and dispute one's irrational beliefs, thoughts, and feelings. (A—Activating Event;

B—Beliefs about Activating Event; C—Consequences; and some have later added D—Disputing Irrational Beliefs—to clarify how and what the belief will do for the person.)

- Journaling
- Relaxation
- Planning

LifeRing is another secular program in which no "steps" are involved. The foundation of this grass-roots, experientially based abstinence program is that members "do not drink or use no matter what." It is founded on positive psychology; each participant is supported in creating a tailor-made recovery program. The main difference from other mutual aid peer groups is that LifeRing participants get and stay sober through their own desire and efforts as well as group support so that they will realize their own capabilities for overcoming their addiction.

Moderation Management is a program started in 1994 designed to serve the needs of "problem drinkers." Of the mutual aid peer groups mentioned in this text, it is the closest to a true harm reduction approach. Meetings and online chat rooms are the source of communication. Nicknamed MM, this program is based on self-management, balance, moderation, and personal responsibility. It is *not* recommended for people with severe substance use disorders (people who are clinically addicted), chronic drinkers, or those who have experienced significant medical symptoms. It is also not intended for former dependent drinkers who are now abstaining. Instead, MM is a viable option for people who want to reduce their drinking because they have encountered moderate to mild alcohol-related problems and would like to make positive lifestyle changes. The MM website notes, "Approximately 30 percent of MM members go on to abstinence-based programs." They conclude, "Outcome studies indicate that professional programs which offer both moderation and abstinence have higher success rates than those that offer abstinence only. Clients tend to self-select the behavior change options which will work best for them."

Celebrate Recovery is described as "Christ-centered" recovery; it is based on the belief that Jesus Christ is the one and only Higher Power. The program utilizes the Bible along with Celebrate Recovery curriculum. The large group lessons are taught from the "Leader's Guide," using the scriptures as key points in the lessons. This is to keep consistency within groups, allowing teachers to be creative with the introduction and conclusion of each lesson. A program called Life's Healing Choices is part of the approved curriculum. The ministry is "group based." All groups are gender specific and use group guidelines and formats. The members believe that each group is accountable to Christ, the local church, and the established model of Celebrate Recovery. The program loosely defines addiction and includes substances as well as process disorders such as sexual obsessions and eating disorders.

JACS (Jewish Alcoholics, Chemically Dependent Persons, and Significant Others) is a Jewish recovery program that encourages recovery in a nurturing, Jewish environment. JACS promotes knowledge and understanding of the disease of alcoholism and addiction as it involves the Jewish community. JACS also acts as a resource center and information clearinghouse on the effects of alcoholism and drug misuse on Jewish family life.

Women for Sobriety (WFS) was created in 1975 by women who felt the AA twelve-step model was not a fit for women. They felt that the general essence of AA was problematic and that a new positive and affirming program was needed. At the heart of WFS is an altered perspective about "powerlessness," emphasizing how powerful women can be in their lives when empowered (and that they ought not be powerless in unjust or dangerous situations). This is a very small program based as a non-profit business.

The concept of multiple "roads to recovery" (Kelly & White, 2012) is one that has begun to gain new traction in the current iteration of the large-scale recovery movement in the United States, and worldwide. It is now most commonly cited as multiple "pathways to recovery" and is deeply rooted in the principles of client self-empowerment, self-efficacy, and motivational interviewing (meeting clients "where they are," promoting advancement through the Stage of Change Model, etc.). Traditionally, as has been discussed earlier, it was considered that to find yourself in recovery, either emerging or long-term, you would have to be completely abstinent from all mind-altering substances. Although this is true for those that follow an abstinence-based, mutual aid peer group (SMART, AA, NA, etc.), it is not true for those that follow alternative "pathways" to find recovery, such as Celebrate Recovery, MAT, harm reductionism, and the like. How then, if recovery communities have long considered abstinence and sobriety to equate to recovery, is this possible? A further exploration of an increased capacity for the definition of recovery is needed to answer that question.

Now what of the issue of "process disorders" or "compulsive illnesses"? Whether speaking of those with substance use disorders, disordered eating, process and behavioral addictions, mental health illnesses (which often present as co-occurring disorders), the notion of recovery goes far past the traditional viewpoint of "sobriety." Recovery is now largely considered to be a process of empowering individuals to find self-efficacy and improve their quality of life overall. Even twelve-step founders gave a nod to this mentality. The *Big Book* explains that substance use is but a manifestation of symptoms and that relieving those symptoms is only a step in the right direction.

Recovery advocate Robert Ashford notes the following critical point: "Defined in this way, we can then begin to see how the framework of multiple 'pathways' to recovery can exist symbiotically with all traditional views of sobriety and abstinence. The key to recovery is in identifying, respecting, and exploring an individual's truth, and then proceeding to actively engage the individual in their chosen pathway of wellness (recovery)." He notes that, for many in the United States, roughly 17 million, this path is not twelve-step programs or other mutual aid peer groups. These individuals utilize their own experiences, harm reductionism, and other unreported resources to find recovery. For another large portion of the population, roughly 2.5 million, this is a mutual aid peer group such as Alcoholics Anonymous, which focuses on complete abstinence. Other successful accounts of programs of recovery include medication-assisted therapy, counseling, and harm reduction.

Ashford concludes: "The major benefits of this emerging mentality, which invokes respect and empowerment of all individuals regardless of their 'truth', is that all individuals on the spectrum of substance use disorders, and other quality of life concerns, can receive the benefits from an active program of recovery. Too often when a shortsighted view of recovery is given (those ascribing to sobriety only), individuals who seek and need assistance are turned away. By expanding the consciousness of our field, we begin to treat humans as humans, giving them access to all aspects of the helping professions that they inherently have a right to."

• •

Recovery can be defined as "the processes that an individual utilizes to actively cope, seek self-improvement and self-efficacy and to expand their individual quality of life."

Robert Ashford

• •

ADDRESSING CHALLENGES FOR THE PRACTITIONER

Building a relationship with an adolescent is typically challenging even when substances are not a part of the picture. As noted earlier, the most important ingredients for a helping relationship with a young person with issues around drugs and/or alcohol are encapsulated by the acronym "HOW." Here is the HOW of working with this population: Honesty, Open-mindedness, and Willingness. An honest approach is key. Adolescents have what they often call a "bull sh*+" meter. As one client noted, "I am a master liar, manipulator, and player. I can spot b.s. from a mile away." This is why it is not enough to recommend that clinicians focus on the client's strengths. The strengths must be true and capture something that can build a foundation for the youth's self-respect, respect of the therapeutic alliance, and eventually respect for others in the process.

Some practitioners encounter difficulties with clients and declare, "That is a resistant client," or, "That client isn't ready for help." These two responses, although natural reactions to frustration, are not therapeutically useful or even accurate. First, consider the concept of "resistance." As Miller and Rollnick (2002), founders of motivational interviewing, have noted:

> The term "resistance" seems to have a pejorative quality to it, as if the individual is refusing to do "what is best" for himself or herself in an intentional, stubborn manner. Labeling counter-motivations as "resistance" may tend to promote urges on the part of the counselor to confront or argue with the client about the client's "resistance." (Miller & Rollnick, 2012, http://www.motivationalinterview.net/clinical/traps.html)

The founders of MI conclude, from experience and research, that it is better to replace the concept of "resistance" with consideration of individual "ambivalence," take all motivations as serious viewpoints or alternatives for the client to fully consider, and approach this consideration in a non-threatening manner. While clients are weighing the payoffs and downsides of change, and engaged in "change talk" (conscious consideration and discussion of the value of change), a lack of honoring of their reservations as well as long-established protective mechanisms, fears, and habits may result in a deterioration of the client-helper relationship on which you might build powerful change.

● ●

Desire: Why would you want to make this change?

Ability: How would you do it if you decided?

Reason: What are the three best reasons?

Need: How important is it? And why?

Can or Commitment: What do you think you'll do?

● ●

This stance, coupled with the Transtheoretical Model as a backdrop, allows clients to be honest where they are when they enter the therapeutic relationship, establish trust in the clinical interactions, and make natural shifts in the decisional balance based on growthful awareness drawn from the nonjudgmental nature of the therapeutic relationship. This perspective also implies a more balanced relationship in which the clinician is more of a partner in change than a "counselor" or "expert" per se. This leveling of the power differential, in itself, creates a safe space for clients to feel empowered and in control of their own destiny. This fits with a social work value base in which the clinician "facilitates" rather than "fixes." Clients are seen as capable of change, imbued with strengths as well as areas for work, and not as "sick," "broken," or in need of repair. This stance of respect, appreciation for the holistic person, and hope are a solid foundation for change to occur. The "holding environment" for change is fertile.

There are times when a clinician has to reconcile safety and therapeutic goals. For example, clients may come to you presenting with substance-related issues and convey (either verbally or nonverbally) safety issues such as abuse. If a client's physical safety is compromised, it would be unethical to ignore that situation in order to address the drug and alcohol concern alone. Other complicated safety issues can arise in working with adolescents with substance use issues. For example, self-injury has become more readily recognized as a maladaptive coping mechanism, often concurrent with adolescent substance use (Lloyd-Richardson, Perrine, Dierker, & Kelley, 2007). This is not a surprise, as the research shows that young people's primary motivations for self-injury are: "to try to get a reaction from someone", "to get control of a situation", and "to stop bad feelings" (Lloyd-Richardson et al., 2007, p. 1,183).

Suicidality is also a huge concern for clinicians working with adolescents and young, emerging adults who misuse substances (Shucheng Wong, Zhou, Goebert, & Hishinuma, 2013). Research has supported the finding that alcohol misuse often accelerates the transition from suicidal ideation to suicide attempt in adolescents with low levels of depressed mood (McManama O'Brien, Becker, Spirito, Simon, & Prinstein, 2013). Because it is very difficult to differentiate attempters from seriously suicidal adolescents, as noted earlier (it warrants repetition), a clinician does best to treat all suicidal thoughts as serious concerns and build bridges for professional screening and psychiatric intervention. Those in the field of social work and other helping disciplines may find it necessary to set aside their client's right to self-determination if there is a chance that the client's life may be in danger.

KEY TERMS

Twelve-step

Spirituality

Secular Organizations for
Sobriety (SOS)

SMART

Rational Emotive Therapy
(RET)

Suicidality

DISCUSSION QUESTIONS

1. As different as college campuses and cultures are, what are some of the mores and manifestations common in "college culture"?

2. Brainstorm some healthy sober activities that young people could engage in in all the areas of the bio-psycho-social-spiritual model.

REFERENCES

Bruns, E. J., Walker, J. S., Zabel, M., Matarese, M., Estep, K., Harburger, D., & Mosby, M. (2010). Intervening in the lives of youth with complex behavioral health challenges and their families: The role of the wraparound process. *American Journal of Community Psychology, 46*, 314–331.

Kelly, J. F., & White, W. L. (2012). Special issue: Broadening the base of addiction mutual support groups: Bringing theory and science to contemporary trends. *Journal of Groups*

Kelly, J. F., Myers, M. G., & Brown, S. A. (2002) Do adolescents affiliate with 12-step groups? A multivariate process model of effects. *Journal of Studies on Alcohol, 63*, 293–304. *in Addiction & Recovery, 7*(2–4), 82–101.

Kurtz, L. F., & Chambon, A. (1987). Comparison of self-help groups for mental health. *Health & Social Work, 12*(4), 275–283.

Lloyd-Richardson, E. E., Perrine, N., Dierker, L., & Kelley, M. L. (2007). Characteristics and functions of non-suicidal self-injury in a community sample of adolescents. *Psychological Medicine, 37*(8), 1183–1192.

MacMaster, S. A., Holleran, L., & Chaffin, K. (2005). Empirical and theoretical support for non-abstinence-based prevention services for substance using adolescents. *Journal of Evidence-Based Social Work, 2*, 91–111.

McManama O'Brien, K. H., Becker, S. J., Spirito, A., Simon, V., & Prinstein, M. J. (2013). Differentiating adolescent suicide attempters from ideators: Examining the interaction between depression severity and alcohol use. *Suicide and Life-Threatening Behaviors, 44*(1), 23–33.

Minuchin, S. (1974). *Families and family therapy.* Cambridge, MA: Harvard University Press.

Room, R., & Greenfield, T. (1993). Alcoholics Anonymous, other 12-step movements and psychotherapy in the US population, 1990. *Addiction, 88*(4), 555–562.

Rowe, C. L. (2012). Family therapy for drug use: Review and updates. *Journal of Marital and Family Therapy, 38*(1), 59–81.

Shucheng Wong, S., Zhou, B., Goebert, D., & Hishinuma, E. S. (2013). The risk of adolescent suicide across patterns of drug use: a nationally representative study of high school students in the United States from 1999 to 2009. *Social Psychiatry and Psychiatric Epidemiology, 48*(10), 1611–1620.

Szapocznik J., Hervis O., & Schwartz S. (2003). Brief strategic family therapy for adolescent drug abuse. *NIDA Therapy Manuals for Drug Abuse No. 5,* NIH Publication Number 03–4751. Rockville, MD: National Institute on Drug Abuse.

PART V

Current Issues

This culminating section will wrap up all that you have learned in the dynamic, new vehicles that allow a variety of roads to recovery. In the late 1980s, clinicians believed everyone had to "hit bottom," "be willing to go to any lengths," and "be totally abstinent from all mood- and mind-altering substances." These statements were defined quite rigidly. Bottom meant serious desperation. Going to any lengths meant following any and all directions from the counselors. And total abstinence meant that if you were still using anything to feel differently (sometimes even medications as prescribed), you were not clean and sober. The field has come to understand that there are as many roads to recovery as there are people with substance use disorders. And there are even individual definitions of abstinence. Clinicians don't flinch when they see this with eating disorder recovery, in which some define abstinence as "no sugar or white flour" and others define it as "weighing and measuring food amounts" and still others define it as "eating three meals a day." They understand that people's eating disorder recovery has to fit the dynamics of the disorder and their visions of their wellness. For years, clinicians have rigidly defined and judged the varied roads to recovery for substance use disorders; fortunately, that is finally changing. Some young people will decide on twelve-step recovery, with total abstinence as their goal. Others choose a more "harm reduction" related path; they work to give up the most problematic substance(s) first and they may not need to go beyond this step (especially if they don't have the "disrupted pleasure pathway" explained early in this book). Still others will need medication, such as Antibuse or Suboxone, in order to achieve their recovery goals.

Addictions treatment and recovery for adolescents are complicated by the multiple needs of teens and families, the spectrum of presenting problems, levels of willingness to change, and access to resources. Although many individual treatments are evidence-based, there are still often holes through which adolescents fall when the network of services in not a tight web. This section delves into new and innovative techniques for creating wraparound services for youth in recovery: collegiate recovery programs (CRPs), alternative peer groups (APGs), recovery high schools, medicated assisted recovery programs, and other advances in caring for this population of young people.

Chapter 9

Young People in Recovery— A New Life

The emergence of new addiction recovery resources within American educational campuses is historic and marks a trend toward injecting such supports into the very heart of abstinence-hostile environments. To accomplish this while also building traditions of recovery stability, academic excellence, and service to other students experiencing alcohol and other drug problems is a remarkable achievement within the history of recovery in the United States.

William White (1998), *Slaying the Dragon: The History of Addiction Treatment and Recovery in America*

Many substance-use texts fail to illuminate the miraculous light side of the darkness. The truth is that many young people recognize their problem with substances and make a powerful change. This tends to happen at younger ages than ever before. Whether because of the impact of the illicit substances resulting in powerful consequences at younger ages or a trend of reducing stigma about recovery itself, the fact is that there is a huge, and growing, population of young people in recovery throughout the country. The frustration is that the energy, the brilliance, and the joy of this culture of recovery for young people is hard to capture in words. It is palpable and has to be seen to be appreciated. Consider witnessing the ICYPAA (International Conference of Young People in AA). Or attend an open young peoples' twelve-step meeting. Where else might you witness the phenomenon?

RESOURCES AND SETTINGS

Collegiate Recovery Programs (CRPs)

Earlier chapters noted that substance misuse is a national problem for young adults; more than 40 percent of youth report having tried an illicit drug by the time they finish high school (Johnston, O'Malley, Bachman, & Schulenberg, 2010). This may be a conservative estimate, and the problem grows into another animal on college campuses. Norms of drinking, availability of substances, and large numbers of young people who have just left their parents . . . these factors add up to the common image of the "party school."

SAMHSA's National Survey on Drug Use and Health (2011) found that 22 percent of full-time college students were current illicit drug users, while 39.1 percent were binge drinkers and 13.6 percent met criteria as heavy drinkers. Perhaps even more alarming, an estimated 18.6 percent of young adults aged eighteen to twenty-four and 6.9 percent of adolescents aged twelve to seventeen had a diagnosable substance use disorder. Although some studies have found that nationally there has been a drop in young people's alcohol and cigarette use, other substance use has remained constant or increased, especially prescription pills such as Adderall and Oxycontin, used by students as "study drugs" and for "recreational highs" (Hamilton, 2009). The needs of college students who have already started using alcohol and/

or drugs are often beyond basic prevention efforts, and yet intensive addiction treatment may be premature (Eggert & Randall, 2003). Furthermore, use and misuse of drugs and alcohol during late adolescence and emerging adulthood may have particularly grave consequences because this is a significant transition point in human development. Young adults can shift from substance use to dependence during this stage, and the initiation of use of so-called hard drugs often takes place during this period as well. Although some erroneously still refer to the disease of addiction being merely a theory or concept, research in the areas of genetics, neurobiology, and pharmacology have unequivocally established addiction as a chronic, potentially fatal brain disease (Leshner, 1997; Erickson, 2007). Some youth, therefore, are biologically predisposed for addiction. Compared to other life stages, the developmental stage of emerging adulthood confers the highest risk for the onset of harmful alcohol and other drug use as well as substance use disorder (Kelly, Stout, & Slaymaker, 2012).

Substance use and binge drinking by college-aged students in the U.S. is also a serious problem (Wechsler & Nelson, 2001). Adolescents and young adults in college often navigate the university environment without individualized, ongoing, and accessible mentoring from professionals. It is especially difficult for students in recovery to find and develop supportive, substance-free social networks (Harris, Baker, & Cleveland, 2010; Perron et al., 2011). College students also have other barriers to wellness, including the following: profound stigma associated with addiction and recovery, increased freedom and substance availability, academic stressors, and mores and norms that include "partying" as an expectation (Grahovac, Holleran Steiker, Sammons and Millichamp, 2012).

● ●

WARNING: DO NOT TREAT A CHRONIC DISEASE AS ACUTE CARE

One innovative intervention is that treatment centers for emerging adults are recognizing that productivity (e.g., college or career) can enhance recovery, sense of purpose, and self-efficacy. One of the leaders in the treatment of emerging adults is Northbound Treatment Services (NTS). NTS aims to provide guidance for people with substance use disorders, with an emphasis on their mission of helping clients achieve a year of sobriety; one of the administrators notes, "We all need a template for living, a talisman to guide (clients) away from the patterns of the past, and into a fulfilling life of recovery." They refer to their palpable culture of recovery and health as the "Northbound Experience" which is, in many ways, beyond the sum of treatment philosophy, theoretical frames, and interventions. The program has special expertise in working with young adults. Historically, young people have been isolated, virtually "quarantined" in "rehab" treatment for acute care and returned to their previous environments with only a conceptual knowledge of how to implement what they learned during treatment. NTS provides "in vivo" support while their young clients continue to live their lives, go to school, work, recreate. The needs of each person are considered and their care is designed according to their needs, strengths, beliefs, and aspirations. The NTS president was the first to create a structured program in which young people can attend college while they are in treatment for addiction recovery (see Holleran Steiker & Alexander, 2014).

● ●

United, students in recovery can overcome the barriers to recovery and transform their lives. Alone, many of them would flounder and relapse, and some would die from their disease

(Perron, Grahovac, & Parrish, 2010). In the mid-eighties, collegiate recovery communities (CRCs) emerged as solutions, providing recovery services and havens of support on campuses throughout the country. The history of a group known as Early Recovery Support on college campuses goes as far back as 1977 at Brown University and 1983 at Rutgers (White & Finch, 2006). Since 2004, the University of Texas at Austin has fostered an active and fast-growing collegiate recovery community through the Center for Students in Recovery (CSR).

The University of Texas at Austin CSR is a program grounded in social work values and ethics that aims to provide a safe, healthy, and welcoming environment for students to cultivate life skills and celebrate recovery successes. The formal mission of CSR is "to provide a supportive community where students in recovery can achieve academic success while enjoying a genuine college experience free from alcohol and drugs."

It has been the philosophical stance of the UT Austin CSR to meet the students in need "where they are" and approach them from a transtheoretical perspective, or stage of readiness for change model which, as you already have learned, contends that

Figure 9.1: Collegiate Recovery Programs

it is normal for people to be in varied stages of readiness to make lasting change. It is CSR's contention that services can be provided to a student who is scarcely more than a potential substance user all the way to those who have a clear sense of their addiction or have been working a recovery program for years. It is important to note that this model recognizes that relapse is, for some, a necessary part of the growth and change process, as opposed to a failure. As highlighted in the Harvard "Health Watch" (March, 2012), "Relapse is common" and can be "an integral part of the process" (https://www.health.harvard.edu/newsletters).

Historically, some collegiate recovery programs have opted to assess for abstinence and have prerequisite lengths of sobriety in order for students to receive support services (i.e., attend programming, partake in community activities, etc.). In contrast, the University of Texas Austin's social-work-based program does not exclude any student interested in participating in the collegiate recovery community and exploring recovery as a possibility for their lifestyle and wellness. CSR also recognizes how difficult it is for students to completely commit to abstinence while still being situated in a university-based substance-using subculture. Studies of people who have recovered from addiction indicate that they usually had to break all ties with other using addicts and develop new interests and social networks to promote long-term drug abstinence (DeJong, 1994).

With the bio-psycho-social-spiritual model as a backdrop, CSR provides a holistic refuge on campus for students to explore, understand, and experience recovery while still pursuing their academics in an otherwise abstinence-hostile environment. As a result, programming takes place throughout the campus community and in the greater community as a whole. Students address their physical health by running and working out

212

together. A yoga studio situated near campus provides free "recovery yoga" on the weekends for the Center's students in recovery. Within the UT community, students attend twelve-step meetings at the Center, as well as in other campus buildings and faith-based community locations on and off campus. To address spiritual aspects, in addition to twelve-step meetings, students are encouraged to attend a Friday night meditation group. The meditation group's leader also comes to the center to teach meditation and build relationships with the students outside of the regular meditation meeting. To augment their psychological health and understanding of addictions and recovery, students are given access to professionals and faculty experts in a variety of disciplines including pharmacy, neurobiology, social work, psychology, nursing, and public health. Socially, the students have a calendar that is packed with fun activities (e.g., roller skating, dances, and road trips) to draw them together in fellowship and community activities.

The Center for Students in Recovery functions not only as a support but as a grounding identity for students, reframing their narratives from those of marginalized and afflicted members of society to uniquely useful recovering individuals poised to serve their peers and communities. The University of Texas CSR students also engage in service activities, adhering to AA's principle of the twelfth step ("carrying the message, and practicing these principles in all of our affairs"). The Center supports and encourages student efforts to organize service opportunities and create formal student groups that will promote recovery lifestyles on campus, establish meetings on campus, and do outreach and recovery-themed social events on campus. The CSR meets as many needs as possible for students in recovery to help them persist with their academic efforts while engaging in recovery-

213

oriented activities needed to sustain sobriety (Laudet & White, 2008).

By virtue of having a warm and welcoming physical place to gather, by being a noteworthy part of the organizational chart of the university, and through the utilization of recovery terminology and culture in the university lexicon, students have the opportunity to take ownership of an authentic identification with a positive aspect of college experience that rivals the Greek system (Holleran Steiker, Grahovac, & White, 2014). Stigma breaks down as students proudly wear their CSR t-shirts, win university-wide awards for courage in the face of extreme adversity, and get accepted into world-renowned graduate schools upon graduation.

As noted by Tinto in his Model of Student Departure, there are three major sources of student attrition from college: (1) academic difficulties, (2) the inability of individuals to resolve their educational and occupational goals, and (3) their failure to become or remain incorporated in the intellectual and social life of the institution. Therefore, his model states that "to persist, students need integration into formal (academic performance) and informal (faculty/staff interactions) academic systems and formal (extracurricular activities) and informal (peer group interactions) social systems" (Tinto, 1993). The UT CSR attends to all of the elements of this model.

One of the most transformative mechanisms of recovery is the re-storying that addicted individuals do as recovering individuals. The original narrative goes like this: "I was okay. I started using. I made really bad choices. I couldn't stop. I kept getting worse. I hurt everyone around me. I hated myself. I used until all I cared about was alcohol and drugs and even that didn't make me happy. I am sick, bad, maybe even evil. The world would be better off without me."

As painful and abysmal as this sounds, these sentiments reverberate in the heads and hearts of young addicts and alcoholics all over the planet. But recovery offers a chance to restore and re-story.

The recovery narrative sounds like this: "I was sick. I tried to get well on my own and couldn't. I gave up and reached out for help. I didn't think I belonged but I stuck around because I was desperate. I came to my counseling sessions and support group meetings even when I didn't want to, even when none of it made sense. After a while, in spite of myself, I started feeling a little better. I followed direction and one day I woke up and realized that I no longer hated myself. I saw that I could have value in the world. In fact, I realized that my horrendous life experiences had made me uniquely suited to help others like me. Everything I went through had value in that it was a springboard for growth, gratitude, and service. Today, I have learned to love myself and others. I have never been more content."

Young people in recovery share their stories of transformation at twelve-step meetings, in classes such as University of Texas Austin's undergraduate studies "Young People and Drugs," and at institutes such as the Waggoner Center for Alcohol and Addiction Research. The social work foundation for the Center has facilitated positive reframes of the student stories, from the hopelessness of addiction to the discovery of sobriety and sustained recovery. For example, one student says:

> As a result [of my addiction], I relapsed and withdrew from the university to focus fully on recovery. During those years away from school, I stayed connected to CSR, attending meetings and social events. The constant support I received from the students and staff helped me to eventually come back and earn two hard-fought degrees in Studio Art and in Radio-TV-Film. I am sincerely

indebted to CSR for making my overall college experience a good one. Even though many of my college years were marred by drug addiction, with a lot of work I was able to pull through and graduate sober. I continue to support CSR because I know there are people just like me who need help and I want CSR to be there for them as it was for me.

CSR conducts an annual assessment of students' recovery perceptions, actions, and utilization of services (Kaye, Stuart, Grahovac, Holleran Steiker, & Maison, 2012). The research team, composed of CSR staff members, advisory faculty, and the University of Texas at Austin Office of Assessment, conducted the survey. A total of 44 responses were received. Two-thirds of respondents were male and most were upper classmen or graduate students. Nearly half began their college careers at UT Austin, and one-quarter transferred there from another campus. A great majority of respondents (86 percent) were currently enrolled. The average GPA for undergraduate respondents mirrored that of the university as a whole.

Over three-fourths of respondents reported that CSR was helping them to succeed academically, and many students associated with the Center reported that their grades had improved since they started their recovery during college. Students commented that CSR was providing a convenient location for sobriety meetings and a quiet place to study and that the recovery support provided by CSR translated to academic success. One student stated, "I sincerely doubt that I would have been able to make it to graduation, or lived an enjoyable life the past two years, without the fellowship of the students and staff of CSR."

Respondents reflected a spectrum of characteristics, including their length of time affiliated with CSR, length and support mechanisms of sobriety, and program service utilization. About

216

half of respondents had been coming to CSR for less than one year; 20 percent had been coming for between one and two years; and 25 percent had been coming for between two and four years. Over half reported attending twelve-step meetings at CSR, and nearly 40 percent reported attending the Tuesday night weekly CSR meetings. Eighty percent also reported attending twelve-step meetings off-campus. When asked what they were seeking when they first came to CSR, over half reported seeking help with sobriety and a supportive environment for living a healthy, sober life. Respondents also mentioned seeking sober friendships and activities, fellowship, service opportunities, and hope. Over 85 percent of respondents indicated that they got what they initially sought from participation in CSR. Over 78 percent reported that CSR is "always" or "often" helping them to experience a safe and supportive recovery community. Over 70 percent reported that they have a home group. Most do some sort of service work either inside or outside CSR, and over half sponsor other people. Eighty-three percent reported they have been able to stay free from their addiction since joining CSR.

When asked how to improve CSR programming, many students indicated that there was not a need for change. However, some indicated the need for mechanisms for continued open communication with current members and augmented focus on newcomers. When asked what the biggest challenges are as a student in recovery on the UT Austin campus, students mentioned maintaining balance, the challenge of interacting with people who are not in recovery, time management, loneliness, and having to deal with faculty and others who do not understand addiction.

One of the most salient findings is that these data indicate that students who continue to participate in CSR programming over a longer period often develop new reasons for participation.

Respondents who had new reasons for attending CSR functions were more likely to go to CSR to make and maintain relationships with other sober students and to give support to newcomers just discovering this resource. This finding supports a flexible model without strict affiliation expectations and assessments. The study found that members of CSR are recovering from a variety of issues, not only drugs or alcohol, and for those students, CSR was providing support. Along similar lines, over half of respondents to the survey indicated that they had experienced issues other than their addiction that affected their educational functioning. These findings support the need for CSRs to maintain a broad scope of support for many kinds of addiction-related issues.

Medication-assisted Recovery

Opioid addiction is a chronic disease necessitating community-based recovery management approaches for increased chances of patient recovery (CCBHO, 2013). Medication-assisted treatment (MAT) is the use of medications in combination with counseling and behavioral therapies to provide a whole patient approach to the treatment of substance use disorders. SAMHSA notes that MAT has been shown to: improve patient survival, increase treatment program retention, decrease illicit opiate use, decrease hepatitis and HIV seroconversion, decrease criminal behaviors, increase employment, and improve birth outcomes with perinatal addicts (SAMHSA, 2013). Research shows that MAT is the most effective mode of treatment for opioid addicted individuals (CSAT, 2005). However, the 2010 National Survey of Substance Abuse Treatment Services documented that only 25 percent of people admitted to treatment facilities were in methadone programs (SAMHSA, 2011). Opioid treatment programs (OTPs) and non-OTPs with a specially trained physician on staff began offering medication-assisted therapy for opioid dependence and addiction with buprenorphine starting in 2002. The number of OTPs offering buprenorphine increased from 11 percent of OTPs in 2003 to 51 percent of OTPs in 2011. In non-OTPs the numbers are rising as well; in 2003, about 5 percent offered buprenorphine services and by 2011, the percentage of non-OTPs that offered buprenorphine services increased to 17 percent (SAMHSA, 2013.)

This dialogue is a critical one for the social-work profession. Social workers represent a significant share of the substance misuse treatment field and are often the ones who may have the power regarding treating or referring clients for the use of MATs and in policy realms (Bride, Abraham, Kintzle, & Roman, 2013). In addition, and perhaps more important, social workers have tremendous influence on client attitudes towards MATs and their ultimate success rates (Bride et al., 2013).

Alternative Peer Groups (APGs)

Alternative peer groups (APGs) are defined as settings where youth and their families have access to other youth and families on the road to recovery and wellness, with recovery support staff and at times clinical services. Houston, Texas, has a model worthy of replication. They have a long-standing and well established alternative peer group (APG) network as a mechanism for adolescent addiction recovery. For those teens who are surrounded by using peers, early research shows that the APG model enhances teen and emerging adults' chances at successful recovery. The APG model surrounds hundreds of involved youth with: peer support, social skills, resiliency training, family recovery, fun/healthy out-of-school activities, and accountability in a socially reinforcing environment (Morrison & Bailey, 2011).

The national relapse rate for teens in recovery is very high, ranging between 50 and 90 percent post-intervention. However, in Houston, one study of adolescents participating in an APG showed relapse rates were as low as 8-11 percent. According to the Institute of Chemical Dependency Studies, since APGs have been in existence, they have yielded a recovery rate over 85 percent versus a nationwide recovery rate of around 30 percent (Rochat et al., 2014). Research shows that positive peer influences lower chance of drugs and alcohol relapse, increase chances of abstinence, improve school performance, improve socio-developmental task acquisition, and improve mental health (Newman, Lohman, & Newman, 2007; Ramirez, Hinman, Sterling, Weisner, & Campbell, 2012). All APGs hold the goal of providing a new, positive environment to replace the old dependence on addicted systems.

• •

The APG model integrates important peer connections with clinical practice through intervention, support, education, and parent involvement. The foundation of this model is the basic assumption that peer relationships, much like the ones that initiate and support drug and alcohol use, are necessary to facilitate recovery. The ultimate goal is to remove the teen from a negatively pressured environment and offer them a new group of friends that exert positive peer pressure and provide support for the necessary changes they need to make in order to recover.

Morrison & Bailey (2011), *The Alternative Peer Group: A Recovery Model for Teens and Young Adults*

• •

Over the past decade, adolescent treatment providers have recognized that their services must resemble the "wraparound services" in mental health (Kutash et al., 2013). It is not enough that young substance users attend eight hours of school in a sober setting; they must receive support after school, in the evenings, and on weekends as well. APGs provide this peer support outside of school along the continuum of care. There are various models that span from youth mutual support groups meeting a few times a week to intensive peer support plus clinical services and even residential peer settings resembling half-way houses. The models vary depending on community needs, culture, and resources (especially financial). They aim to help individuals in recovery develop a new peer group that consists of those who also are in recovery (Cates & Cummings, 2003). APGs provide recovery support and access to family and clinical services. Developed initially for teens in the early 1970s at the Palmer Memorial Episcopal Church in Houston, Texas, APGs take into account the developmental focus of adolescents and the importance of peers in shaping identity.

Other APGs grew from the model in Houston. Lifeway International, created in 1985 by some of the Palmer Drug Abuse Program (PDAP) originators, incorporated the APG model (Morrison and Bailey, 2011). Cornerstone and Teen & Family Services in Houston, Texas, also grew from the APG model, adding clinical services and more intensive therapeutic components to the peer support. APGs are rooted in a twelve-step philosophy, which suggests "old friends" are something to be "given up". Thus, APGs allow teens to recover within a safe version of typical adolescent development with a new set of peers. These peers give honest feedback and accountability to promote change and help develop a new set of behaviors. APGs help teens learn to stay away from substances and substance users, interact appropriately with peers and adults, and have fun while abstinent from substance use. Today, APGs include twelve-step involvement as well as groups facilitated by schools, treatment programs, and other health and social service organizations (Cates & Cummings, 2003).

Although there is limited research on the impact of APGs, there is extensive research on the impact of peer groups. The literature supports the idea that behaviors may be more likely to be successfully socialized in the presence of a positive peer culture (Lynch, Lerner, & Leventhal, 2013). Mejias, Gill, and Spigelman (2014) found that a peer support group had a positive impact on young women with disabilities. In fact, students who participate in peer support groups in schools score higher on general, social, academic, and parental self-esteem than non-participants. Aspects of behavioral peer culture are correlated with individual achievement, and components of both relational and behavioral peer culture are related to school engagement (Lynch et al., 2013).

SAMHSA, in a meta-analysis of research that derived guiding principles of systems of care from findings, indicates that a network of personal connections with peers is critical to recovery and that poor social support is a major factor in the return to substance use following recovery initiation. Peer support helps a person in recovery see or visualize others in similar circumstances doing well, which increases a belief in that individual's own abilities. Peer support also helps those in recovery build or rebuild healthy relationships and play constructive roles in their communities (SAMHSA, 2007).

Although limited, there is some research on APGs that shows similar outcomes. Cates and Cummings (2003) indicate that teens do better in groups with other teens as opposed to groups with adults. Nowinski (1990) describes the concept of the "therapeutic tribe" with adolescents, suggesting the need to create a highly connected peer group with a common identity. Nash (2013) conducted a qualitative study of alumni from Houston-area APGs.

She found that successful alumni described their process in recovery as a quest-like journey, citing the importance of role models in recovery as keys to their success. She also found that full engagement in successful recovery requires more time than current treatment allows. Her research shows an 8 to 11 percent relapse rate for adolescents participating in Houston APGs between January 2007 and 2010, with a recovery rate greater than 85 percent (Morrison and Bailey, 2011). Scott Basinger, director of the Addiction Scholars Program at Baylor College of Medicine, notes that although national results show that a 50 to 90 percent relapse is typical for teens in recovery programs, Houston APG's intensive out-patient programming (mostly with youth in Cornerstone APG) results showed relapse rates to be under 10 percent when associated with the APG (Rochat, Rossiter, Nunley, Bahavar, Ferraro, MacPherson, & Basinger, 2014).

Innovative substance use disorder treatment programs have attempted to fill in post-intervention gaps by incorporating APGs as part of aftercare plans. These groups vary by type and structure, but the main idea is to connect young people with their point of reference, other young people. In many communities, the continuum of care that is available to recovering teens and their families includes residential treatment, out-patient treatment groups, and twelve-step or other recovery mutual aid groups, some of which are connected with APGs.

Although APGs in Texas provide significant support, adolescents still are faced with spending the majority of their waking time each week in school settings that not only put them in contact with peers who do not support sobriety, but may also add stressors as they try to balance recovery and school success. To provide a complete continuum of care, some thirty recovery high schools have been established (Moberg & Finch, 2009). They vary from separate high schools to embedded programs for students in recovery that provide a combination of academic coursework and recovery support.

In spite of the fact that some teens participate in APGs in their communities, they still find it challenging if they are in a public school environment, since teens spend the majority of their waking hours in school. Many students leaving inpatient or residential treatment are offered alcohol or other drugs by their friends the first day they return to school. That's where recovery high schools come in.

Recovery High Schools

The history and diversity of recovery schools have been outlined within the professional literature. According to White and Finch (2006) and Finch and Wegman (2012), the first documented recovery high schools were Phoenix Schools I and II in Maryland, which opened in 1979 and 1982, respectively. In the mid-1980s, there were fewer than ten such schools in operation. Both campuses had ceased operations by 2006, though, and the oldest currently operating recovery high school is PEASE (Peers Enjoying a Sober Education) Academy, which opened in Minneapolis in 1989. Just as models of APGs vary by community need, culture, and resources, so do recovery high schools. Some emerged as partners with treatment centers, some sprang up from church-based APGs, some grew and partnered with charter schools or independent school districts, and others remained as private schools. The Association of Recovery Schools, which began in 2002, originally consisted of both recovery high schools and collegiate recovery programs. There have only been about seventy recovery high schools ever, and the most open at one time has been around thirty-five. In 2011, there were 31 recovery high schools (also called sober schools) operating in ten states in the

U.S. The leadership of these schools split from the collegiate programs organization (the Association for Recovery in Higher Education) and the Association of Recovery Schools (ARS) narrowed its focus to the success of recovery high schools. NIH funded the first national study of recovery high schools in 2006. This was a descriptive study of seventeen recovery high schools in ten states (Moberg & Finch, 2009). NIH is currently funding a second national study, which is the first rigorous outcomes study of recovery high schools, to be completed in 2016.

The biggest issue facing recovery high schools is the cost of running them. Because many recovery high school students have co-existing disorders (both substance use and mental health) (Moberg & Finch, 2009; Finch, Moberg, & Krupp, 2014), they require extensive academic and emotional support, resulting in a low student-to-teacher ratio. Four states—Indiana, Massachusetts, Minnesota, and Texas—have passed or proposed specific legislation to support recovery high schools since 2009. State and federal legislation such as the charter school legislation in Texas and the Minnesota Graduation Incentive Act allow school districts flexibility in providing education to special groups of students such as those who are pregnant, emotionally impaired, or chemically dependent. Most recently, senators from Rhode Island, Ohio, Vermont, New Hampshire, and Minnesota introduced the Comprehensive Addiction and Recovery Act of 2014 (S. 2839). The aim of the legislation is to address the opiate epidemic proactively. The proposed law would authorize new programs that would embrace recovery support, prevention, law enforcement, and treatment strategies. Over a six-year period, approximately $42 million would be appropriated for expansion of recovery high schools, collegiate recovery programs, and recovery community organizations.

Nonetheless, as funding for public education has become limited across the U.S., some recovery high schools have been forced to close (Chmelynski, 2002; Levy, 2011). Transforming Youth Recovery, a non-profit organization primarily funded through the Stacie Mathewson Foundation, in conjunction with the Association of Recovery Schools, has made the creation and building of infrastructures for recovery schools (high school and collegiate recovery programs) its mission. The agency's market study notes that several historical factors will increase the interest in and viability of recovery high schools. These factors include high-profile incidents related to schools and mental health, the revised *Diagnostic and Statistical Manual* (DSM-5) (which increases the number of qualifying youth), and a broadening of services through the Affordable Care Act (ACA) (Stacie Mathewson Foundation, 2013).

Although qualitative information suggests that recovery high schools are a critical component for adolescents' successful recovery, there is limited research indicating which models are most effective. Moberg and Thaler (1995) conducted an evaluation of Albuquerque's recovery high school in the mid-1990s. They found that the program had a highly committed staff and improvements in abstinence rates with the students it served. However, the school, initially conceptualized as a transition program with the idea that students could return to their home schools, did not expect the severity of problems that they found among the student body. Most of the students were dually diagnosed and had severe psychological problems in addition to being in recovery for a substance use disorder. Relapse rates were 40 percent, viewed as high by many but well below the 90 percent reported among students in recovery attending traditional public schools. Because of the multiple needs of its students, the program became more of a day treatment program

226

and could maintain only a small enrollment. It also operated independently and was not well known within the community. Due to conflicts, problems in funding, and the fact that the program could not grow in enrollment, it was dismantled before the researchers could publish their evaluation (1995).

More recently, Lanham and Tirado (2013) conducted research on Serenity High School in McKinney, Texas. The oldest recovery high school in Texas, it began operation in 1999. Lanham and Tirado's research found that 64 percent of adolescents who went through treatment relapsed within three months, 79–85 percent relapsed within one year, and 93 percent relapsed by the end of four years. Additionally, 25–90 percent did not follow recommendations from treatment programs after they were discharged. Like other researchers, Lanham and Tirado believe that returning to a traditional school is one of the greatest threats to a teen's sobriety. Serenity High School, like many other recovery high schools, incorporates a twelve-step model and a self-paced educational curriculum. Serenity reports that 80 percent of its students decline in their use of substances and 71 percent report improvement in academic areas. Lanham and Tirado identified short-term goals, which included "regular attendance, reestablishment of consistent learning patterns, daily sobriety, respectful behavior toward others, biweekly attendance at on-campus AA meetings, and completion of weekly community service activities"; intermediate goals, which included "ongoing sobriety, completion of a high school degree followed by post-secondary education, military service, or employment"; and long-term goals, which included "maintaining sobriety, contributing to the betterment of society by holding down jobs, performing community service, staying out of the criminal justice system, and passing on what they learned to their children and future generations" (2013, p. 250–251).

227

Lanham and Tirado's primary focus was on graduation rates. At the time of their study, more than 90 percent of the seventy-two alumni who responded to the survey reported enrolling in college and six had graduated. However, many reported struggling with their sobriety once graduating from the recovery high school. Most were no longer participating in twelve-step programs, 40 percent had reentered treatment at some point after high school graduation, 40 percent had remained sober, and 60 percent were no longer using illegal drugs.

● ●

Maximizing Sustained Sobriety—Percentages with Intervention Components

Treatment alone = 3%

Treatment + APG = 52%

Treatment + APG + Parent Involvement = 63%

Treatment + APG + Parent Involvement + Recovery High School = 75%

Rochet & Basinger, 2014

● ●

Although more research is needed, the evidence that exists appears to support the notion that recovery high schools are an important component of the continuum of care for teens (Finch, Moberg, and Krupp, 2014). Recovery high schools can link with other APGs in the community, creating an empowering, sober environment that helps teens develop a positive sense of identity and be proud of who they are, rather than viewing their former substance misuse as a stigma (Holleran Steiker, 2014; Mackert et al., 2014). Such high schools can also teach skills for resisting peer pressure and reduce the social acceptability of using alcohol and other drugs (Sussman, Skara, & Ames, 2008). Research by Rochat et al. (2014) had statistically significant results showing that youth who participated in APGs had better perceptions of peer relationships than those who did not take part in APGs. Such enhanced perceptions may serve to build bridges as teens graduate from high school. Efforts need to be made to continue a continuum of care that supports them during their college/early adult years.

Implementing University High School, Austin, Texas: A Case Study

The University High School (UHS) founders in Austin collaborated with a network of substance use treatment programs, other social service agencies, and community supporters to establish the first recovery high school in the Austin area. The inspiration for this school came from the Association of Recovery Schools Conference in 2012 (held at Archway Academy, the largest recovery high school in Texas). The founders of University High School were a diverse mix of people from academic, recovery, and professional realms—the director of Houston's Archway Academy, the director of the Center for Students in Recovery, addictions experts, recovery community members, parents, and professionals. Over thirty community members attended the group's first meeting. Attendees included several young people who had attended Archway Academy and were committed to helping Austin create its own recovery high school. The leadership team met with charter school and other educational experts at the university, local school districts, and online schools for high-risk youth. Individual committees and task forces prepared for funding, facilities, operations, policies and procedures, staffing, marketing, and constituent relations. Initial approval was obtained

229

through the University of Texas Charter Board, but ultimately the decision was made to open as a private non-profit with an online component to allow for the student diversity (i.e., ninth-twelfth graders, from learning challenged to Advanced Placement ready students).

University High School is innovative in the following ways: (1) It incorporates a mentorship program with linkage to a ten-year-old collegiate recovery program, the University of Texas's Collegiate Students in Recovery (UT CSR) and mutually advantageous collaborations with undergraduate and graduate students in diverse departments. (2) It provides numerous opportunities for participatory research to learn more about what is effective in working with teens in recovery.

Austin, Texas, is one of the fastest growing cities in the U.S. The death rates for overdose in Americans aged fifteen to twenty-four more than doubled from 2000 to 2010, and Texas high school students were more likely than their peers nationally to report lifetime use of alcohol, cocaine, Ecstasy, and methamphetamines (Maxwell, 2014). Austin has a number of collaborative programs that provide supportive substance use disorder treatment programs for teens. Two APGs exist in Austin (Teen and Family Services and the Palmer Drug Abuse Program), and several residential and out-patient adolescent substance use disorder treatment settings have helped to create a recovery community of adolescents and a network with a variety of organizations, including some public schools, to provide supportive services once teens leave treatment programs. In addition, a thriving community of young people in recovery, primarily youth associated with a peer-run group, the Texas Conference of Young People in AA (TCYPAA), extends recovery beyond therapeutic settings.

Many students who are active in UT's CSR attended recovery high schools elsewhere, and several of them and others served as sponsors for teens in the Austin area. The leadership team of University High School determined that the formal mentorship of UHS high school students by collegiate students at the UT Center for Students in Recovery could be a powerful innovation. This idea was met with enthusiasm, and other key people were quickly identified and included. As others became involved, collaboration was extensive and the turf issues that often surface when these kinds of efforts are undertaken did not take place. The main barrier was people's busy schedules, but because of their commitment, plans quickly fell into place.

A model that ensures a nonlinear continuum of care and collaboration with community allies is an important key to youth's success in recovery. In addition to creating a service that fills the gap and enhances the continuum of care for residents in Austin and surrounding areas, assessment and research will set the stage for this school's impact on both state-wide and national models for life/college preparation via recovery high schools. A clear framework for baseline measures has been established, in accordance with the UT Institute of Public Schools Initiatives Quality Framework for Charter Schools as well as the Standards for Accreditation of Recovery High Schools published by the Association of Recovery Schools (ARS). Evaluation of the students' progress will be conducted using instruments including the NWEA-MAPS measuring academic growth, Recovery Capital Scale to measure recovery tools and progress, the GAIN-SS for mental health issues, and the Personal Health Questionnaire (PHQ). Work is under way to utilize innovative and youth-culture-friendly mechanisms for evaluation delivery, including wireless technology (e.g., smart phone apps).

CONCLUSIONS

Research suggests that adolescents who are in recovery from a substance use disorder are at great risk of continued substance use and related problems if they return to their high schools. Even if they participate in continuing care programs that include APGs, spending eight hours a day five days a week in school with peers who may be users of alcohol or other drugs makes them especially vulnerable to resumption of substance use. If students in recovery participate in an APG that also provides a quality education with an emphasis on preparation for college, they are less likely to relapse and more likely to develop behaviors that will lead to a better quality of life. However, graduating from a recovery high school and going to a college that does not continue to support sobriety places adolescents and young adults at risk of relapse, even if they remained sober while in high school.

Austin's University High School is unique for two important reasons. First, the link to a university with a strong APG for its students who can also provide mentoring prolongs the safety net for teens and young adults and reduces risk of continued substance use problems. Second, opportunities for research in a university-based school will increase evidence-based practice knowledge that will strengthen intervention strategies for teens and families, particularly in this area where current research is limited. This case study leads to the following considerations for future replication efforts, community needs assessment and planning, and salient points for researchers:

- Community collaborations are critical. Agencies and organizations serving adolescents and their families need to communicate and determine ways that they can work together rather than compete for resources.

- It is important to have creative brainstorming around innovations that will resonate in a particular community. At the same time, clinicians need to learn from the recovery school and APG settings that already exist in order to avoid pitfalls and build on solid foundations. For example, the Association of Recovery Schools Accreditation rubric is an excellent checklist for those starting new schools.
- Passionate and charismatic "launch teams" who have connections in overlapping communities of interest (e.g., twelve-step programs, local universities, children and youth coalitions, and treatment centers) must meet prior to the creation of the school to build an effective mission statement and business strategy for a successful launch.
- Staff and recovery coaches who open the school should have at least some experience in recovery school and/or APG settings so that the youth know that they identify and are addressing key components and barriers for the school.
- Marketing is important, but the first year should be devoted to building the culture of recovery rather than numbers of students. The vision should grow according to the board-determined strategy, and not be haphazard.
- The students (and family members) who are a success within the new school are the best advocates and promoters of the model.

The field related to recovery schools is dynamic, with new information unfolding regularly. Those who are interested in starting or growing a recovery school should utilize the growing literature around recovery schools (Finch, 2005; Holleran Steiker, Counihan, White, Harper, & Nash, in press), follow the Association of Recovery Schools website (https://www.recoveryschools.org/), attend related conferences, and learn from the existing schools to incorporate new developments.

Recovery high schools, APGs, and CRPs provide holistic "holding environments" for students at any stage of readiness with regard to recovery. Overwhelmingly, students who are surrounded by positive, recovering peers and those that frequent CSRs and other supportive peer groups tend to stay clean and sober and perform academically at levels equal to, and sometimes surpassing, other students. Students note that there is no replacement for a safe community where they find hope and support for their recovery. These environments also provide sober activities and other options in the midst of a world that often is not alcohol- and drug-free. The vast majority of students involved in recovery high schools, APGs, and CSRs have adopted positive recovery habits such as having a home group, participating in service work, and helping others.

Recovery schools, APGs, and CSRs are growing exponentially as the need for such settings grows and as leaders in the field advocate for these communities (White, Kelly, & Roth, 2012). Since these newly emerging recovery-support institutions constitute new referral sources for social workers, the presence of these settings must be made visible and part of the cultural lexicon. Although systems must be in place to protect students' confidentiality, recovery centers on college campuses should not be hidden entities. To break down the existing stigma and shame, such centers must be accessible, open, and the subject of conversation across campus constituencies.

It is important that those embracing this model recognize that there is not a one-size-fits-all program for students in recovery. For example, CSR survey respondents reported interacting with CSR in diverse ways. Many attended as many CSR and twelve-step meetings as their schedules allowed; others dropped by occasionally or kept in touch with individuals they met through CSR on a more infrequent basis. Social, recreational, and health-related activities appear to be a valued component to students' recoveries. Ultimately, CSR students should be "met where they are," viewed within a strengths orientation, and given the opportunity to build relationships that can grow and transform. The presence of CSRs and the size of existing CSRs have both been growing since their inception; presently, over thirty schools have professionally run CSRs in university settings, and they are being disseminated rapidly to other schools (Laudet, Harris, Kimball, Winters, & Moberg, 2014). For example, due to the powerful successes of the Center, the administrators at the University of Texas at Austin have recently determined that the UT CSR will be implemented at all nine UT locations. There is no doubt that the presence of CRCs is a growing and needed area for research. Evidence clearly supports recovery high schools and CSRs on campuses for youth in recovery. The real challenge and payoff of progress is in the continuum; the gaps are finally being filled.

KEY TERMS

Collegiate recovery programs
   (CRP)
Relapse
Tinto's Model of Student
   Departure
Re-storying

Medication assisted treatment
Opioid treatment programs
Alternative peer groups
   (APGs)
Therapeutic tribe
Recovery high schools

DISCUSSION QUESTIONS

1. Go to the websites for the Association of Recovery Schools (ARS) and the Association of Recovery in Higher Education (ARHE) and determine what the collegiate and high school recovery organizations have in common and how they are different. What issues make them distinct?

2. Consider the resources in your community and design a model for a recovery high school. Where would it be held? Would it be private for-profit, private non-profit, associated with a charter school system, associated with an independent school district, or attached to a treatment center or APG? Why would you make the choices you are making?

3. There is a great deal of stigma associated with medication assisted recovery services. Methadone, Suboxone, and other medications that enable people to live without their life threatening drugs are often erroneously thought of as "substitute highs"—how can stigma be broken down?

REFERENCES

Association of Recovery Schools (2013). *The 2013 market study for recovery schools*. Reno, NV: Stacie Mathewson Foundation.

Bride, B. E., Abraham, A. J., Kintzle, S., & Roman, P. M. (2013). Social workers' knowledge and perceptions of effectiveness and acceptability of medication assisted treatment of substance use disorders. *Social Work in Health Care, (52)*1, 43–58.

Cates, J., & Cummings, J. (2003). *Recovering our children: A handbook for parents of young people in early recovery*. Lincoln, NE: i-universe, Inc.

Center for Substance Abuse Treatment (CSAT) (2005). *Medication assisted treatment for opioid addiction in opioid treatment programs*, treatment improvement protocol (TIP) series 43, DHHS Publication No. (SMA) 05–4048). Retrieved from http://www.ncbi.nlm.nih.gov/pubmed/22514849

Chmelynski, C. (2002). "Sober" high schools rate sobriety high. *Education Digest, 68*(4), 56–59. Community Care Behavioral Health Organization (CCBHO) (2013). *Supporting recovery from opioid addiction: Community care best practice guidelines for buprenorphine and Suboxone®*. Pittsburgh, PA: Community Care Behavioral Health Organization.

Community Care Behavioral Health Organization (CCBHO) (2013). *Supporting recovery from opioid addiction: Community care best practice guidelines for buprenorphine and Suboxone®*. Pittsburgh, PA: Community Care Behavioral Health Organization.

DeJong, W. (1994). Relapse prevention: An emerging technology for promoting long-term drug abstinence. *The International Journal of the Addictions, 29*(6), 681–705.

Eggert, L. L., & Randell, B. P. (2003). Drug prevention research for high-risk youth. In W. J. Bukoski, & Z. Sloboda (Eds.), *Handbook of drug abuse prevention theory, science, and practice* (pp. 473–495). NY: Plenum.

Erickson, C. K. (2007). *The science of addiction: From neurobiology to treatment.* New York: W.W. Norton and Company, Inc.

Finch, A. J. (2005). *Starting a recovery school: A how-to manual.* Center City, MN: Hazelden.

Finch, A. J., & Wegman, H. (2012). Recovery high schools: Opportunities for support and personal growth for students in recovery. *Prevention Researcher, 19*(5), 12–16.

Finch, A. J., Moberg, D. P., & Krupp, A. L. (2014). Continuing care in high schools: A descriptive study of recovery high school programs. *Journal of Child and Adolescent Substance Abuse, 23*(2), 116–129.

Grahovac, I., Holleran Steiker, L. K., Sammons, K., & Millichamp, K. (2011). University centers for students in recovery. *Journal of Social Work Practice in the Addictions, 11*(3), 290–294.

Hamilton, G. J. (2009). Prescription drug use. *Psychology in the Schools. Special Issue: Psychopharmacology and the Practice of School Psychology, 46*(9), 892–898.

Harris, K., Baker, A., & Cleveland, H. H. (2010). Collegiate recovery communities: What they are and how they are supported. In H. Cleveland, K. Harris, & R. Wiebe (Eds.) *Substance abuse recovery in college: Community supported abstinence* (pp. 9–22). New York, NY: Springer.

Holleran Steiker, L. (2014). *Helping teens into addiction recovery.* Austin, TX: University of Texas at Austin School of Social Work. Available at http://www.utexas.edu/ssw/featured/helping-teens-into-addiction-recovery -unive rsity-high-school/

Holleran Steiker, L. K. & Alexander, P. (2014). Addiction Treatment Coupled with Higher Education. *Journal of Social Work Practice in the Addictions, 14*(1), 117–123.

Holleran Steiker, L. K., Counihan, C., White, W., Harper, K., & Nash, A. (in press). Transforming Austin: Augmenting the system of care for adolescents in recovery from substance use disorders. *The Journal of Alcoholism and Drug Dependence.*

Holleran Steiker, L. K., Grahovac, I., & White, W. (2014) Social work and collegiate recovery communities. *Social Work, 59* (2), 177–180.

Johnston, L. D., O'Malley, P. M., Bachman, J. G., & Schulenberg, J. E. (2010). Monitoring the Future national results on adolescent drug use: Overview of key findings, 2009 (NIH Publication No. 10–7583). Bethesda, MD: National Institute on Drug Abuse.

Kaye, A. D., Stuart, G., Grahovac, I., Holleran Steiker, L. K., & Maison, T. (2012). *The center for students in recovery, spring 2012 assessment.* Unpublished report. Austin: University of Texas.

Kelly, J. F., Stout, R. L., & Slaymaker, V. (2013). Emerging adults' treatment outcomes in relation to 12-step mutual-help attendance and active involvement. *Drug and Alcohol Dependence, 129*(1–2), 151–157.

Kutash, K., Acri, M., Pollock, M., Armusewicz, K., Olin, S., & Eaton Hoagwood, K. (2013). Quality indicators for multidisciplinary team functioning in community-based children's mental health services. *Administration and Policy in Mental Health and Mental Health Services Research, 41*(1), 55–68.

Lanham, C., & Tirado, J. (2013). Lessons in sobriety: An exploratory study of graduate outcomes at a recovery high school. *Journal of Groups in Addiction and Recovery, 6,* 245–263.

Laudet, A. B., & White, W. L. (2008). RC as prospective predictor of sustained recovery, life satisfaction and stress among former poly-substance users. *Substance Use and Misuse, 43*(1), 27–54.

Laudet, A. B., Harris, K., Kimball, T., Winters, K. C., & Moberg, D. P. (2014). Collegiate recovery communities' programs: What do we know and what do we need to know? *Journal of Social Work Practice in the Addictions, 14*(1), 84–100.

Leshner, A. I. (1997). Addiction is a brain disease. *Science, 278,* 45–47.

Levy, P. (November 13, 2011). Sober outlook for famed school: Sobriety High has won plaudits for transforming lives but faces enrollment and fiscal problems. Minneapolis, MN: *Minneapolis Star and Tribune,* B1.

Lynch, A. D., Lerner, R. M., & Leventhal, T. (2013) Adolescent academic achievement and school engagement: An examination of the role of school-wide peer culture. *Journal of Youth & Adolescence, 42*(1), 6–19.

Maxwell, J. (2014). *Substance abuse trends in Texas.* Community Epidemiology Work Group, June 2014.

Mejias, N., Gill, C., & Shpigelman, C. (2014). Influence of a support group for young women with disabilities on sense of belonging. *Journal of Counseling Psychology, 61*(2), 208–220.

238

Moberg, D. P., & Finch, A. (2009). Recovery high schools: A descriptive study of school programs and students. *Journal of Groups in Addiction and Recovery, (2)*, 128–161.

Moberg, D. P., & Thaler, S. (1995). *An evaluation of Recovery High School: An alternative high school for adolescents in recovery from chemical dependency.* Milwaukee, WI: University of Wisconsin Medical School Center for Health Policy and Program Evaluation.

Morrison, C., & Bailey, C. (2011, March). The APG: A recovery model for teens and young adults. *Recovery Today Online.* Retrieved from: http://www .recoverytoday.net/articles/286-the-alternative-peer-gr oup-a-recovery -model-for-teens-and-young-adults?format = pdf

Nash, A. (2013). *The APG: What can "winners" from this program teach us about recovery from adolescent substance use disorder?* Houston, TX: University of Texas Health Sciences Center–Houston.

Newman, B. M., Lohman, B. J., & Newman, P. R. (2007). Peer group membership and a sense of belonging: Their relationship to adolescent behavior problems. *Adolescence, 42*(166), 241–63.

Nowinski, J. (1990). *Substance abuse in adolescents and young adults: A guide to treatment.* New York, NY: W.W. Norton and Company.

Perron, B. E., Grahovac, I. D., & Parrish, D. (2010). Students for recovery: A novel way to support students on campus. *Journal of Psychiatric Services, 61*, 633.

Perron, B. E., Grahovac, I. D., Uppal, J. S., Granillo, T. M., Shutter, J., & Porter, C. A. (2011). Supporting students in recovery on college campuses: Opportunities for student affairs professionals. *Journal of Student Affairs Research and Practice, 48*(1), 47–64.

Ramirez, R., Hinman, A., Sterling, S., Weisner, C., & Campbell, C. (2012). Peer influences on adolescent alcohol and other drug use outcomes. *Journal of Nursing Scholarship, 44*(1), 36–44.

Rochat, R., Rossiter, A., Nunley, E., Bahavar, S., Ferraro, K., MacPherson, C., & Basinger, S. (2014, unpublished manuscript/PPT). *APGs: Are they effective?*

Substance Abuse and Mental Health Services Administration. (2007). *Guiding principles and elements of recovery-oriented systems of care: What do we know from the research?* Rockville, MD: U.S. Department of Health and Human Services. Retrieved from http://www.facesandvoicesofrecovery .org/resources/guiding-principles-and-eleme nts-recovery-oriented -systems-care-what-do-we-know-research

Substance Abuse and Mental Health Services Administration (SAMHSA) (2011). *Results from the 2010 national survey on drug use and mental health: Summary of national findings.* NSDUH Series H-41 (HHS Publication SMA) 11–4658). Retrieved from http://www.samhsa.gov/data/NSDUH/2k10 ResultsRev/NSDUresultsRev201 0.htm/

Substance Abuse and Mental Health Services Administration (SAMHSA) (2013). *The N-SSATS report: Trends in the use of methadone and buprenorphine at substance abuse treatment facilities: 2003 to 2011.* Rockville, MD: U.S. Department of Health and Human Services. Retrieved from http://www.samhsa.gov/data/2k13/NSSATS107/sr107-NSSATS-Buprenorph ine Trends.htm

Sussman, S., Skara, S., & Ames, S. L. (2008). Substance abuse among adolescents. *Substance Use and Misuse, 43,* 1802–1828.

Tinto, V. (1993). *Leaving college: Rethinking the causes and cures of student attrition (2nd ed.).* Chicago: University of Chicago Press.

Wechsler, H., & Nelson, T. F. (2001). Binge drinking and the American college students: What's five drinks? *Psychology of Addictive Behaviors, 15*(4), 287–291.

White, W. L. (1998) *Slaying the dragon: The history of addiction treatment and recovery in America.* Chicago, IL: Chestnut Health Systems.

White, W. L., & Finch, A. (2006). The recovery school movement: Its history and future. *Counselor, 7*(2), 54–58.

White, W. L., Kelly, J. F., & Roth, J. D. (2012). New addiction-recovery support institutions: Mobilizing support beyond professional addiction treatment and recovery mutual aid. *Journal of Groups in Addiction & Recovery, 7,* 297–317.

Chapter 10

Substance-Misusing Youth in the Juvenile Justice System

Although the word "delinquency" is commonly utilized in the research, literature, and legal world, it is not particularly helpful rhetoric for helping professionals. The stigma and attitudes towards adolescents as delinquents are injurious at best, and paralyzing or even fatal at worst. However, according to the Office of Juvenile Justice and Delinquency Prevention (OJJDP, 2011), there is an undeniable link between adolescent substance misuse and delinquency. There is no doubt that many youth engaged in substance use will experience being arrested, adjudicated, and intervened upon by the juvenile justice system. According to experts, a causal link is not clear (OJJDP, 201). Yet a strong correlation exists between substance misuse and the following: school and family problems, involvement with negative peer groups, a lack of neighborhood social controls, and physical or sexual abuse (Wilson and Howell, 1993).

Substance misuse by adolescents is primarily related to violent and income-generating crimes. Although the media highlights gangs, drug trafficking, prostitution, and growing numbers of youth homicides as the social and criminal justice problems linked to adolescent substance misuse (OJJDP, 2013), it is important to keep the bio-psycho-social-spiritual frame in mind throughout this discussion. Hoards of young people are caught, tried, and adjudicated for substance-related crimes and behaviors. Although it is important that they be held accountable for choices, the picture gets muddled when one considers that many of the youth in such situations were under the influence of mood- and mind-altering substances, some perhaps even in blackouts with no memory of the events for which they are accused or punished. This is a tricky area of inquiry. Many legal experts are starting to value joint degrees such as MSW-JD for mediation work, which considers the psychosocial history of clients in addition to their illegal behavior(s).

The Drug Use Forecasting (DUF) Study measures levels of and trends in drug use among persons arrested and booked in the United States. The data address the following topics: (1) types of drugs used by arrestees (based on self-reports and urinalysis), (2) self-reported dependency on drugs, (3) self-reported need for alcohol/drug treatment, (4) the relationship between drug use and certain types of offenses, and (5) the relationship between self-reported indicators of drug use and indicators of drug use based on urinalyses. DUF found the highest association between positive drug tests of male juvenile arrestees and their commission of drug-related crimes (e.g., sales, possession). However, a substantial rate of drug use also was found among youth who committed violent, property, and other crimes (Miller, Cohen, & Wiersema, 2006).

There is a variety of intervention models for adjudicated youth with substance use disorders. There are advantages and disadvantages to mandated treatment. Descriptions of clients "going through the motions" of treatment without actively engaging or participating in the therapeutic process have been documented as common incidents of non-compliance in both adults and adolescents mandated to treatment (Sung & Feng, 2001; Schacht Reisinger, Bush, Colom, Agar, & Battjes, 2003). These findings indicate that, although physical presence in treatment may form part of client engagement, it does not guarantee meaningful participation (Schacht Reisinger et al., 2003; Sung, Belenko, Feng, & Tabachnick, 2004).

The American Probation and Parole Association Project (APPA) serves as an exemplar for those hoping to address the juvenile justice system's punitive nature in regard to adolescents with substance misuse problems. The APPA aimed to accomplish several objectives through its project "Identifying and Intervening with Drug-Involved Youth." The first was to develop a training and technical assistance curriculum reflecting sound principles for identifying and intervening with drug-involved youth. Providing training and technical assistance for juvenile justice agencies, based on the curriculum, was also a major goal of the project. A final project purpose was to evaluate the effectiveness of the curriculum and its application with training participants and technical assistance sites. Although juvenile probation and aftercare agencies were a key focus of the APPA, the program's efforts were not limited to juvenile community corrections. The curriculum, training, and technical assistance were developed broadly to apply to juvenile justice service providers generally. The APPA project had three major phases: (1) curriculum development, (2) training delivery, and (3) technical assistance provision and evaluation.

During the curriculum development phase, the project assembled an advisory committee that met periodically to provide recommendations to staff, review project products, and provide feedback. With input from the advisory committee, project staff researched and drafted a curriculum document, *Identifying and Intervening with Drug-Involved Youth* (Crowe & Schaefer, 1992), a fifteen-chapter, 274-page text. Parts of the curriculum were based on earlier projects APPA had conducted, including the development of a training curriculum on using drug recognition techniques in juvenile probation agencies and the development of the document *Drug Testing Guidelines and Practices for*

Juvenile Probation and Parole Agencies (1992). The project delivered five comprehensive training programs based on the curriculum. These four-day programs were held in regional sites around the country to encourage the broadest participation by juvenile justice professionals. The 209 participants in these training sessions represented twenty-nine states, Washington, D.C., and Puerto Rico. Participating agencies were encouraged to send teams composed of both administrators and line personnel to the training programs.

The content of the training sessions provided an overview of the problem of substance-abusing youth and program development processes and concerns (including legal issues). The training concentrated on methods and technologies for identifying illicit drug use, including the use of assessment instruments and techniques, drug recognition techniques, and chemical testing (primarily urinalysis). Throughout the training, the need for appropriate intervention following the use of drug identification measures was emphasized. To maintain focus, the time available to delve into treatment strategies and other intervention methods was limited. Five demonstration sites were selected to implement or enhance a drug identification and intervention program with the assistance of the APPA. The technical assistance process included three major tasks: (1) site selection, (2) on-site and other training and technical assistance for program development, and (3) evaluation of the programs.

DRUG COURTS

In the field of youth and substance use disorders, there are two concurrent beliefs, which are sometimes harmonious and at other times conflicting: (1) Youth need natural and meaningful consequences to prompt changes in behavior. (2) Youth need more than coercion to recover and become well. As noted by Urbanoski (2010), those who criticize the evidence base for the effectiveness of addiction treatment under social controls and coercion miss the potential value of incorporating client perspectives on coercion. Reviewing empirical and theoretical literature, Urbanoski makes a case for greater accuracy in representing the complexity of "coercive" experiences and events in research. Such accuracy will help to align the measured concepts with actual processes of treatment entry and admission. There are undoubtedly connections between coercion and decision-making. Work is being done using theoretical perspectives on motivation and behavior change, including self-determination theory. According to these perspectives, workplace and school sanctions, drug testing, drug courts, and mandatory treatments are not the same to all people. Ultimately, at present, it is still unclear to what extent many of the commonly employed methods for getting people into treatment may be beneficial or detrimental to the treatment process and longer-term outcomes. Urbanoski (2010) concludes: "The impact of coercion upon individual clients, treatment systems, and population health has not been adequately dealt with by addiction researchers to date" and "It remains to be demonstrated whether the exposure to treatment among coerced clients is ultimately beneficial or harmful in the long run for the individual and for the public" (p. 7).

Drug courts are an excellent bridge between the juvenile justice realm and the road to wellness and recovery. They provide an alternative to punitive or custodial interventions. Research on juvenile drug treatment courts (JDTCs) has not received as much attention as adult drug courts, but evidence is growing to support the effectiveness of JDTCs in reducing delinquency and substance misuse. However, much work still needs to be done to discern effective from ineffective programs (Marlowe, 2011).

Recent review articles and meta-analytic studies show that JDTCs produced an average reduction in recidivism (return to crime) of only about 3 to 5 percent—which, although marginally statistically significant, is relatively small in magnitude (Shaffer, 2011). It's important to note, however, that the size of the effects varied considerably across programs, with some JDTCs having no effects whatsoever on recidivism and others reducing recidivism by as much as 8 to 10 percent. According to Marlowe (2011), when JDTCs have made substantial efforts to incorporate evidence-based treatments into their curricula and reached out to family and other caring supports in the youths' natural social environments, reductions in delinquency and substance use have been reported to be as high as 15 to 40 percent (Shaffer, 2011).

KEY TERMS

Delinquency

American Probation and Parole
   Association Project (APPA)

Juvenile drug treatment courts
   (JDTCs)

Recidivism

DISCUSSION QUESTIONS

1. Why is delinquency a problematic term in the realm of substance misuse?

2. What else might improve the lives of adolescents caught in the juvenile justice system and recidivism?

3. Explore the difference between punitive and custodial programs and juvenile programs focused on restorative justice and rehabilitation and recovery. How do they differ? What are the pros and cons of each side? Which do you endorse and why? If you think your state's policies and incarceration techniques are flawed, how might they be improved?

REFERENCES

Crowe, A. H., & Schaefer, P. J. (1992). *Identifying and intervening with drug-involved youth*. Washington, DC: Office of Juvenile Justice and Delinquency Prevention.

Marlowe, D. B. (2011). Adult and juvenile drug courts. *Handbook of Evidence-Based Substance Abuse Treatment in Criminal Justice Settings: Issues in Children's and Families' Lives, 11*, 123–142.

Miller, T. R., Cohen, M. A., & Wiersema, B. (2006). *Victim costs and consequences: A new look. A final summary report presented to the National Institute of Justice*. Washington, DC: U.S. Department of Health and Human Services.

Schacht Reisinger, H., Bush, T., Colom, M., Agar, M., & Battjes, R. (2003). Navigation and engagement: How does one measure success? *Journal of Drug Issues, 33*, 777–800.

Shaffer, D. K. (2011). Looking inside the black box of drug courts: A meta-analytic review. *Justice Quarterly, 28*(3), 493–521.

Sung, H., Belenko, S., & Feng, L. (2001). Treatment compliance in the trajectory of treatment progress among offenders. *Journal of Substance Abuse Treatment, 26*, 315–328.

Sung, H.E., Belenko, S., Feng, L., & Tabachnick, C. (2004). Predicting treatment noncompliance among criminal justice-mandated clients: A theoretical and empirical exploration. *Journal of Substance Abuse Treatment, 26*, 315–328.

Urbanoski, K. A. (2010). Coerced addiction treatment: Client perspectives and the implications of their neglect. *Harm Reduction Journal, 7*, 7–13.

Wilson, J. J., & Howell, J. C. (1993). *Comprehensive strategy for serious, violent, and chronic juvenile offenders. Program summary*. Washington, DC: U.S. Department of Justice, Office of Justice Programs, Office of Juvenile Justice and Delinquency Prevention.

Chapter 11

Current Issues, Policies, and Future Directions

The topic of young people and substance misuse is constantly evolving. Exploring adolescent substance use, prevention, intervention, and recovery can feel like trying to staple Jell-O to a tree. Youth are dynamic, as are times and trends. As Rosenbaum, Carreiro, and Babu (2012, p. 15) have noted, "Despite their widespread Internet availability and use, many of the new drugs of abuse remain unfamiliar to health care providers." In particular, herbal marijuana alternatives (commonly known as K2 or Spice) contain a mixture of plant matter in addition to chemical grade synthetic cannabinoids. The synthetic drug commonly called "bath salts" has resulted in emergency rooms across the nation being flooded with young people experiencing severe agitation, toxicity, and death. Other new drugs include Kratom (a plant product with opioid-like effects for pain relief), Salvia (a hallucinogen with therapeutic potential banned in many states due to dangerous psychiatric effects), Methoxetamine (aka "legal ketamine" or "Special K" on the Internet), and piperazine derivatives (amphetamine-like compounds such as BZP and TMFPP, which are being revived in the scene as "legal Ecstasy"). These psychoactives have often been accessible via the Internet, sporadically legal, and even erroneously perceived as safe by the public. These substances have effects ranging from minimal to life-threatening. Helping professionals must be familiar with these important new classes of drugs and should keep one ear to the ground as new substances emerge.

INFLUENCE OF THE MEDIA AND ROLE MODELS IN SPORTS AND ENTERTAINMENT

Despite the ugliness of addiction, many still associate substances with glamour and prestige. Popular and rap music, television shows, media, and advertising have tremendous alcohol and drug content. Some researchers have found that elevated popular music involvement is a risk factor with respect to younger adolescents' substance use behavior (Slatera & Henry, 2013).

● ●

Rave Culture Terminology

Dreads or cyberlox: real or fake and often playful form of the dreadlocks hair style, often made with brightly colored, tubular, crin decorative ribbons

Drum and bass: a genre of electronic dance music (EDM) focused on the bass and sub-base line

El wire: electro-luminescent wire that has many decorative purposes

Glover: a raver who uses rave gloves to give light shows

Glow stick: a plastic container filled with liquids that have a chemical reaction, causing it to emit a bright neon light

Hardcore: a fast and upbeat genre of EDM

House: a funky and soulful genre of EDM

Jungle: a rhythm-filled genre of EDM that holds African and Caribbean roots

Kandi: bracelets or other jewelry, often made of plastic pony beads, that many ravers wear and trade at events

LED lights: light emitting diodes that have many purposes in the rave scene due to their small size, lack of heat, and bright light

Leg fuzzies: leg warmers that are made with thick, furry fabric and often brightly colored

Light show: an improvised display of moving light given from one raver to another

PLUR(R): rave credo or mantra that stands for "Peace Love Unity Respect (Responsibility)"

Rave gloves: gloves, used for light shows, that have LEDs in the fingertips

Raver: a person who goes to raves

Rollin': a term for someone who is under the influence of drugs, especially Ecstasy

Techno: a genre of EDM that focuses on rhythms

Thizz: a slang term for Ecstasy

Trance: a genre of EDM that focuses on melody, build ups, break downs, and progressions

● ●

Large groups of young people are involved with the "party culture" or "culture of intoxication" (Measham & Brain, 2005). Anderson (2009) describes an extreme example of the unique world of drugs in *Rave Culture*. Although some young people attend raves and do not use substances, one law official was quoted to have said, "A rave without drugs is like a rodeo without horses. They don't happen." (Penman, 2013). The prominent drug of use at raves is Ecstasy. Large raves have resulted in overdoses, accident-related deaths, and injuries (Weir, 2000). The culture, when studied ethnographically, appears to be the modern version of Woodstock, with the underlying credo P.L.U.R. (Peace, Love, Unity, and Respect). Numerous traditions and practices

250

characterize rave culture, including the attribution of nicknames, unique dances, light shows, music, and exchanging of bracelets called kandi.

POLICY ISSUES

Marijuana legalization involves removing prohibitions on production, distribution, and possession of marijuana. Legalization can—but need not—involve regulation and taxation. Contrary to popular belief, marijuana was not legalized in the Netherlands; there, it is not legal to sell to the coffee shops. However, now, in Colorado and Washington, proprietors can sell to the shops. The College on Problems of Drug Dependence (CPDD), the longest standing group of researchers addressing problems of drug dependence in the United States, held its annual conference in California (summer 2013). A panel of top policy researchers presented the critical points for consideration with regard to youth and substances in light of the movement towards legalization. In order to understand and attend to the complex policy issues of marijuana legalization, Beau Kilmer recommended consideration of what he called "the Seven P's," which are as follows:

1. *Production*: This consideration revolves around concepts including reduction in risk, economics of scale, and changes in technology. As growers move from basements to industrial farms, production costs inevitably go down. If marijuana could be farmed like other goods, or even produced using indoor growth systems, prices would undoubtedly plummet (RAND, 2010). At present, the federal response is unknown, but costs are expected to go down. Testing for organic vs. chemical make-up and mold testing is also an area of production yet to be determined.

2. *Profit Motive*: If you want to make changes, you don't have to let profit-maximizing companies into the picture. Is the U.S. alcohol model desirable? One might want to remember that, currently, with alcohol, 20 percent of consumers are responsible for 80 percent of consumption. Another option is state monopoly. This could allow more aggressive pursuit of violators who pretend to be legitimate distributors or retailers. State monopoly would also allow prices to be set by government at levels higher than otherwise possible. The challenge is that monopolies are hard or impossible to implement.

3. *Promotion*: Allowing competition and profit creates incentives for commercialization. Experiences with alcohol and tobacco raise concerns. Countering promotion can be difficult.

4. *Prevention*: How will youth messaging change now that consumption is legal for adults? Ideally, this is something that would have been in place before states began legalizing. Advocates need to move quickly to insure that plans exist now that legalization is a reality.

5. *Potency*: Should THC levels be regulated? THC is the main intoxicant in marijuana. It is responsible for increasing anxiety and panic attacks (Hall & Pacula, 2003: Room, 2010). THC ranges tend to be between 10 and 25 percent. Regulators are thinking about capping THC at 50 percent in Washington and Colorado. They are not allowing hash oil, shatter, or wax (extracts) to be put in edibles. In access points in Washington, retailers are selling items other than marijuana weed such as new vaporizer pens (like e-cigarettes) and butane hash oil, which can be preloaded into "o-pens" and which may have THC levels greater than 80 percent. CBD is now getting more attention: CBD is cannabinoid that offsets some of the THC effects. There is now a great deal of discussion of THC:CBD ratios. Manipulating these ratios through regulation or taxation may be one way to control potency.

6. *Price*: A 10 percent decline in price is likely to lead to about a 3 percent increase in marijuana initiation (Pacula, 2010: Gallet, 2013). Price influences consumption and revenues. At present, there are not good data on total price elasticity. The retail price of marijuana will be a function of several factors: production choices, demand, federal response, and taxes. A tightly enforced government monopoly could keep prices artificially high. There are alternatives to taxing by weight, such as taxing by the percentage of THC or by the THC:CBD ratio. The use of such alternatives might be a good way to set retail prices as well.

7. *Permanency*: How easy will it be to change policies once they are put in place? According to the experts, no one will get it absolutely right the first time. Early adopters will likely want to be able to respond to "growing pains." Kilmer suggested another idea: a "sunset clause," which would give pioneering jurisdictions an escape clause.

Policy expert Rosalie Liccardo Pacula has evaluated the impact of marijuana decriminalization and medicalization on marijuana use among youth. She has analyzed gender and racial differences in response to particular substance use policies, assessed the impact of higher cigarette and alcohol prices on demand for illicit substances, and conducted cost-benefit analyses of school-based drug prevention programs. Pacula and her colleagues have helped to measure the size of illicit drug markets and prices. As part of this larger research agenda, they have done in-depth policy analyses of state-level parity legislation, medical marijuana policies, and decriminalization policy in the United States and abroad. They have concluded that it is important to focus on four public health objectives:

- Prevent youth access and use.
- Prevent drugged driving.

- Regulate the content and form (potency and quality) of marijuana.
- Minimize the concurrent use of marijuana with alcohol. (The potentially harmful effects of marijuana are much greater when combined with alcohol. The effect is not just additive. It's a multiplicative effect.)

How do we reach these four objectives? The experts (Pacula, Kilmer, Wagenaar, Chaloupka, & Caulkins, 2013) made the following recommendations (but discussions are still warranted about cutting-edge perspectives and mechanisms):

1. Keep the price of marijuana as high as possible (which will be difficult when production costs drop, as they undoubtedly will). Despite movement towards legalization, it is still hard to guarantee that an underground market in marijuana will not continue to exist. The experts recommend tough sanctions against those that are not compliant (but they note that this may be harder with marijuana than alcohol).

2. Consider adoption of a state monopoly. This could allow more aggressive pursuit of violators who pretend to be legitimate distributors or retailers and would allow prices to be set by government at levels higher than otherwise possible. There are a number of challenges, because monopolies are hard or impossible to implement.

3. Restrict and carefully monitor licenses. Such restrictions will allow the government to track and trace all products, ensure they meet minimum quality standards, and monitor the sale of products in terms of excess or insufficient supply. By reducing the number of outlets, one can reduce availability and public health harm. The experts also suggest restricting access, such as making sure that density is not near schools or after a certain time of day, like with alcohol.

4. Limit the types of products sold. The more variations, the more the risk exists that some will produce anxiety attacks or psychosis in those who use it. There is much yet to learn about warnings needed on cannabis. Other questions include: What additives and flavorings should regulators allow? Should they require retailers to reduce molds, metals, and other problems? If there is no regulatory mechanism in place, policy implementers' hands will be tied when these issues arise.

5. Limit all forms of marketing (advertising, promotion, and sponsorship). Pop tarts and lollipops with THC exist and these are kids' products! In limiting promotion, comprehensive bans are the most effective strategies. Advocates need to do what they can to make sure broad-scale advertising is not used for cannabis.

6. Prohibit consumption in public places. It is hard to make a case for banning public smoking of marijuana because there is little research showing the evidence of harm from secondary marijuana smoke. The better argument is to reduce youth initiation by banning people from smoking marijuana, for example, in malls, public parks, and restaurants.

7. Give serious consideration to the problem of drugged driving. This problem is not as easy to solve as drunk driving because there is no test like an alcohol "breathalyzer" that can capture an impaired level effectively. For cannabis, blood testing is the gold standard, but this is considered invasive and expensive and not feasible to use with drivers (and urine screening is not a very good option). Oral fluid tests are not yet accurate enough; research is improving regarding this technology.

Another complicating issue is that one cannot equate exposure to intoxication. However, for youth, one cannot deny the neurocognitive effects and the established impact on neurodevelopment. Unfortunately, within the Colorado initiatives, the policy developers did not put aside money for a prevention component. In Washington state, policymakers are trying to address these issues, but they are not likely to have much in place in time for legalization processes. The mistake is having prevention efforts as a function of the tax revenue; this is a perfect example of putting the cart before the horse. Politically, science has not been too much a part of the discussion. NIDA is trying to get the messages to the public. This discussion is not confined to Colorado and Washington state. Discussions are going on in the White House, and twelve other states are considering legalization of marijuana. Youth advocates need to be educated members of these planning discussions.

• •

Join Friends of NIDA—http://www.thefriendsofnida .org/default.php

Help teach researchers how to translate the research on marijuana to the public! Know how your system works, where to go, and whom to talk to!

• •

WHERE WE GO FROM HERE

What are the implications for the future? Clinicians must find ways to communicate so that they are not operating in silos and so that there are no longer gaps between clinical interventions, prevention, community recovery connections, dissemination of findings, and teaching/scholarship. There are new community-based groups called ROSC (recovery oriented systems of care) that exist in each local area, with state networks and national connections. Adolescent ROSCs are beginning to proliferate, but there are still holes in systems that can be much more effective.

One must think in terms of systems of care rather than isolating prevention from intervention, policy from practice, and harm reduction from other paths to recovery. Draw upon what you know and what you have learned to connect aspects of recovery from beginning to end. Remember that one cannot treat this chronic, potentially fatal disease with an acute care model (White & Kelly, 2011; White & McClellan, 2008). There must be ongoing attention to individuals in need throughout the continuum and beyond the initial crisis. Can you imagine if someone with cancer was treated acutely without any follow-up chemotherapy, ongoing support, continued assessment and evaluation, and attention to life beyond the crisis? Addiction is no different; it requires continued support beyond the initial life change of recovery. Be acutely aware of the community around you, and mobilize resources towards the greatest impact (White, 2009).

KEY TERMS

The Seven P's
Decriminalization
Medicalization

DISCUSSION QUESTIONS

1. What new drug trends have you heard about in the news media? TV? Your schools or workplaces?

2. In dyads, debate marijuana legalization. Note all the pros and cons on each side and tally them to see where the debate takes you. Where do you stand? Now extend the debate to arguing that all drugs be legalized. Do you still feel the way you did before?

REFERENCES

Anderson, T. (2009). *Rave culture*. Philadelphia, PA: Temple University Press.

Gallet, C. A. (2013). Can price get the monkey off our back? A meta-analysis of illicit drug demand. *Health Economics, 23*(1), 55–68.

Hall, W., & Pacula, R. L. (2003). *Cannabis use and dependence: Public health and public policy*. Cambridge, UK: Cambridge University Press.

Measham, F., & Brain, K. (2005). Binge drinking, British alcohol policy and the new culture of intoxication. *Crime, Media, Culture 1*(3): 262–283.

Pacula, R. L. (2010*). Examining the impact of marijuana legalization on marijuana consumption: Insights from the economics literature*. Santa Monica, CA: RAND Corporation.

Pacula, R. L., Kilmer, B., Wagenaar, A. C., Chaloupka, F. J., & Caulkins, J. P. (2013). Developing public health regulations for marijuana: Lessons from alcohol and tobacco. *American Journal of Public Health, 104*(6), 1021–1028.

Penman, J. (2013) Interviewed in article, "Raves: Records show deadly toll of drugs among concertgoers." *Los Angeles Times,* February 4.

RAND Annual Report (2010). *Focus on making a difference*. Santa Monica, CA: RAND Corporation. Accessed May 20, 2015, at http://www.rand.org/pubs/corporate_pubs/CP1–2010

Room, R. (2010). *Cannabis policy: Moving beyond stalemate*. Oxford and New York: Oxford University Press.

Rosenbaum, C. D., Carreiro, S. P., & Babu, K. M. (2012). Here today, gone tomorrow . . . and back again? A review of herbal marijuana alternatives (K2, Spice), synthetic cathinones (bath salts), Kratom, Salvia divinorum, methoxetamine, and piperazines. *Journal of Medical Toxicology, 8*(1) 15–32.

Slatera, M. D., & Henry, K. L. (2013). Prospective influence of music-related media exposure on adolescent substance-use initiation: A peer group mediation model. *Journal of Health Communication: International Perspectives, 18*(3), 291–305.

White, W. L. (2009). The mobilization of community resources to support long-term addiction recovery. *Journal of Substance Abuse Treatment, 36*(2), 146–158

White, W. L., & Kelly, J. F. (2011) Recovery management: What if we really believed that addiction was a chronic disorder? *Addiction Recovery Management: Current Clinical Psychiatry,* 67–84.

White, W. L., & McClellan, T. (2008). Addiction as a chronic disorder. *Counselor. 9*(3), 24–33.

EPILOGUE

Now that you have read and studied this book, embrace the responsibility to help shift the stigma, to raise awareness, to build bridges between services over the deep chasms (not cracks) that youth might fall through. If you yourself have not been touched by an adolescent in recovery, witness the miraculous life-changing experience by connecting with your local agencies, or visit a recovery high school, or at least watch the recovery high school videos that are popping up all over the Web. Be a recovery advocate no matter what aspect of this work you are engaged with. You can make the difference.

The field of adolescent substance use, misuse, and recovery is growing daily. You must always keep your eye on your youth and communities, your ear to policy, your mind to the research, your mouth to advocacy possibilities, and your heart to the young people who need you. Always notice new mechanisms for helping. Avoid contempt before investigation. Advocate for recovery. And never lose hope.

INDEX

Note: Page numbers followed by "f" refer to figures.

Lori Holleran Steiker (MSW, *University of Pennsylvania*; PhD, *Arizona State University*) is a renown addictions therapist and professor of social work at the University of Texas at Austin. With more than a decade of experience working with youth and families, she has served as a clinical social worker, clinical supervisor, and outpatient group and family therapist. She conducts federally and foundation-funded research in the area of adolescent and emerging adult substance misuse prevention, intervention, and recovery with an emphasis on peer-to-peer mentorship. She is proud to identify as a person in long-term recovery, and she is the driving force behind University High School—Austin's first recovery high school. Professor Holleran Steiker serves actively as the faculty liaison for the University of Texas at Austin's Center for Students in Recovery (CSR) as well as the founder and liaison for the university's Drug and Alcohol Public Awareness (DAPA) student group. She designed and teaches the course Young People and Drugs, working with hundreds of students each year. Professor Holleran Steiker has more than ninety publications in the area of substance use disorders and has received numerous academic, career, and civic honors, including being selected as one of *Social Work Today*'s Ten Dedicated and Deserving Social Workers and receiving the 2015 CSWE Distinguished Recent Contributions in Social Work Education Award.